LIN⬤LEUM
BETTER BABIES &
THE M⬤DERN
FARM WOMAN

1890–1930

MARILYN IRVIN HOLT

UNIVERSITY OF NEBRASKA PRESS
LINCOLN AND LONDON

∞

First Nebraska paperback printing: 2005

Library of Congress Cataloging-in-Publication Data
Holt, Marilyn Irvin, 1949–
Linoleum, better babies, and the modern farm woman, 1890–1930 /
Marilyn Irvin Holt.
p. cm.
Originally published: Albuquerque: University of New Mexico Press,
1995.
Includes bibliographical references and index.
ISBN-13: 978-0-8032-2436-0 (pbk.: alk. paper)
ISBN-10: 0-8032-2436-2 (pbk.: alk. paper)
1. Rural women—United States.   2. Rural women—Education—United
States.   3. Home economics—United States.   4. United States—Social
conditions—1865–1918.   5. United States—Social conditions—1918–
1932.   6. United States—Economic conditions—1865–1918.   7. United
States—Economic conditions—1918–1945.   I. Title.
HQ1419.H65   2005
305.42'0973—dc22   2005015879

To my sisters and brothers
(The Walpole kids)
Cathy, Teresa, David, and Joel

Contents

Acknowledgments

For their help and advice in locating research materials for this study I am grateful to Virginia Lee Clark, former dean and professor for the College of Home Economics, South Dakota State University (now dean of the College of Human Development and Education, North Dakota State University); Anthony Crawford, director, University Archives, Kansas State University; staff at the University Archives, Texas A & M University; and Carlene Aro, archivist, Briggs Library, South Dakota State University. A special thank you also must go to staff at the South Dakota Historical Society, University of Kansas Library of Government Documents, Kansas Collection at the University of Kansas, and Kansas State Historical Society. Staff at the National Archives and Records Administration, Washington, D.C., and National Archives–Central Plains Branch, Kansas City, Missouri, offered helpful suggestions and aid regarding materials on the Children's Bureau and Bureau of Indian Affiars. A special acknowledgment must also be made of the time generously given me by Marsha Weaver, home extension agent, Dickinson County, Kansas, and the members of several home extension units who offered their stories and viewpoints of farm living. Last, but certainly not least, I want to thank Paula Nelson, Bernadine Barr, Gilbert Fite, and my husband, Daniel Holt, for commentary, suggestions, and conversation.

LINOLEUM, BETTER BABIES, AND THE
MODERN FARM WOMAN, 1890–1930

Introduction

THIS VOLUME WAS CONCEIVED AS A STUDY OF the domestic economy movement and the rural women it targeted during an era of significant cultural and economic change in American life. The study, spanning the years 1890 to 1930, was built around the movement and its relationship to the duties, roles, lifestyles, and living space of women. The framework for the investigation incorporated the context of the times, the challenges women faced, the ways in which women appropriated the movement, and the contemporary farm scene. Essentially, the domestic economy movement grew out of, and was a reflection of, the era's push for progress and reform. It centered on rural women and their education. It intended to transform and redirect agrarian society with women's cooperation. It meant to improve women's lives.

Any discussion of the movement must begin with the understanding that the women involved made a clear distinction between "housekeeping" and "homemaking." Housekeeping was home maintenance; homemaking was that and much more. An 1890 home reference guide explained what homemaking entailed: reducing labor by using methods discovered by "practical and progressive women"; saving time and money; preventing disease; and creating an attractive home.[1] Homemaking functions and goals were often described by other terms—

domestic arts, domestic science, home economics, home economy, and domestic economy. Used interchangeably over time, the terms have lost any distinct definitions they once may have had. Domestic arts, for example, once meant mastering the art of cooking or sewing but eventually conjured up the image of niceties such as flower arranging or embroidery. Domestic science, originally a reference to instruction or training in the domestic arts, came to mean the application of scientific principles to homemaking. Thus, the movement to engage farm women in transforming themselves and their world never had one name assigned to it, as did the "scientific farming" movement, which aimed at improved land management and farm production. Because several terms were used, I chose to identify the movement by the name that seemed best to embody its goals—domestic economy. Consistently, what the movement hoped for was economy in time, money, and work. The other terms, however, cannot be overlooked because commentators employed them and, in the case of home economics, used them to identify a particular form of education within the movement.

During the years under study, every facet of American life was a cause for reform. Rural areas witnessed transformations in education, health care, community cooperation, production, and labor. Calls for reform came at the same time Americans, including rural families, were looking to science to improve the quality of life. Tremendous faith was placed in technology's ability to expand communication, transportation, and the availability of material goods and conveniences. "Progress" was the byword of those years, and the individual who explained its implications and applications for everyday life was the "expert." These people were, in fact, interpreters of newly gained knowledge in the social and physical sciences. Each discipline had its own language, and these increasingly became incomprehensible to laymen. The experts explained research and plans for change in the context of both social reform and material and physical modernization. Their presence changed society. As Lawrence Levine noted,

"Americans at the turn of the century were learning to defer to experts in a wide range of activities that had been relatively open during the nineteenth century and that were being professionalized and codified at its close."[2]

Both experts and laymen believed that improvements could come if everything were better managed. Land and livestock management meant improved production. People could manage themselves for better cooperation. The environment—home and field—could be managed for the benefit of all. Women, as well as men, could be managers. They could manage their homes and work roles for greater efficiency; oversee their children as industrialists managed employees; manage local communities for social and educational improvements; and work in partnership with men as co-managers or outright managers. For women in agriculture, reform messages, experts, and science came together to preach a new form of education in domestic economy.

I do not intend to suggest that every woman accepted the movement. After all, farm people were not just one thing. Some were progressive, wanted to fit into the twentieth century, and were willing to use the movement if it meant progress. Others did not want to hear the message in the first place and, when they did, rejected it or felt unable to act because of personal circumstances. Nevertheless, domestic economy became a force in agricultural life because of the numbers that responded.

Many voices, often with conflicting interests, attempted to extend a multitude of reforms upon the rural landscape. Because the nation was becoming more urban and reformers often focused on urban problems first, the push for rural change was as likely to come from outside agricultural districts as from inside. Reformers generally agreed that farm women were the glue that held the rural world together. They were the catalysts for change. Thus, programs grounded in the domestic economy movement attempted to enlist farm women at home and in their communities to introduce social engineering and economic growth. Proponents of domestic economy recognized women's labor, production potential, and contributions to the farm economy. For this reason, changes in agriculture as an occupation and economic force cannot be separated from the roles of rural women or the movement that engaged them.

A challenge to agricultural commentators and experts, as well as a question for historians today, was to define and understand the broad category of "rural women." Then, as now, women were labeled by landownership, race, ethnicity, and region. In today's discussions, various fields of study treat these rural women differently. Traditional agricultural history generally assigns the rural woman a fixed role. As such, her place often is ignored within the larger questions of government programs, ownership, and economic stability. Meanwhile, women's history often minimizes the agrarian environment, assuming that rural women were shaped and molded by precisely the same social forces that influenced their urban counterparts. I will argue that the urban paradigm cannot be transposed wholesale onto rural women, although during the time under study rural women were asked to imitate the social and material culture of urban females. (The very fact that imitation was encouraged suggests that rural women had not followed the urban model too closely in the past.)

Women's historians have not reached clear agreement. Some writers underscore agrarian subjugation and oppression of women, whereas others stress women as partners or see them as part of an egalitarian society. Thus far, writings in women's history have demonstrated both a desire narrowly to confine and broadly to explore interpretations. Some belabor the point that no single interpretative model exists, but, notes historian Paula Nelson, "there would be no great harm in that. It is important that the lives of women in the West, as elsewhere, be understood in all of their diversity and complexity and that no rigid interpretive framework be forced on to the study." I agree.[3]

Interpretations continue to differ and collide, but one thing is certain: Both agricultural and women's historians are giving more notice to rural women. Nevertheless, the two areas of study continue to neglect each other when analyzing and translating the rural experience. It is my contention that the agrarian environment and cultural fabric are basic to understanding what the domestic economy movement hoped to achieve. It does little good to discuss home extension lessons in nutrition and child care unless one realizes the state of rural health care at the time. If there is to be any understanding of why women found any promise in the movement, the times and those who experienced them must be allowed to speak for themselves.

It is also essential to raise the question of class, if only because feminist studies often turn on class attitudes and expectations. Defining class in agrarian society is, however, difficult. Laboring by hand or with heavy equipment is, by urban definition, working class, blue collar; owning the land and means of production is not. Those engaged in agriculture—not only as farmers and ranchers but also as homemakers—were both laborers and capitalists. A rural woman who owned a cow, separated cream from milk, and then sold that cream for profit was a capitalist because she owned the means of production and benefited from sale of a product. In the early 1900s agricultural and economic experts grappled with rural class systems. A person's or family's local standing often was based more on cooperation with neighbors, church attendance, or interest in education than on financial assets. It was quite possible for someone to be considered among the "better class of farmers" without being among the wealthiest or largest landholders. This concept was not isolated to white Anglo ruralists; it was at work among immigrant and nonwhite farm residents as well. The term "farmer," in fact, is non–gender specific, because women, as well as men, engaged in agricultural pursuits. Today, class definition remains a prickly question. For this study, it is far more relevant to consider the cultural definition of middle class, which suggests participation, or attempted participation, in the general culture. This conveys the sense that cultural definitions of class and status recognized unmeasurable qualities that did not depend on income or labor.

The domestic economy movement was created by educated, predominantly middle-class professionals and experts (male and female).
Some, but certainly not all, were farm reared. The majority were white
Anglos, but there were also nonwhite experts who reached out to
minority communities with the same messages conveyed in the dominant culture. Collectively, these experts were intent upon educating
a population group they identified by gender—female—and placed
into one class—rural. Programs generally did not categorize women
by region. Thus, western farm women were not seen as distinctly different from their counterparts in Indiana, Connecticut, or Maine.
Perhaps influenced by the 1890 U. S. census that claimed that the
frontier was gone, experts saw rural women as sharing common needs
and experiences, despite the near-frontier conditions that often still
existed for western women.

The categories of rural and female do not suggest that all racial
and ethnic groups were treated equally. Hindsight makes it easy to
condemn the movement for its sometimes halfhearted attempts to
enact full participation; however, to understand the movement's significance and intent, the times must be kept in mind. American society was complex and diverse. Enforced segregation, racial violence,
and anti-immigrant feeling coexisted with a blithe, if not naive, belief that acculturation and assimilation would turn everyone into
"Americans." The movement reflected the times. It expected to dilute ethnic and racial traditions, creating *American* homemakers. It
extolled a homogeneous society, and movement supporters seemed
quite willing to downplay ethnicity and accept racial segregation. For
example, Kansas home extension agents were careful to specifically
note work among blacks or Mexicans but failed to mention immigrant groups such as the Mennonites, Russian-Germans, or Swedish.
This does not mean that such groups were excluded—in many counties they were the majority and had to be involved if home extension
was to be organized at all. Rather, the agents did not bother to note
this diversity because ethnic origin meant less than the fact that *rural*

women, no matter their backgrounds, were being reached. The fine lines drawn between race and ethnicity, inclusion and exclusion, were contradictory and illogical. Nevertheless, the movement did not see itself as anything other than in step with the best reform impulses of the period.

The domestic economy movement was not confined to one agricultural region. It did not concentrate on western women. For this study, however, the general focus is west of the Mississippi River, specifically on women and programs for them in the Dakotas, Nebraska, Kansas, Oklahoma, and Texas—successive tiers in the nation's midsection. I concentrate on Euro-American and African American women because they were the ones most often targeted by the movement. Though Native Americans or Hispanics are only modestly referred to, this is not a slight. During the era under study, reservation and Indian school programs taught Euro-American domesticity, and Hispanics were noticed intermittently. (It must be remembered that Hispanic populations in the Plains states were small, and those that emigrated from Mexico during the early 1900s usually were not farmers but town residents, working for railroads and packing houses.) It was not until the New Deal of the 1930s that the movement turned its considerable attention to education and self-help programs for Hispanics and Native Americans.

The Depression era is a logical ending point for this study. With New Deal recovery projects, domestic economy programs such as home extension, 4-H, and rural beautification projects were overlaid by programs of the Works Progress Administration, Public Works Administration, and Civilian Conservation Corps. Domestic economy activities provided the groundwork for many federal recovery programs, serving as essential building blocks for community canning kitchens, mattress factories, and child care centers. This is itself an important point for students of the Depression. Programs established by the Roosevelt administration were not created out of a void. Some writers, including Joan Jensen, have noted that lessons learned before the Depression served rural families during the 1930s and helped them survive before federal aid arrived. As a Texas worker in black home extension put it, "The gray of the cloud of depression that hovered over us at the dawn of 1932 has been tinted with rose" because of strategies women already had at hand.[4] During the Dirty Thirties, the nucleus of the domestic economy movement remained, but its appropriation by government projects changed women's and rural communities' involvement.

In the pre-Depression years, the nation's collective mind-set featured a belief in scientifically formulated solutions for farm problems and the challenges faced by women. Agricultural America could be pushed into the twentieth century. Between 1890 and 1930, women were noticed for their contributions in agriculture, their maintenance of the farm home as an economic and social unit, and their influence in enacting changes in local communities. Stressed was rural women's importance in sustaining agrarian traditions yet at the same time adopting new ideas and innovations was stressed. In its attempt to educate rural women and enact change, the domestic economy movement began with nineteenth-century ideals of the Victorian woman. However, it was not entrenched in the Victorian era's separate-sphere dictates for women, in part because the roles of rural women and men did not always fit sphere expectations. Moreover, definitions of domestic economy for farm women occurred at the same time popular culture began to recognize and idealize the emerging, progressive New Woman and the Outdoor Girl. These images most often were meant to represent the urban female, but they were significant in deciding who and what rural women were supposed to imitate. Just when rural women were asked as never before to parallel urban females, those women were breaking out of the Victorian mold. Products of changing social patterns and attitudes, female ideals and images evolved. The domestic economy movement vowed that farm women could change, too, and that whatever resulted would be for the better.

In the chapters to follow I consider the application of the domestic economy movement to the lives of rural women, what reformers and experts wanted, and the ways in which women chose what was workable in their world and for their circumstances.

1 The Farm Scene

EACH GENERATION IS MARKED BY ITS ACHIEVE-
ments and failures, identified forever with easy generalities that neatly
describe a period in American life. The Gay Nineties, Roaring Twenties, Age of Flight, and Progressive Era quickly identify and define
times in which America faced the uncharted world of the twentieth
century. Between the conspicuous materialism of the elite during the
Gay Nineties and the "anything goes" recklessness of the Roaring
Twenties there emerged other visions of America, tied together by their
emphasis on science and progressive reforms. John M. Cooper, Jr., called
these the "pivotal decades"—pivotal in the country's involvement with
international affairs and in its handling of domestic issues.[1]

As important, although Cooper did not elaborate, this period was a
turning point for American agriculture. The age of machines altered production methods, and the age of science reshaped traditional beliefs about
the land and its resources. The pivotal decades also brought major changes
for farm women, especially in how they went about their work and how
they defined themselves and their families. A movement based on domesticity and farm roles evolved whose ultimate design was to alter
women's thinking and to transform their environment.

The lives of rural women can not be evaluated outside the environment in which they lived. Agriculture was diverse, and so were

the females who bore the title "farm woman." To some observers of the time, these women were literate, forward thinkers. They were not to be overlooked in discussions of the New Woman, who had taken center stage in that period and had begun to contradict idealized Victorian images of gender. The New Woman was not stifled; she sought self-improvement and greater personal freedom than was deemed acceptable under nineteenth-century social dictates.

The popular media reflected this change. Women's magazines began to feature stories with New Woman heroines. Most centered on women who lived in cities or who left small towns for bigger, brighter places. Yet occasionally, as in the 1926–1927 *Woman's Home Companion*'s "Call of the House," rural women were represented. True, "Call of the House" cast rural women as secondary characters, but they had the crucial role of electing a prosperous ranch woman to the state senate. Although described as "lean, workworn, and sun-burned," these women shared the same outlook as the New Woman senator. Hand in hand with the New Woman image came the athletic, fresh-faced Outdoor Girl, who donned bloomers, swimsuits, and knickers and was often portrayed as a camper, hiker, or sports star. Farm girls and young, adventuresome, single homesteaders shared Outdoor Girl status in women's magazines and popular fiction. Two good examples are "Trail's End: The Story of a Girl's Experiences in Her Log Cabin on the Plains" (1915) and "The Loafer of the Paladora: The Story of a Girl's Pluck and Courage" (1903). In the first, the "city-smothered" heroine found freedom in homesteading; in the second, a west Texas girl "of ease and grace" claimed a wolf bounty to get the money needed for a "neat little dwelling built on her land."[2]

There were, in fact, early-twentieth-century women who homesteaded alone. In 1900, Rosa Kately left Minnesota at age twenty-five and took a claim near Anamoose, North Dakota. To fund the land improvements required under homesteading laws, she taught school and did domestic work. By 1902 she reported, "Have one more cow. My hens laid the first egg for me yesterday." Like Rosa Kately,

Mattie Gordon also put her modest teaching salary into her claim, located near Miller, South Dakota. By 1906 she owned a house, a well, and fencing and rented additional pastureland. Whether these individuals saw themselves as New Women or Outdoor Girls is debatable, but they filled those descriptions as popularized by the media.[3]

Single homesteaders were only a small portion of the group labeled "rural." A woman could belong to a succession of generations living on the same farm, or she could be a tenant like Ida Cross, who oversaw a Kansas farm from 1899 to 1910 and kept its accounts for another woman, an absentee landowner living in Illinois. Poor farming years mixed with better ones, but Cross was proud of the results: "I wish you could come and see for yourself that I have good farming done on the land." Cross was not exceptional. In 1900 an estimated 300,000 women made their living as farmers, tenants, or overseers; farming was the sixth largest occupation for women. Women's presence was recognized and worthy of comment. Said the *South Dakota Farmer* in 1917: "As a rule women make successful farmers. Many cases might be cited and names given of women who have developed great business ability in this line." Woman suffrage advocates agreed and held up rural women as an argument for female voting rights: "They are making no noisy or threatening clamor for equal rights. They are simply showing by what they do [in farm work and community involvement] that they are the equal of man, and that the ballot in their hands would not only be safe, but wisely used."[4]

Defining rural women depended largely upon individual perspective. Some saw women in terms of ethnicity—particularly as immigrants, insulated and following Old Country traditions. Some women were defined by their work, either as farm domestics or as migrant or day laborers. Immigrants, American-born whites, and Asian and Hispanic women worked in truck gardens and orchards, and in 1900 about 440,000 black women earned wages as field laborers, especially in cane, tobacco, and cotton cultivation and harvesting.[5]

One historian has written that it would be reasonable to assume that farm women's work and its importance to the national economy gave them a status superior to that of urban, middle-class females. The reality, however, wrote the historian, was not borne out by the women themselves or by any blurred divisions of responsibility between male and female labor. This analysis of women's status is based on the heavy, demanding work—men's work—performed by many women. It cannot be denied that such work occurred; its presence drew comment and various explanations.[6]

Some closest to agriculture echoed the long-standing belief that only immigrant women worked in fields. Writing of her North Dakota neighbors, Mary Woodward observed: "Elsie is plowing for her father, a stingy old German who makes the women work out of doors. He thinks an hour long enough for them to prepare a meal, and affords them only the necessities of life, though he owns a half section of land." Expressing similar sentiments, a Kansas woman looked with disgust at men who allowed, or forced, women to perform outdoor labor: "I have never worked outdoors as a regular habit and feel my husband has done as well financially as those men whose wives work in the field." One man remembered that his mother never worked outside "like some other neighboring women [who] did the milking and nearly all of the gardening." The reason was simple: "She had all she could do to try to cook and wash and iron and mend clothes."[7]

Nevertheless, women did perform outdoor work, either because they were paid field hands or because, on the family farm, there was no one else to do it. Wrote an observer of recently arrived Japanese farmers in Texas, "On the truck farms, where women are found, they aid materially in the cultivation of the garden crops, helping their husbands to weed, cultivate and harvest the vegetables." Outdoor life was also the norm for Ozetta Sullivan, who bluntly said what she thought of it: "Well, I've had my equal rights all of my life, and I don't think much of it. I said if a woman wants to get out and work like a man, that's all right, but I had to do it whether I wanted to or not. I worked in the fields. I plowed. I cultivated. I disked. I done every-thing a man does, and I wasn't enjoying it one bit."[8]

Many women, however, voiced few if any complaints. When im-migrant and American-born hands on Chicago-area truck farms were interviewed by social workers in 1924, most said they liked the work. One even called it a "vacation" from the stench of her city neighbor-hood. (Considering that the neighborhood bounded the Chicago stockyards, it probably was a relief to get away.) The investigators were shocked. From their perspective, these women were exploited laborers, not unlike those who worked long hours in factories. The women, however, saw the situation differently; they had escaped fac-tory work for something better. If the interviewers were surprised by this attitude, they may have had the same reaction at encountering women such as Carrie Miller, who homesteaded with her family in South Dakota in 1907, or Josephine Boltz, whose family moved to a western Kansas farm in 1910. These women did not seem to mind outside work. Remembered Boltz: "I always helped with the teams when [my father] came in at noon and in the evenings, and one sum-mer I helped cultivate a good-sized acreage of cane—I was much more at home outdoors than in the kitchen and it fell to Virginia [my sis-ter] to help mother there."[9]

Conflicting observations and testimony both support and contra-dict the assertion that farm women had, or expected, no special sta-tus. The difference may be that, although women may not have enjoyed a particular task, they saw beyond it to their contributions for economic survival. Their labor was essential, and they knew it. True, some women had no choice other than to work outside, but others chose the outdoors over housework. Perhaps the problem in definition results from historical interpretations that allow too little latitude for individual experiences, that picture women as subjugated by gender, and that assume that nineteenth-century dictates for ur-ban women permeated rural life.[10] For farm women, gender did not necessarily determine experience. The multitude of ways in which women engaged themselves in agriculture suggests that Victorian gender roles had limited applications in a world where distinctions between male and female labor often failed.

Personal accounts also suggest something else. Unlike many town women who knew little of their husbands' work or business affairs, rural women were intimately involved. They were aware of farm operations and market prices, and they generated income. Louise Ritter, writing from Nebraska to relatives in Switzerland, outlined the year's assets for 1906: "The corn we sold last Monday yielded $610. In addition, we sold this summer 100 hogs and 45 head of cattle (42 bulls, 3 cows), all fed with corn we raised. We received $4000 for them." Ritter did not record how much she personally contributed to the planting of corn or raising of stock, but many women did. Grace Fairchild in South Dakota was instrumental in devising innovative production methods for her farm's operation. She was not alone; other women planned and implemented money-making projects. Mabel Hickey McManus remembered that during her South Dakota childhood it was her job to churn butter, which her mother then prepared for sale: "Butter for sale was molded in a pound mold, and wrapped in wet sterilized white cloths. Delivery to customers was made early in the morning before the heat of the day and because of this careful process our butter was sold for four or more cents a pound more than other butter. The top price we ever received for butter was twenty cents a pound." And there was the woman who, as a ten-year-old, had been responsible for taking eggs to town for sale. Crated eggs were tied to a buggy, which she drove alone, twelve miles round-trip. "And mom would give me a list of the things she needed. And then oftentimes she would tell me if there was extra money. . . . [T]hen I could buy something extra . . . [a] treat, maybe like raisins or canned fruit or something special that we didn't have." Neither she nor her parents questioned her self-reliance or ability to carry out the task.[11]

Not unlike pioneer women of earlier generations, farm women of the early 1900s were viewed contemporaneously, and now with hindsight, in a generally positive light. Perhaps the only difference is that women of the frontier have been assigned more heroic attributes, such as stalwartness and bravery. Farm women as a group, and certainly those of the early twentieth century, have not received such praise, perhaps in part because paid field workers were invisible and beneath comment except to a few reformers and women who evoked the more traditional images of farm wife and girl were considered "settled."

This idea of being established on the land itself presumes much about farm living. Somehow it is expected that conditions for women during the settlement of a particular region had little relationship to later periods. In reality, there was no great leap. Improvements in material and financial status came slowly for most; for some, they came not at all. Differences had more to do with the availability of material goods at a certain time and place and how they shaped domestic tasks. A writer of settlement in Oklahoma Territory noted that most homesteaders owned cast-iron stoves. Thus, it was unlikely that even the most primitive first homes had open fireplaces for cooking; they simply were not needed. The same was true in other areas; a Kansas woman, "writing in my far western home," supplied the information, "This morning I sawed a new stove-pipe hole through the roof [of the dug out] and put up a tin to run the pipe out through." The picture of a country woman at the turn of the century working over an open fire, pulling iron skillets from the coals, did not conform to what most women experienced. Home chores remained consistent, however. Tools evolved, but daily tasks remained the same across time. Raising a garden, struggling to do the most basic chores with no ready water supply, sewing, and seasonal work such as butchering were no less familiar to settled farm women than they had been to the first pioneers in an area. Wrote a Nebraska woman in 1922, long after the state's frontier period: "We butchered this week, and yesterday I rendered down thirteen gallons of lard."[12]

Regionalism itself is a question. Certainly, location determined forms of agriculture. Climate, geography, and soil composition affected not only what could be raised and cultivated but also how people lived on the land and adapted to their surroundings. Across regional lines, however, rural women shared many of the same experiences. Thus, although cotton reigned as a crop in the South and wheat dominated sections of the central Plains, women in these areas exhibited similar living patterns. Regionalism played a smaller role in defining these women than did the fact that they were rural. As Elizabeth Hampsten points out in *Read This Only to Yourself*, regionalism does not spring from the pages of rural women's writings. Often it is difficult to identify the state or section of the nation in which the writing occurred.[13] The same point is made by Eleanor Arnold in discussing an oral history project conducted by the National Extension Homemakers Council:

> Perhaps the most outstanding finding of the research has been the simple fact that [rural] homemaking experiences are so universal. Butchering in Hawaii and Alabama is so much the same; washing by hand on a washboard knows no state limits. . . . Backgrounds vary from ranches to farms; from treeless prairies to sandy swamps; from old established communities to new settlements; but the homemaker still fulfills the basic function of keeping the family intact.[14]

There were constants in rural life, but the agrarian environment was not static. The farm scene evolved in the first decades of the twentieth century. Advances in science, technology, and the dissemination of information and goods directly influenced rural America. Changes in material culture and social thinking dramatically affected landscape and people. They certainly influenced women and their surroundings. A Kansas woman in 1929 remarked: "Kansas kitchens in the sodhouses of the nineties were very different from the well equipped laboratory-like kitchens of today. They were different because they belonged in different types of houses, to a different people, and filled a different need." The comparison is important. In this woman's lifetime, women not only reacted to unbelievable changes but embraced them, becoming "different people" from their mothers and grandmothers. The Kansas woman saw these changes as positive, as did a South Dakota woman who wrote that whatever the challenges in rural life, she had no higher ambition than that her daughters "become the wives and mothers of good, intelligent, independent farmers. In fact I cannot see that there is any higher goal that any woman can attain."[15]

This statement is an example of agrarian boosterism, but it is also eyewitness testimony to a changing environment. Whatever her own circumstances, this South Dakota woman saw something important happening. At the beginning of the twentieth century, agriculturalists looked increasingly to technology and science to improve the quality of life and to solve every problem. They investigated electricity for the conveniences it could bring. Of interest too were the telephone and radio, both capable of reducing isolation and expanding access to information. For women, the benefits were basic: "To one who has never experienced the solitude of the farm it is hard to realize the joy of the wife and mother at being able to consult [by telephone] a friend about the cut of the baby's coat, the recipe for mince pies or the dose of cough syrup."[16]

Rural Free Delivery, aided by improved roadways and mechanized transport, brought the outside world closer. Where such delivery was unavailable, U.S. Postal Service contractors ran the Star Routes, delivering letters, newspapers, and magazines directly to patrons or to outlying postal stations. These services also brought clothing, household utensils, books, farm implements, and poultry ordered from catalogs and transported by railroad to the nearest town. It was not unusual, said one rural Kansas mail carrier, for his local post office to be filled with crates of cheeping baby chicks ordered from Sears, Roebuck and Company. The crates were lashed onto the mail car and delivered to waiting farm families. Accessibility to goods expanded as businesses used a laboratory approach to create mass production and marketing strategies. These methods found application in areas as diverse as canned food and precut frames for buildings. Technology, new and improved products, and scientific research opened the door to a new age.[17]

One newspaper called these material changes nothing short of a revolution for rural residents. Such transformations meant that women's "lot has been improved. . . . The 'separator' and the creamery have relieved her of the severest toil of the dairy. The rural free delivery brings magazines and newspapers to her door. Lately the telephone has put her within distance to her neighbors." Women, along with men, could see changes unimagined a generation earlier.[18]

Science, its products, and a growing business in advertising to promote those goods were becoming powerful forces in national culture. As important was the emergence of experts, specialists in an increasingly complex world that no longer seemed to yield easy answers. Experts in everything from business management to child rearing looked to the sureness of science and evolving technology to plot work, business, and play. America entered an age of increased mechanization and new inventions. People talked about having a "get up and go" attitude. Ignoring the way of the future meant being left behind economically and socially.

This was the Progressive Era, when reformers were bent on sweeping away old ideas and social structures that allowed abuses. Suffrage, temperance, child labor, urban reform, agrarian reform, and control of big business all had their supporters and detractors. Theodore Roosevelt preserved land for national forests and parks; Jane Addams worked to improve the lives of the immigrant poor. Americans were intent on correcting ills brought on by the industrial age and solidifying the national culture under an umbrella of progress and reform. Experts in the developing specialties of sociology, social work, medicine, psychology, education, economics, and business management attempted to define what the world should be. Authorities on agriculture and rural life teamed with urban social workers and reformers. Knowledge was empirical, not intuitive. There was less room for leadership from laymen; more often, it was expected to come from trained experts and specialists. These new professionals were sure of their approaches to problem solving and better living.

For agriculture, this trend brought an influx of experts preaching the virtues of scientific farming. Certainly, the idea of being a "book farmer," of following science-directed methods rather than traditional ones, was not new. Throughout the nineteenth century, farmers were encouraged to learn the rudiments of science and to apply these in eradicating farm pests, improving soil, and raising better stocks of animals and plants. The message, however, did not gain a wide audience until the end of the century. By then, farmers and ranchers had faced boom markets and bust years. Grasshopper plagues and droughts on the central Plains drove many off the land during the 1870s. By that decade's end, boosters conceded that "land broken this year may hardly provide for the body's nourishment, and it may do little better next year." The optimistic urged farmers to wait, and little by little "we shall reach a greater degree of condition and excellence." For many, however, the promise failed. The 1890s were as devastating as the 1870s with droughts, crop failures, and grasshopper plagues. As historian Gilbert Fite noted, the drought of the 1890s "laid to rest for all time the idea that rainfall followed the plow." At the same time, a national economic depression brought low market prices and an agrarian revolt over freight rates and market incomes. Farmers not only organized but also began to see themselves as part of an economic whole. To stay on the land, to exploit and develop it to its full potential, and to earn a living, farmers must realized that new techniques were needed.[19]

At the same time, additional lands opened for settlement. Frederick Jackson Turner, using the 1890 census as his source, declared the frontier closed, but emigrant trains continued to deliver settlers to the western Dakotas, eastern Colorado, Wyoming, Montana, and Idaho. The open lands that still remained were the most inhospitable to traditional farming methods. For would-be farmers and ranchers to succeed, they needed the assistance of specialists in "dry farming" and irrigation, as well as hardy livestock and seed strains adapted to the environment. Farm families in the already settled regions of the country were equally in need of advanced knowledge. Those who had survived pioneer days and sustained several generations on a single piece of ground realized the need for innovative methods. Improved machinery and scientific knowledge presented new possibilities for making a living from the land.[20]

Thus, beginning in the 1890s, the scientific farming movement gained momentum. Likened to a religious crusade, it was a new gospel seeking converts:

> Fifty years ago the circuit rider, a bible in his saddlebags, was a familiar figure in the woods, making his house to house visits among the settlers, to look after their spiritual welfare. His place today is taken by a missionary of another type, the government farm demonstration agent, who, often similarly mounted, calls from farm to farm and whose mission ultimately results in spiritual betterment through improvement of material conditions. Instead of the bible, the modern messenger of the gospel of better farming carries government bulletins and a little record book, in which he enters the names of those who desire to turn over a new leaf and lead a better cultural life.[21]

Scientific farming encompassed many things. Better seed, improved livestock strains, and controlled soil treatments spelled greater productivity, but agriculturalists also learned basic business principles of production, marketing, and distribution. Rural families were encouraged to think of themselves as capitalists, not simply laborers. The point was essential for changing mind-sets. Additionally, farm families, regardless of whether they owned the land they worked, were directed toward mechanization and conveniences that added to home life. Both became important themes for homemaker education. For rural residents in general, the lessons were clear.

Agricultural colleges, organized under the Morrill Act of 1862 and supported by legislation in following years, naturally promoted the scientific farming movement. Professors from these colleges conducted farmers' institutes, published bulletins on specialized subjects, and gave on-site talks and demonstrations. Considered a part of land-grant schools' extension service for those unable to attend college, these forms of education reached thousands. By 1920 every state and territory except Alaska had an agricultural college or a state university providing agricultural courses, and seventeen states had such an institution for blacks only. (Beginning in 1890, these received federal money.) All schools, including those for blacks, engaged in extension work. Tuskegee Institute, for instance, hired its first farm extension agent in 1906 and fitted up a special wagon with seed and fertilizer samples, examples of farm equipment, and appliances such as butter churns and cream separators. The Tuskegee agent traveled throughout Alabama giving talks and demonstrations to black farmers, but he also attracted a number of whites with his message of scientific farming.[22]

In every region, extension work was a primary function of agricultural schools. In this they were supported by the American Farm Bureau, which evolved from private local groups into county and then state federations. The Farm Bureau's ties to extension work were so close that it was often difficult to separate its programs from those of agricultural colleges, which began to send teaching faculty into communities before the turn of the century. In 1915 a national magazine, the *Country Gentleman*, praised extension services in general and defended agricultural schools against those who called them provincial. They, their staff, and their programs were the "backbone of America" making available "service education for every last man and woman, son and daughter." A South Dakota–based farm magazine vehemently agreed: "The old type of farmstead must go and the State College is in the foremost ranks of those who are waging the fight. The time has come when the farm must be run efficiently in all departments."[23]

Through agricultural colleges, the federal government, and the Farm Bureau (with almost seven hundred county units by 1919), male extension agents served at the grassroots level. When a report from Texas spoke of a Walker County couple who sought and then followed an agent's advice, the results were called typical for those striving to be scientific. The couple expanded production, added purebred cattle to their herd, and planted an orchard; these, in turn, brought enough financial stability to pay for material comforts, house remodeling, and the addition of "waterworks and a bath tub." This case, along with others cited by agents or the agrarian press, illustrated what could be achieved. In 1906, for example, the *South Dakota Farmer* offered the story of two Minnesota brothers who had the most perfect "horseless farm"; tractors had replaced horses in the fields, and the brothers "even go to town and market with a motor car." Then there was the Brown County, South Dakota, family that installed electricity and running water and enjoyed "all the conveniences of city life with none of its drawbacks."[24]

The federal government sanctioned extension activities with the 1914 Smith-Lever Act. Meanwhile, the U.S. Department of Agriculture (USDA), railroad companies, agricultural schools, and various farm groups established traveling education programs known as demonstration trains. Innovative in their approach, these trains appeared at the turn of the century, crisscrossing their respective regions to spread the word of better farming. With names such as the Opportunity Special, the Diversified Special, and the Alfalfa Special, these trains, not unlike Tuskegee's traveling wagon, were "movable schools of agriculture." As early as 1898, Iowa's agricultural college sponsored "farm and home excursions," bringing visitors to the campus for a first-hand look at agricultural programs and research experiments.

Most trains, however, went out to the people. All regions of the country, including the Plains states, saw demonstration trains. In 1912 the Rock Island Railroad crossed Kansas with a Wheat Train. The next year the Atchison, Topeka & Santa Fe Railroad reported that it had cooperated with Oklahoma's agricultural school to teach that state's farmers "the need and value of better poultry, hogs, kafir corn, the advantages of silos, and how best to increase the acreage of al-falfa." The numbers visiting demonstration trains were at times stag-gering. Between 1912 and 1923, the Union Pacific Railroad operated five Livestock Specials in Kansas, with a total attendance of over 58,000. In 1924 alone, the Santa Fe's Cow, Sow, and Hen Specials in Kansas, Texas, Oklahoma, and New Mexico attracted almost 400,000 visitors. And the Union Pacific's Kaw Valley Potato Train ran for only five days in 1922, but it instructed almost 3,000 in Kansas.[25]

The ability of traveling classrooms to reach thousands was not lost on the federal government. The USDA called demonstration trains one of the most promising forms of rural education. As early as 1901 the department, along with the National Good Roads Association and the U.S. Bureau of Public Roads Inquiries, sponsored a Good Roads Special. The government hoped to convey the idea that "upon the prairies of the west admirable roads can be constructed at com-paratively small cost." When these were built in Texas, they were designated "farm-to-market" roads; no matter where road building occurred, the plan was to improve access to marketing points and to reduce isolation. Later, in 1914, the USDA sponsored a Poultry and Egg Demonstration Car that began in Texas and worked its way through Oklahoma, Kansas, Missouri, and Arkansas. This train showed how to cut waste and spoilage in eggs and poultry sent to market. It was of special interest to women, who often were responsible for these products.[26]

Demonstration trains were designed to educate farmers and ranch-ers, but the sponsors had a selfish interest: If production rose, more farm goods would be shipped to market by rail. Thus, railroads prof-ited from increased freight activity, and in new settlement areas they gained from the sale of their lands. The Northern Pacific, for ex-ample, launched demonstration trains to attract more buyers for its Montana acreage. Demonstration trains allowed agricultural schools to carry out their mandate and educate thousands, not just the hundreds that attended the standard farmers' institutes or college short courses, which lasted just a few weeks. For the federal government, trains provided an opportunity to educate the rural population, increase agricultural production and quality, and encourage improvements such as paved roads, which the government was unwilling to undertake until 1916 when Congress passed the first Federal Aid to Roads Act.[27]

During this era, colleges and the USDA added faculty and staff. These included architects devoted to improving the physical structure and environment of farm homes and rural schools; community planners concerned with building neighborhood parks in rural areas, where few community centers existed; and education specialists. Along with these experts came sociologists intent on studying the interactions and living patterns of country folk. Social workers, medical staff, and child care providers augmented these specialists.

One result of this infusion of trained professionals was a structured sociological evaluation of the rural population. After all, experts had to identify and isolate problems peculiar to the group under analysis. As a field of study, sociology was almost nonexistent until the 1890s, when the Academy of Political and Social Sciences organized, paving the way for specialization. Most sociologists concentrated on elements of the urban world, but some delved into the new subject of rural sociology. An emerging part of academic curricula, this discipline was taught in approximately forty-four colleges by 1917. There were, however, varying interpretations of what the subject actually meant. A University of North Carolina professor considered rural sociology "a study of the group actions and reactions of human nature under country conditions," whereas a University of Utah scholar said it was "exposition of the social problems of rural life with suggestions for home and neighborhood amelioration." Whatever its definition, rural sociology became a course of study in Kansas, Iowa, Oklahoma, Texas, Wisconsin, and Minnesota agricultural schools.[28]

Agricultural colleges and farm organizations used sociological studies to evaluate what rural families did and did not have. A 1925 study
by the Kansas Committee on the Relation of Electricity to Agriculture, for example, found farm families extremely interested in apply-
ing electricity to kitchen and laundry. However, another study of
farmhouses and their "proper equipment" found that only 15 percent
of those surveyed had home generating plants for electricity. The gap
between what families hoped for and what they had could be staggering. Undaunted by the differences, a number of professionals used
study results to identify directions for educational programs, especially in extension services.[29]

On a more esoteric level, researchers attempted to decipher social
and cultural relationships within a community, often in the vain belief that any bit of information could yield mountains of truth about
a people. In one case, two sociologists studied motion picture preferences among country people. From information gathered in four rural communities in New England in 1926, the investigators made
sweeping generalizations about the farm population at large. Finding
that New England farmers favored action-packed Westerns—Tom Mix
was the favorite actor—but hated the films of Charlie Chaplin, the
sociologists determined, "Sophistication confuses them [rural people],
and psychological nuances are either ignored or resented. They are
accustomed to action rather than implication, objective events rather
than emphasis upon motives and mental processes." The authors did
not explain why the dramatic and sophisticated Gloria Swanson was
preferred over Lillian Gish and "America's Sweetheart," Mary
Pickford. Ambivalent conclusions also prevailed when Columbia
University, with *Woman's World* magazine, tried to learn how closely
rural women imitated the "fads and habits" of their metropolitan counterparts. In 1930 ten thousand questionnaires went out to rural community leaders, and about three thousand replies came back. From
this exercise, it was decided that an overwhelming majority of rural
women approved of Prohibition but that smoking, growing in popu-

larity among city women, was almost unheard of among farm women—
except, that is, among girls who had "been away to school" and among
women of the South, where the tobacco tradition predated urbane
sophistication. Wrote one respondent, "We women have too many
interesting things to do . . . so we do not want to reach for a sweet or
a Lucky." Meanwhile, it was found that farm women were as concerned as those in town with staying up to date in dress styles. In
conclusion, the survey decided that rural women in "practices and
ideas" made "intelligent selections" from the urban culture. The im-
plicit assumption was that rural women were influenced by urban
America but not vice versa.[30]

The ongoing rush to dissect America's rural population began with
President Theodore Roosevelt's 1908 Country Life Commission. Not
overwhelmingly accepted by the USDA and some farm organizations,
the commission drew mixed response. A South Dakota farm paper
spoke for many when it called the commission "distinctly novel, if
not paternalistic" in its attempt to "study conditions on the farm and
suggest ways of improving the business and social life of the rural
districts." Nevertheless, over half a million questionnaires went to
farmers and rural leaders. Responses, numbering about ninety-four
thousand, were used to identify problems and suggest improvements.
Based on these data and the commissioners' own fact-finding work,
the final report underlined two basic handicaps in country living—
handicaps decried many times over by reformers.[31]

One major shortcoming, said the commission, was a lack of "organized rural society"; farmers were too much the individualists. The
conclusion itself was startling. After all, "rugged individualism" was a
valued American trait and exemplified the agrarian myth of frontier
settlement. Additionally, it can be argued that by the late 1800s individualism had diminished. Farmers had united to form the Grange,
collectively protested through the People's Party, and later joined the
Nonpartisan League and Green Corn Rebellion. The commission,
however, overlooked these facts. The questionnaire asked if farmers

and their wives were "satisfactorily organized to promote their mu-
tual buying and selling interest." The answer was a resounding "no."
Respondents intended to signal that more work was needed to establish farm co-operatives, but the commission made a broader interpretation. Overlooking agrarian protests and strides made toward creating
co-operative enterprises, the commission declared individualism and
the inability to work together rural faults. Dwight Sanderson, a noted
rural sociologist at the University of Chicago and later Columbia
University, repeated the sentiment. He was not alone. Many others, including fiction writers, often portrayed farmers as willing to help their
neighbors but suspicious of joining thousands in a common cause.[32]

Educators at agricultural colleges agreed with this view. Among
the more scathing analyses to appear was that of L. L. Bernard, a
University of Missouri professor of rural sociology. Labeling farmers
emotionally unstable, impulsive, and lacking any interest in social
welfare, Bernard declared that they failed in teamwork because they
were too bent on doing things their own way. Bernard may have over-
stated, if not wholly misinterpreted, the agrarian mentality, but both
the USDA and agricultural schools generally agreed that individualism was an obstacle to cohesion in rural society. Kansas State Agricultural College concurred in 1915 with its published findings on
"community welfare," determining that country districts had not taken
adequate steps to organize economically or socially. Using a USDA
publication as its guide, the report called for a "uniform national plan"
to bring about organization.[33]

The Kansas experts accepted the argument that individualism was
a blight, but they had no corrective proposal. The USDA, however,
had definite ideas. One was the creation of community centers where
instruction, club meetings, church services, local fairs, and Americanization classes would erase individuality, induce conformity, and
bring a "revival of the spirit of cooperation." More important, in 1914
the USDA outlined a comprehensive organizational plan based on
interlocking local committees. These would develop marketing and

distribution strategies, find financing and suppliers of farm materials at reasonable rates, and establish sanitation, beautification, and social programs. The USDA would have disavowed suggestions that it favored a model for communal living, with each individual responsible for the good of the whole. Its plan, however, argued that individuals were served when community uplift came first. The agency believed its idea would solve problems, preserve the small farm, and shape the rural population into a team. Ultimately, the agency predicted, the way would open for "city" ideas.[34]

The second great defect in rural life, decided Roosevelt's commission, was education. Farmers were asked if local schools satisfactorily trained boys and girls for life on the farm. The answer, by only a slight majority, was "no." In this case, country schools and teachers became the scapegoats for much that afflicted agriculture in general. Poor education, the commission said, produced "ineffective farming, lack of ideals, and the drift to town." To reverse the situation, schools would have to address the world in which rural youngsters lived. Instruction should teach the importance of farm life, instill the American vision of agriculture—more aptly stated, the agrarian myth—and bring a level of academic excellence found in progressive urban environments.[35]

In addition to focusing on what it called the two greatest problems, the commission noted secondary concerns. These included a declining number of seasonal laborers (at the same time that nonresident landownership was on the rise), depletion of soil quality where one-crop agriculture prevailed, lack of paved roads, and inadequate health care. Rather incidentally, the commission noted heavy work performed by women as an issue bearing further scrutiny.[36]

Following the commission's work came a series of rural life conferences at the end of World War I. These were organized because so many forces were working for rural progress that agencies were actually in each other's way. National Country Life Conference organizers hoped to integrate programs and reduce overlap. Voices most often heard at these meetings were those of academics, the majority of them from the eastern United States. At the 1918 conference only two speakers came from west of the Alleghenies—a University of Wisconsin professor, who spoke on rural sociology, and a professor from the University of North Dakota, who addressed improved communication's effects on rural life. Generally, experts talked to experts at these gatherings, excluding the population with which they seemed so concerned. Perhaps this lopsided representation was recognized, for in 1923, when the annual meeting became known as the Conference of the American Country Life Association, nonacademics were invited. The theme that year was "The Rural Home"; a woman from Ames, Iowa, spoke on farm boys and girls, and one from Missouri presented the "farm woman's viewpoint." Generally, however, conferences included only professionals. The list of attendees at the 1924 National Council of Agencies Engaged in Rural Social Work provides a good illustration: The National Catholic Welfare Conference, Russell Sage Foundation, National Congress of Parents and Teachers, USDA, American Home Economics Association, American Red Cross, and Young Woman's Christian Association all participated. The meeting concluded that agencies were seeing little success in "really reaching the people who actually live on the farms." Although no effort was made to include rural residents in the conference, meeting participants expressed genuine confusion as to what was wrong. It was, said professor A. R. Mann of Cornell, the experts' problem. They overlooked the possibility that "superimposed organizations are usually doomed to failure because they express the judgments of those without the community rather than those within whom they are intended to serve."[37]

Mann was correct, but rural residents were not immune to change. Many jumped on the progressive bandwagon. Communities formed neighborhood improvement clubs, which addressed everything from economic development to health care. Some rural districts concentrated on establishing a community building. The new center in Kittson County, Minnesota, became a theater in which "plain common, everyday farm folks may display their musical and dramatic talents"; a similar edifice in Fairfield, Montana, was the site for community sings and chautauquas. Many rural Americans wanted to feel that they, too, could have city culture and entertainment, even if in most cases it was homemade. More important, farm families wanted telephones, electricity, and better schools. They knew that such amenities would not come immediately, though. Electrification and water systems were far in the future for some areas. So was telephone service. The 1920 agricultural census showed that two out of every five farm families had telephones. Nevertheless, in some remote areas and in the western mountain states, rugged country and great distances made phone service nearly impossible to provide. Perseverance was the key. As one farm newspaper observed, "The impatient reformer can not hope to bring about the millennium over night." Professor Mann agreed and cautioned colleagues: "In dealing with rural affairs it has long been a common mistake to underrate the validity of the farmer's own judgment as to what is good for him."[38]

Farmers and ranchers did decide what was good for them. They read informational bulletins from state colleges and the USDA and attended farmers' institutes and demonstration train visits. Scientific farming's message was accepted, and although its cumulative effects are incalculable, it can be said that the movement showed the farm population the possibilities for a better life and higher agricultural productivity. Growth in yields per acre and the rise in market and farm values may have been direct results, although it must be remembered that federal government hopes for education and productivity were accompanied by economic support. Well before World War I, the government gave financial aid to irrigation projects, promoted privately run farm co-operatives, and provided limited subsidies as well as direct payments to agricultural colleges and extension programs.[39]

No matter how it was achieved, a feeling of prosperity and optimism reigned in the early 1900s. Of the Kansas farmer, a periodical said: "In 1897, the Kansan stopped talking about wanting to sell out that he might go back East; in 1898, he was better contented; in 1899, he raised the price of his real estate and built a porch and bay window; in 1900 other improvements followed, and he congratulated himself on his foresight in having remained while so many left the state." A case in point was the Pratt family of western Kansas. When Jennie Pratt married in 1888, she became a "housekeeper, mother, wife and sheepherder," and by the mid-1890s the family's hard work produced dividends. The ranch flourished, and the Pratt home contained stained-glass windows, furniture from England, and a piano. Culture and finer material things were to be found in the isolation of open prairie. What was said of Kansas in general and the Pratts in particular also could be written of other states and their residents. In fact, though Roosevelt's commission found much to decry, it also observed, "There has never been a time when the American farmer was as well off as he is today."[40]

Signals were mixed. The years between 1900 and 1920 have been called a golden age in agriculture, full of hope and productivity. However, rural life conferences and pronouncements by rural sociologists seemed to think American farmers were in a terrible fix. The characterization of farmers as rubes and rustics, suspicious of each other and the world, seemed appropriate, especially when it was argued that their shortcomings left them "destitute of the ordinary provisions of life." World War I generated agricultural growth, but the aftermath brought economic woes. Inflated prices dropped significantly after the war, and a growing disparity existed between farm prices and production costs. In addition, rural America was losing its population to urban migration. Many blamed the war for luring young men off the farms, giving real meaning to the popular tune, "How 'Ya Gonna Keep 'Em Down on the Farm (After They've Seen Paree)." Concern turned to alarm when the 1920 U.S. census showed that, for the first time in the nation's history, urban residents outnumbered rural ones.[41]

For some, all of this augured an immediate collapse of agricultural America. Many foresaw the impending decline of the farm family.

Dwight Sanderson worried that, although the farm family seemed to be holding together as an economic unit, the social component was threatened. Among the culprits was one of the day's great innovations—mechanized transport. The automobile made the city and its "away-from-home" entertainments closer and more enticing to farm families, particularly impressionable youngsters. Sociologists and reformers found themselves in a bind. They encouraged modern inventions like the automobile and hailed radio and film as educational tools, but these same items might lure young people from home. If the siren song of modern life became too strong, it might cause a breakdown of the family and a rise in juvenile delinquency. Social workers had seen this happen in urban neighborhoods. They wondered if agrarian society was next.[42]

It suited any number of commentators to present the worst interpretation as an argument for reorganization and change. Conditions offered the experts an opportunity to preach scientific farming as a form of retrenchment, and reformers in general offered formulas for preventing social ills and creating economic success. The experts' hopes often were skewed. They expected rural residents to hold fast to the agrarian culture of the past yet, at the same time, to accept values imposed by a growing urbanized world. The message was stay on the farm, but imitate urban life.

Despite real problems and often contradictory expert opinion, there was optimism. Especially before World War I, positive agricultural statistics inspired confidence. In the central Plains, new varieties of seed were introduced, and sorghum grains joined wheat and corn as money-making crops. Production became not only more extensive in some areas but also generally more intensive per acre. "The aim of the farmer," said one newspaper, was not "to see how much he can cultivate, but how well he can do it, and how much he can make each acre produce." Farmland increased in value nationally.[43]

A side benefit to increased production and land values was diversification and growth in agriculture-related businesses. Companies manufacturing farm implements and small machinery such as milking machines saw advances. So, too, did the fledgling automobile companies; by 1920, 2.1 million cars and trucks were on farms, an average of one for every three farmers. Meanwhile, beef-packing and hybrid-seed industries boomed. Overlooked in this economic growth were the women who held stock in companies tied to agriculture. By 1930, 14 percent of the stockholders in Allis-Chalmers Manufacturing (producer of tractors and other farm equipment) were women; female stockholders in American Sugar made up 46 percent of the total; and 40 percent of those with stock in Swift and Company (meat packers) were women. Usually identified as "housewives," these women did not necessarily live on farms, but they were akin to female absentee landowners with a stake in agriculture's profitability.[44]

For those preaching the benefits of scientific farming, agricultural statistics and the growth of connected businesses seemed to bear out their faith in what could be accomplished. A USDA spokesman painted a rosy picture when he wrote, "The farmer is becoming more and more expert in using this scientific knowledge when it gets to him. The reward is not his alone; the Nation reaps a harvest in more meat from farms and ranges, more crops in fields, and better all-round development of its agricultural resources." This was certainly all well and good for the nation, but of most importance to farmers and ranchers were the positive results of better production and marketing methods.[45]

Amid the swirl of sociological studies, extension and science-directed education, new technology, and industrial growth, the role of farm women was evolving. For them, the Progressive Era brought changes in domesticity. Much of this change was material, but when means of production change, so do the workers. Women now had more choices in how to perform their chores. The wooden-tub washing machine (patented in 1863) evolved into newer, improved models and replaced the scrub board; the wood- or coal-burning stove was refined and competed with the oil- or gas-burning stove and then by the electric one; and installation of water pumps inside the kitchen or utility closet brought running water, although in 1950 more than half of America's farm homes still lacked complete water or sewage disposal systems.[46]

Although not every rural home had modern amenities, their existence suggested alternatives. Electricity, indoor plumbing, and the fixtures that came with them reshaped domestic chores. As important, these new conveniences influenced attitudes about what was important. Women began to see themselves and their work in a different way. Sentiment for the traditional ways of doing things held little allure if new ones eased their lives. In the words of Florence Ward, a USDA employee, the country woman was often "conservative and inclined to question the value of things new and untried," but she expressed an "openmindedness and a forward-looking spirit" when convinced that new methods brought desired results.[47]

With the dawn of the twentieth century, American society saw itself on an upward spiral of progress and modernity. For experts, the domestic economy movement was simply part of the nation's advancement. Some women actively pursued the movement's goals; others passively absorbed its messages. Not all women understood how the movement would change their lives or what it would demand of or mean to them and their families. As never before, rural women drew the attention of experts and reformers. In part, they placed themselves in the limelight by complaining of inequitable educational opportunities and a widening gap between urban and rural amenities. They demanded recognition at a time when a multitude of interests were addressing agrarian society. Women were not to be ignored during this pivotal era.

𝒵 A Life of Domestic Economy

OLIVE CAPPER, A YOUNG WOMAN LIVING WITH her family on a farm in north-central Kansas, kept a diary in which she recorded her activities and those of family members. She noted social gatherings and her work for two nearby families that occasionally hired her to help with domestic chores. No self-examination or introspection filled Olive's 1895 diary. Only concrete realities of daily life and work appeared.

> August 30—I cleaned some pie plant [rhubarb] ironed some
> & sewed some and helped peel peaches in the evening.

> November 12—Pa shucked corn Ma sewed and patched I
> ironed and baked 7 loaves of bread in afternoon.[1]

For Olive and her family, life was a round of chores broken by neighborly visits, trips to town, and social activities. Her mother made butter for sale; her father threshed wheat and planted corn. They were a typical farm family, representing just the group that agricultural colleges and education professionals hoped to reach and influence with the message of scientific farming.

If men saw benefits in following farm experts' advice, so, too, did their wives and daughters. Many women were as interested as men were in learning about the correct feeding of livestock, the possibili-

39

ties of electric incubators for baby chicks, and how to fight insects that attacked their gardens. Scientific farming attracted both male and female followers. Experts, however, began to argue for an organized movement directed at women, something that could coexist with the scientific farming campaign. The result was the domestic economy movement, devoted to improving and streamlining women's labor through the application of scientific strategies to everyday chores. Whereas scientific farming emphasized mechanized equipment, land management, and purebred livestock, the domestic economy movement focused on home utensils, mechanized appliances, and an improved work environment. These were essential components of women's contributions to the family's economic well-being and stability. By rethinking basic work habits and learning to manage time and environment, women would be more effective and exert greater control over their labor and expenditure of energy. What scientific farming offered agriculturists, domestic economy emphasized for women.

Professionals in several fields—from home economics to business management—joined the movement, offering advice and direct interaction, but it was a woman's choice to be involved. At its beginning and through its maturation, the domestic economy movement was a self-help program. It gained acceptance because rural women believed that it had something to offer and that they had the intelligence and ability to apply its lessons.

The domestic economy movement relied on modern approaches, but it borrowed from female education traditions established in the 1800s. Nineteenth-century domestic training was directed at all socioeconomic groups, with differing intents for each. Young women of the middle and upper classes were advised to pursue domestic studies in preparation for marriage and the running of a household. For those of lower socioeconomic status, as well as immigrant and nonwhite populations, domestic training taught skills needed to work as domestic servants or to become "American" housewives. In the latter case, there was a missionary quality to lessons. Certainly, many in-structors saw themselves as ministering to uninformed masses.

Domestic economy instruction occurred in places as diverse as the women involved. Before the Civil War, some progressive girls' schools already included domestic studies; by the late 1800s land-grant colleges had added classes. During this era, schools for native Americans attempted to instill white culture by teaching agriculture and domesticity. When South Dakota's Pierre Indian School or North Dakota's Fort Totten Indian Industrial School reported that girls learned table etiquette and preparation of "good wholesome food," the emphasis was on transmitting white values. The same was true of attempts to educate specific groups of new settlers. Jessie Hoover, a home economist, wrote that European immigrants arriving in west-ern states were "anxious to learn not only the methods of farming presented by the agricultural college, but also the customs of the home." She assumed Native Americans and blacks felt the same way. Indeed, soon after the black settlement of Nicodemus, Kansas, was established, a white woman visited in 1879. This individual, Mrs. Elch, went from house to house teaching "domestic science [that] included making patterns for clothing, brading [sic] grass to make hats or mats, sewing, crocheting, and embroidering." She was "kindly re-ceived," despite her tendency to "preach" rather than to instruct. Undoubtedly, Mrs. Elch was influenced by urban charity schools that attempted the same sort of education with newly arrived immigrants and the destitute classes. New York's Association for Improving the Condition of the Poor sent home economists into tenements, and the Young Woman's Christian Association provided domestic instruc-tion in city night schools. Institutions such as the Boston Domestic Reform League School of Housekeeping and the Chicago School of Domestic Arts and Sciences served the complementary purposes of training domestic servants and preparing middle- and upper-class women to work as teachers and social workers in settlement houses and charity schools.[2]

In rural areas, the domestic economy movement was an extension of well-established avenues for female education. The movement sometimes carried overtones of Indian education, which for almost a century forced assimilation. It also borrowed from schools for the urban poor, which meant to change household patterns and dilute ethnicity. As defined by urban advocates, the movement emphasized domesticity in terms of middle-class nineteenth-century ideals for women's roles. It adhered to traditional notions of masculinity and femininity, which assumed that men and women existed in separate spheres of work. Women were considered dependent and did not work outside the home, as doing so betrayed their husbands' masculinity and ability to play the role of provider. This, of course, was a point of view under revision with the onslaught of the New Woman image, but Victorian remnants remained.

Some rural women may have articulated such views of femininity, but these were often unworkable, if not artificial. The necessities of getting a crop harvested or a garden planted precluded dependent femininity. The realities of rural life could not, and did not, accommodate Victorian expectations. Therefore, the urban domestic economy movement was modified by experts in the USDA, agricultural colleges, farm organizations, the agrarian press, and women themselves to include the real world of rural domestic chores, farm labor, and contributions to an agricultural economy. As important, experts generally presented themselves as allies of and advocates for rural women. They believed that this approach made them and their message more acceptable. As experts and farm women interacted, portions of the movement's urban baggage were discarded. These had no use in a rural setting.

The domestic economy movement intended to reach rural women of all classes and backgrounds. Its first audience was found among blacks and American-born or European immigrant whites because they were the most likely to attend farmers' institutes. (There were some instances of institutes for Native Americans, but the direction taken for education at Indian schools and on reservations set Indian groups apart as having their own forms of education.) Domestic economy instruction was first provided by farmers' institutes, which were sponsored by farm organizations and agricultural schools and attempted to educate at the local level. Lectures, demonstrations, and sometimes visits to model farms and households provided information. Occasionally an institute included a female lecturer who dealt with such topics as diet, beekeeping, general home improvement, poultry care, or cleanliness in the dairy. Scientific farming topics overlapped with homemaking lessons. That some programs reached a female audience was encouraging, but colleges, the federal government, and rural specialists decided that this was not enough. They argued for consistent programming that related to homemaking and the outdoor chores that were most often within women's domain—care of the garden, dairy, and poultry.

Because rural women already attended farmers' institutes, these seemed a natural forum in which to build the domestic economy movement. Such institutes could serve a dual function: While men were treated to a lecture on the perils of hog cholera, the women could hear their own speakers. There would be direct contact between women and experts in specific areas. The topics themselves concerned women's work in the home and on the farm or ranch. With that in mind, Kansas State Agricultural College in 1906 announced that an "experiment will be made this year in many counties of having a separate meeting of women at the same time that the men are discussing some topic not of special interest to women." In the same year, South Dakota's agricultural school began women's programs.[3] These states, of course, were not alone. Institutes were utilized in a number of regions.

One of South Dakota's first institutes, held in Howard, was entitled, "The American Girl and the Home." It advised farm women "to learn the necessary and useful things that would make the home what it should be," leaving subjects such as Latin or music for last, if they were studied at all. After all, a little piano music would never take "the place of a good loaf of bread for a hungry man." Practical advice followed at later institutes. In January 1907 about two hundred women met in Sioux Falls to hear "what Mrs. Howie had to say about poultry": Mrs. Howie, in fact, admonished women for considering their hens only in "odd moments" and insisted that raising chickens could be a glorifying and financially rewarding experience. In this, as well as in other institutes that dealt with dairy or gardening, scientific farming strategies were not divorced from domestic chores. Mrs. Howie, for example, discussed the importance of purebred chickens, their types, and correct feeding methods. Knowing how to raise healthy chickens was as important as knowing how to cook them.[4]

In 1908 South Dakota's women's institutes took another direction when instructor Jessie Hoover demonstrated the application of science to food preparation. Comparable to institutes in Minnesota, Wisconsin, and Michigan that imitated urban cooking schools, Hoover's presentation focused on "fireless cooking." This was an early equivalent to present-day Crock-Pot cooking. Food was partially cooked in a conventional manner and then put into a porcelain pot, tightly lidded, and placed in a box, with wool, paper, or hay as outside packing. Sometimes small radiators were packed around the container for additional warmth. For women who could afford them, there were commercially manufactured fireless cookers. Whether store-bought or homemade, these appliances insulated food so that it slowly cooked for several hours. Hoover promised that "a woman need not be a slave to her kitchen if she will adopt this system." Food companies agreed. The makers of Royal Baking Powder published a cookbook with fireless-cooking recipes, noting that "while the time required for cooking is longer than in the usual methods, the actual time consumed in preparation of a meal is considerably reduced." It should have been easy enough, but, as one Kansas woman recalled, if the food was not well cooked beforehand or if the food was left in the fireless cooker too long, families faced a bout of food poisoning. Despite possible drawbacks, this method of preparation released work time for other chores and provided a modern approach. For her part, Hoover was proclaimed "a lady who thoroughly understands her subjects and is an interesting talker."[5]

Not every state offered institute programs for women, but the federal government reported that in 1910 alone 5,651 farmers' institutes were conducted in the United States and its territories. Of these, 444 included programs exclusively for women in 16 states. South Dakota's agricultural college reported that during 1913 women attended 168 institutes. The Kansas State Agricultural College continued to give farm women "any aid in institutes or by letters that is within its power," and in 1910 it initiated cooking schools to heighten women's "domestic economy knowledge." Nonetheless, by 1914 and the passage of the Smith-Lever Act, institutes were on the wane. They never reached a full national audience and became less important as new extension service programs were developed.[6]

Farmers' institutes were important first steps for reaching women, and the lecturers, like Jessie Hoover, were often professors in domestic science. Sometimes academically trained by the schools they represented and often members of the American Association for Farmers' Institutes Workers, these women were at the forefront of a rural movement that evolved in the age of science and technology. The movement met the expectations of its early advocates, placing domesticity on the level of a science. Under the direction of such women as nutritionist Ellen Swallow Richards, domestic science became a professionalized field of research and application. Largely because of Richards' work, it also had its own organization, the American Home Economics Association. Devoted to academic excellence and career development for women, this organization had 8,200 members by 1926.[7]

Summing up the movement's professionalization and its recognition as a science as legitimate as botany or zoology, Nellie Kedzie, a professor at Kansas State Agricultural College, wrote:

The question is often asked, Just what is domestic science?
We can only answer, It is classified domestic knowledge. The
classification means the application of knowledge to all kinds
of work, so that one cause will always be the same effect. It
means that cooking is to be done in such a way that good
food will always be the result; that good materials are never
to be ruined for lack of knowledge; that systematic work will
bring good results in the kitchen as well as in the factory; and
that the head of a house needs system and training in her
work as well as does the head of a bank. Domestic science
means the science of home making, and to anyone who has
made a home, the meaning is apparent.[8]

As Kedzie suggested, domestic economy meant successful homemaking achieved through "systematic work." This simple phrase cannot be overlooked. It signaled an essential component of domesticity:
logic in the performance of chores, the desire to place work on a
businesslike basis, the reliance on scientific management guidelines
found in American industry. The reference to "systematic work" was
no accident. It meant much more than keeping books and ledgers of
farm income; it meant imitating industrial strategies for full use of
resources and efficiency.

Scientific management grew out of the sustained economic down-
turn of the 1870s, which affected farmers and manufacturers alike. To
pull themselves out of the morass, industrialists began to examine
their factories and the ways in which resources were controlled, organized, distributed, and used. By 1895 problems and solutions were
analyzed by experts in the emerging field of scientific management.
Among the leaders in this arena was Frederick W. Taylor, who said
that technology brought labor-saving devices and changed work demands but that management methods had not kept pace. Industrial
productivity required that both machines and workers be fully employed. Taylor detailed the importance of trained managerial staff familiar with time and motion studies, which determined how long it

should take to complete a measured performance in output. Later, Lillian Moller Gilbreth, continuing research begun with her husband, studied ways to eliminate wasted motion and industrial fatigue. Results from studies in routings, actual steps taken, and cost per produced unit were used to create effective work management.[9]

Industrial America devoted itself to a modern age of science. In addition to creating new technologies, this sector followed the maxim that anything and everything could be measured. Logical approaches, not guesswork, would stave off economic ills. What worked for industry should serve agriculture, too, and many of the emerging strategies in business management were suggested for farm production. The idea was paradoxical. Farmers who had so recently denounced big business and joined the Populist movement were expected to imitate the very thing they despised. Nevertheless, farm-oriented publications such as *Farmer and Breeder* used the language of business. The magazine noted that farmers had less control than manufacturers over materials and processes because they could not completely control their work environment, especially the weather. If, however, farmers thought of the soil and other environmental factors as an "industrial plant," they could contrive artificial ways to manage more effectively. Farm men and women, said the magazine, had to realize that "the plan of rural life is coming to approximate urban life in its control of materials, plants and processes."[10]

Livestock was an industrial resource; farm implements were manufacturing tools; farm buildings were part of an industrial complex. The farm family was a corporation, with every member a stockholder. For women, this meant that "housekeeping is a business as practical as farming, and with no romance in it." To be successful, women had to grasp the fundamentals of household management, including control over time, work area, and finances. Indeed, control was the key to life. Women were urged to see themselves as business partners, farm managers, and purchasing agents. Observed *Farmer and Breeder*: "As soon as women realize that business principles are necessary for the best results in the management of their homes they will adopt the budget system of expenditure and look with disapproval on the old uncertain, haphazard way."[11]

Putting chores on the same level as business management required that everything be reevaluated. Both the agrarian press and popular media offered ideas. To save time in the kitchen, women were told to label storage tins and keep each in its own special place; to invest money wisely by buying proper utensils; and to keep a notebook of cleaning and household hints. Echoing this advice were Lydia Ray Balderston, a homemaking specialist at Columbia University and author of *Lippincott's Home Manual of Housewifery* (1919), and Christine Frederick, whose 1912 *Ladies Home Journal* articles and 1920 book, *Household Engineering: Scientific Management in the Home*, incorporated industrial management strategies. Also counted among expert publications was C. W. Taber's 1918 *The Business of Household*, which cast homemaking as a business. According to these and other educators, women were supposed to maintain filing systems of household hints, conduct inventories of clothing and larder contents, and analyze chores to better plan work and ultimately save time and labor. It was simply a case, said Margaret Reid at Iowa State College, of dividing work into categories—management and performance.[12] Women were told to organize their work areas and to have the right tools around them. The kitchen was a laboratory; food preparation was a studied calculation of calorie and nutrient intake; sewing and mending were garment construction; and household management in general revolved around efficiency in time and resource control. These were the sermons to be learned.

One could not hope to achieve a businesslike approach, however, with existing technology. To move into the twentieth century, new conveniences were necessary. Mail order and mass merchandising made goods more accessible, and advertisers made them more attractive. Aluminum and Pyrex cookware, for example, were widely touted in women's magazines and offered through mail-order catalogs.

Whether these were better than cast-iron cookware was beside the point; they were "new," modern utensils that no kitchen should be without—at least, so the advertisements said. These small items, however, were easier to obtain than the larger conveniences of electricity and running water. Power and water utilities were not usually close by, and a family incurred substantial costs when it decided to construct its own power plant or build a cistern, install running water, and arrange for sewage disposal. Nevertheless, experts said that such services could and should be put in. In Kansas, for one example, the land-grant college published bulletins that explained how to build self-contained farm electrical plants, how to buy power from a utility (if one was nearby), and how to use appliances correctly. A 1917 Kansas State publication cautioned, "electric ranges, because of their large kilowatt capacity, cannot be used in connection with farm lighting plants. However, socket appliances, such as the iron, the toaster and the percolator, may be used." Home generating plants for electricity, then, had their limitations. Today, the advice may seem oversimplistic, but it was a necessary beginning. As one woman recalled, people "just couldn't realize" the possibilities. Many women, in fact, could only imagine that electric lights would free them from cleaning the glass chimneys used on kerosene or gas lamps.[13]

Some rural residents regarded electricity, indoor plumbing, and powered appliances as creature comforts they had always done without and therefore did not need. Farm agents and agricultural reformers tried to quash this notion by arguing that such conveniences allowed everyone to work more effectively. Time saved in one chore was time freed to do another. When The USDA published a time-efficiency study for use of electricity on the farm, it was not an idle exercise. Pointedly, results suggested that if electricity saved 2.75 hours a week in churning butter and 3.83 hours in running a cream separator, every family should bring electricity into the home. Time would be saved and women would be allowed to work more efficiently.[14]

A further argument was that modern amenities would save women's health. Said one farm report, "All over this broad land we may find in our cemeteries little fresh mounds of earth over which there might appropriately be placed the inscription, 'She worked herself to death.'" Many believed this no exaggeration and concurred that there was little reason for women to labor long hours or perform duties that physically drained them beyond endurance. At a time when powered machinery was finding its way into all phases of agriculture, women should expect to have the same in their homes. "This is the age of machinery," observed one newspaper. "No woman ought to be permitted to break her back over the wash board, carrying water long distances, feeding hogs and calves, running back and forth many times to a cave [cellar for food supplies] several hundred feet from the house. . . . It is not necessary. . . . We must not waste our women as we have in the past." Often men were blamed for lack of home conveniences, but at times women were taken to task. If they made no attempt to learn and practice scientific household management techniques, said some, then women got just what they deserved—drudgery followed by an early death. "It is the duty of every woman, especially a mother, to spare herself as much as she possibly can. But when you come to look into the matter, you will half believe that they are bent on killing themselves." A modern farm woman would not subject herself to overwork when technology combined with careful work habits made it avoidable. Mary L. Bigelow, an editor for *Farm, Stock, and Home* magazine and the expert speaker at a 1919 South Dakota conference on "The Needs of the Farm Woman," summed up the situation: "Woman power is the most expensive kind of power known. A farm woman is not only a wife and mother, as are other women, but she is also her husband's business partner and in this relation alone, she should develop her greatest efficiency. This can only be done by capitalizing her energy most economically."[15]

Rhetoric and grand plans to introduce business ideas for manpower and efficiency did not spring full-blown onto the agricultural scene. In fact, translating industrial management from urban to rural environments could take on a look of the ridiculous. In 1899, the Boston Domestic Reform League School of Housekeeping conducted experiments to learn how long it took to use coal- and wood-burning stoves and then examined how this time could be reduced. Findings reported that in a six-day period, it took one hour and forty-eight minutes to tend fires, two hours and nine minutes to black the stove, and twenty minutes to shift ashes. What did such calculations mean for farm women? For some, like Anna Sorensen in North Dakota, they had little application. Fuel was not delivered to the door, as it was in Boston; Anna used coal, as there were few trees, and when that ran out, "we could get [railroad] ties [and] we went out into the ranch pastures. . . and picked up dried cow chips." Concluded Anna, "There is a saying, 'Out in the West, the wind draws the water, and the cows cut the wood.'" No time and motion studies could translate that homily.[16]

Nonetheless, over a span of years women began to believe that scientific applications for work and labor-saving devices had a place in the country. Slowly, the lessons of domestic economy moved from cooking and sewing and chicken feeding to a myriad of concerns about how people lived and conducted their affairs in the home and within their rural communities. In the beginning the movement stayed with basics, as evidenced by the subjects covered at farmers' institutes. Rightly, agricultural schools' extension programs focused on women's immediate needs and pointed out the best ways to prepare food, raise more productive cows or better gardens, and increase quality in salable commodities.

Application of this knowledge, said the experts, would make adult women better farm wives and mothers and prepare girls for their expected futures as homemakers. In an article suitably titled "While She Waits," a Kansas writer suggested that girls could not necessarily learn modern homemaking from their mothers. In fact, many women in new settlement areas were trying to run households under much more primitive conditions than their mothers had known. Young girls in these homes had little by which to assess living standards. Said Maude Richman Calvert, Oklahoma's state supervisor of home economics, "mother-to-daughter instruction alone cannot be depended upon to train our future homemakers." Taking the position that they were simply waiting for marriage, the author of "While She Waits" concluded that women would benefit themselves and their husbands-to-be by enrolling in college home economics courses until Mr. Right came along. The theme continued in the *South Dakota Farmer*, which claimed that domestic science graduates were desirable wife material, practically swept off to the altar as they walked out the school door. This viewpoint was supported by a home economist who flatly stated that husbands were grateful for any training their wives received. Another commentator, trying to speak sensibly to girls, wrote that they were in "dreamland" if they believed education in the arts would prepare them for a perfect future. The cold facts, cautioned the writer, were that the girl would marry a man who "tears his clothes, snores, and eats unlimited quanities of pork and cabbage" and who would give her a passel of loud, mischievous, and occasionally sick children. For her own good, she should gain "all the knowledge which related sciences can contribute to her intelligence, deftness, and efficiency in that greatest and purest of womanly arts, the art of making a home."[17]

Based on this argument, the domestic economy movement encouraged farm daughters to move beyond attendance at farmers' institutes. They could learn far more by enrolling in home economics classes at agricultural colleges. These colleges were filling an educational void, as few rural elementary and secondary schools early in the century provided domestic science instruction. Young women were not expected to seek degrees, however. After completing one or two basic courses, they were to return home armed with their newfound skills. The call for college work was primarily aimed at the white rural population, but black agricultural schools also offered domestic science instruction.

For those unable to attend college on a full-time basis, there was also the short course of just a few weeks. The 1906 winter short course at South Dakota's agriculture school, for example, offered "instruction in the methods of cooking and the scientific principles underlying the same." It also included sewing classes. A short course offered in 1917 by Iowa's agricultural college dealt with sewing, but lessons resembled those found in manufacturing—they focused on quality control. At the Iowa course, it was advised that scraps of material from homemade clothes be filed away. When the clothing wore out, women should attach notes to the fabrics specifying how well dyes held in washing and how well the materials had worn in general. Then she would know the quality of the fabric and what to buy in the future. No matter how simplistic these lessons may seem today, for the time they were revelations in the modern systematic ways of doing things. Availability of short courses was of great importance for girls, who were as tied as their fathers and brothers to seasonal farm work. Unable to be away from home for too long, the country girl still had some educational opportunities. Wrote Jessie Hoover, who became an instructor at North Dakota's agricultural college: "If the agricultural college is to educate the farmers' children there is but one thing for it to do and that is to arrange a course which will meet the time requirements of the student from the farm."[18]

In the latter half of the 1800s, land-grant colleges offered some form of domestic study. Short courses remained popular, and young women attended college for a few basic courses in homemaking. Eventually, however, schools also developed degree programs that required four years of course work. Kansas State Agricultural College began its first steps toward a degree program in December 1873 when it offered "sewing, dressmaking, and millinery." The Dakota Agricultural College at Brookings followed examples set by Iowa, Kansas, Illinois, and Oregon when it introduced a "Course in Agriculture and Domestic Economy Leading to the Degree of Bachelor of Science for Ladies," as described in the 1884–1885 catalog. The Dakota school did not, however, hire a home economics professor until 1887, when Dalinda Mason, a graduate of Kansas State Agricultural College, joined the faculty. Until the addition of Mason, the school relied on part-time domestic science instructors and faculty in the sciences, especially chemistry. This was not unusual. University of Nebraska in Lincoln created a domestic science department in 1898 and hired an instructor named Rosa Bouton, but it did not have an academically trained home economics professor until 1909.[19]

Land-grant colleges did not develop programs for women as quickly as they did men's programs, but that they recognized women at all before the turn of the century suggests a growing interest in domestic education and the professionalization of home economists. Leaders of the domestic economy movement all seemed to agree upon the importance of training young women for their future role as home-makers. Lou Allen Gregory, the first professor of domestic science at Illinois' land-grant college, was adamant that women's education "bring the aids of science and culture to the all-important labors and vocations of womanhood." Similarly, a Minnesota home economist, Juanita Shepperd, saw the domestic economy movement as a crusade: "If each daughter of the land could have benefit of one or more such courses, but few generations would pass before every woman would thoroughly appreciate the importance and magnitude of the home-maker's profession and be anxious to solve successfully all its problems."[20]

Sometimes achieving a college education was difficult. Leaving the family farm for college, one South Dakota woman recalled, "From White Lakes to Brookings! To go 136 miles from home and never having been in that town of about 3,000 . . . this to a person who got homesick so easily, was a huge hurdle!" Distance, time to be away from home, family approval, and money were all factors affecting full-time attendance. South Dakota, typical among colleges in its home economics program, graduated its first student in domestic science in 1888. In the years that followed, only one or two women a year completed the degree program.[21]

These beginnings were crucial to the rural domestic economy movement and the women involved. The intention had been that college courses would prepare women to return to the farm, trained for their agrarian home duties. This they did, and it is reasonable to assume that these educated women would also expect the local schools and their own children to adhere to higher educational standards. A college degree, however, provided young women with something else. For rural women in particular, domestic education brought a form of liberation by expanding their work opportunities beyond the country kitchen. This was true for black as well as white students.

Some land-grant college graduates found professional work as nutritionists, designers, and researchers in the expanding food and clothing industries. South Dakota's agricultural college noted that, because so many nutrition-related fields existed, the school tried to train as many young women as possible for careers as dietitians, institutional food managers, and caterers. Added to these possibilities were positions with manufacturers who wanted their new lines of washing machines, stoves, or electric sewing machines demonstrated to retailers and prospective female buyers; product demonstrations by a professional home economist improved sales and proved manufacturers' claims of easy home use. A few graduates became radio commentators for women's programs. Others found work as journalists or editors for farm publications or women's magazines. Some took their training to magazines' experimental kitchens. *Modern Priscilla*, for example, had a "proving plant" where home economists "try out every recipe before it is published . . . test all sorts of household ideas and devices [and] foods and methods of food preparation." Careers opened, but many college graduates continued along the more female-oriented path of teaching. This was particularly true after passage of the 1917 Smith-Hughes Act, which gave federal support to home economics as vocational education. Home economics instruction expanded in high schools, state institutions—such as schools for the blind and deaf—and urban industrial schools. Only two women graduated from

South Dakota's program in 1915, but both became high school home economics teachers. One went to a school in North Dakota, the other to Wisconsin.[22]

A 1924 domestic science textbook, *First Course in Home Making*, noted thirty career paths for college women. By the mid-1920s agricultural colleges conceded or celebrated—depending upon their point of view—the numerous opportunities beyond farm living available to graduates. As some of its students moved away from farm communities, Kansas State Agricultural College cautioned that they should at least keep the ideals of domestic education: "After all, the purpose of home economics is to make better homes. . . . You can find ways to promote better homes whether your work be lecturing to society women or Kentucky mountaineers, teaching high school girls to cook, or helping the poor mother stretch her budget."[23]

For a number of graduates, making better homes meant reaching out to farm women as home extension or home demonstration agents. (Both home extension and home demonstration were used to describe agents' work.) Some women without college degrees filled these positions in the early years, but the professionalization of home economics eventually required that all extension agents have degrees and specialized training. In the 1910s and 1920s, extension agent programs became an increasingly important bridge between colleges and rural neighborhoods. Just as agricultural colleges, the federal government, and various farm organizations employed male agricultural agents, these groups began to see the value of hiring women as agents in domestic economy. As a result, home extension gradually became a significant presence in rural life. The agent, closely engaged with rural women, introduced the lessons of domestic economy and their attendant progressive ideals.

It is unclear how many college instructors and women employed in home extension work were themselves from rural backgrounds. In 1928 a Texas home economist responsible for twenty-two counties reported that twenty-five country girls in her district were enrolled in college domestic science courses. The agent implied that all desired a career in home extension, although it is probable that not all finished what they began. Two demonstration agents hired for black extension work in 1932 did come from farm backgrounds and held bachelor degrees from Texas's black agricultural college, Prairie View A & M. In another example, Conie C. Foote grew up in a rural Kansas town and graduated from Kansas State Agricultural College. Although from an agrarian community, she probably had taken on a more urban viewpoint by the time she completed postgraduate work at Columbia University and returned to Kansas State as a nutrition specialist. She, like other home economists, became an instructor in her home state. Other professors, however, came from elsewhere and brought with them attitudes that made students wonder at what they took for granted. Recalled a former student of South Dakota's college in the 1920s: "I remember when instructor Eloise Huskins, who was born and raised in the east, was quite 'shocked' at some of our midwestern ways, such as going to the movies unescorted."[24]

It may be a moot point to wonder if rural women who returned as instructors within their home states or who went to farm districts as home demonstration agents did not necessarily have greater sympathy and understanding than their urban counterparts for the women they were supposed to teach. It might be argued that their familiarity with the rural environment made them better suited for the job. However, the college experience separated the country native from her background, exposing her to influences and training from teachers who may or may not have been farm-reared themselves. Rural women may have more readily accepted agents with farm backgrounds, but the question seemed to be secondary to the idea that educators and extension agents were authorities who could demonstrate a better way of doing things. The emphasis was on making improvements to self, family, and community. Women newly trained in domestic economy had the tools to bring those lessons to agricultural America.

Although home extension agents were a factor in spreading domestic economy ideology and information, there were not enough of them to reach the entire farm population. This was especially true in the movement's early years. Therefore, to supplement agents' work, the farm-based media and women's magazines added a chorus of professional enthusiasm for domestic training. Agricultural newspapers, magazines such as *Farmer's Wife*, government and college publications, and eventually radio acted as informational resources. Either straightforwardly or obliquely, these outlets attempted to influence and enhance rural females' chances for education and the amount of information they had immediately at hand. Newspapers and magazines carried how-to articles detailing better ways to perform the dreariest of chores. A woman living near Sibley, Iowa, offered to *Farmer and Breeder* magazine her time-saving approach to cleaning overalls: Do not immerse them in water but "lay them over a washboard, soap them, and scrub with a brush." Meanwhile, *American Needlewoman* included the letter of a Kansas woman who suggested, "Let those who dislike the task of cleaning washbasins try rubbing them with a cloth that has been dipped in kerosene." Another woman gave this laundry hint in *Modern Homemaking*: "When you clean spots off clothes with gasoline, just put a little salt in it, and it will not leave a circle." Kerosene also was recommended for problem laundry, as evidenced by the "chemical compound" of "common yellow soap" and kerosene noted in *The American Domestic Cyclopaedia*. [25]

Along with personal housekeeping pointers came professional suggestions for performing everyday work with the correct equipment and a scientific mind-set. Explained a 1921 article in *Modern Priscilla*, "Physics teaches us that water boils more quickly in a shallow, broad-based container. . . . Science tells us, too, that certain metals are affected by acids and are therefore not fitted for cooking processes like preserving." A 1929 issue of *People's Home Journal* provided an indepth analysis of dishwashing methods and bacteria growth in dishcloths, with the cautionary words, "the importance of sanitary methods should be regarded seriously." Magazines routinely published articles on food and nutrition. *Woman's World* included one meant to dispel misinformation about the ill effects of combining stewed tomatoes with potatoes, citric juices with milk, or celery with cheese. Discussing food properties and the digestive process, the article concluded that modern-day scientific knowledge of foods and their preparation disproved superstitions, wive's tales, and quackery. Lessons and information appeared in a range of published articles and reached out to all women, including those whose magazines came by Rural Free Delivery.[26]

Numerous sources also perpetuated the idea that the economical woman could seemingly make something from nothing. Annie Gregory's *Woman's Favorite Cookbook* provided recipes for meals, housecleaning solutions, and homemade medicines. All used the "scantiest and plainest material," and Gregory underscored the idea that "thrift [is] the highest art known to domestic science." The message was the same in a *South Dakota Farmer* article, "Tempting Dishes Made of 'Scraps,'" which observed: "Lucky is the housewife who wishes to keep her housekeeping expenses down, if she has facility, either natural or acquired, in making good use of left-overs and remnants, whether of clothing, furnishings or food." With a little imagination and help from advice columns, women could replicate any number of store-bought items from odds and ends. They could construct their own nonelectric refrigerators by using two boxes, packing for insulation, a little charcoal as filter for odors, and some shelves. Similarly, a "cheap durable linoleum" could be made from old carpets or burlap sacks, lots of flour-and-water paste to cover the material, and a little whitewash to finish the job. For decoration, stenciling patterns were suggested. Sometimes women served as examples for those around them. Tired of "an old hoe handle across the corner of my living room which served as my clothes closet," a Texas woman made a clothes wardrobe out of pieces of wood from old furniture, four apple boxes, and some drawers found in a secondhand store and traded for ten baby chicks. If she could scrape together usable materials and show a little initiative in creating what she needed, then surely others could, too.[27]

Detailed, step-by-step directions also appeared in USDA or college bulletins. One home economics professor observed that rural women were more willing to contemplate the information when they knew it came from professionals involved directly with farm women's interests. The federal government agreed. Its USDA publications ranged in topic from "Making and Using Cottage Cheese in the Home" to "Stain Removal from Fabrics, Home Methods." Women also had access to publications from state agencies. In 1915, the Kansas State Board of Agriculture, knowing that women raised poultry not only for home use but also for the sale of eggs and hens, printed some advice on the subject. In a thorough account with illustrations, the agency covered the need for purebred chickens, their attributes, good feeding methods, and henhouse maintenance. "I know what a job it is for the farmer's wife to clean the henhouse when the droppings are allowed to fall and accumulate there," the author wrote. "It takes but a few minutes' use of the hoe to scrape the dropping boards. . . . If you take a little air-slacked lime and sprinkle the boards, your house will be free from odors . . . and from lice." That subject fully discussed, the state board later turned to canning and food preservation, offering drawings, timetables, and a classification chart of fruits and vegetables.[28]

To these sources of information were added newspaper and magazine articles that carried recipes, sewing and millinery patterns, cleaning hints, and beauty tips. One article extolled sunshine as a hair tonic and suggested that women go without hats as much as possible and wash their hair "every three or four weeks," preferably in rainwater. (Considering that water from any source was at a premium in many western rural areas, the suggested interval may have been overly optimistic.) Regarding suitable home attire, one magazine noted: "[Women] think torn, soiled, shirt waists, half-worn, greasy skirts and buttonless, down-at-the-heel boots good enough for the kitchen, or

they wear the cheap, ugly frocks and aprons that are sold in number-
less thousands. They look like slovens; or like scarecrows. There is no
excuse." The message was to shape up and take pride in how one
looked—even, we may suppose, when scraping droppings out of a
henhouse. Appearance was especially important, said the magazine,
for young women. They should be seen in housedresses and aprons
that were "fresh and good to look at." After all, young husbands and
suitors did not want frumps. McCall's Magazine agreed, but its articles
couched the view in arguments for efficiency. If women used potholders
and dishtowels instead of resorting to the "unhousewifery trick" of
using dress or apron hems to remove pots from the stove or clean up
spills, they would reduce wash loads. Observed the author of "Making Wash-Day Easier": "Half of my success in keeping down the amount
of weekly washing is due to the never-failing care I've given things.
. . . Is a roast better if pulled out of the oven with a big apron or a
dress-hem or a nice white dishcloth?"[29]

Instead of offering direct advice and admonitions, some articles
led by example. Farmer's Wife magazine was partial to this form, carrying stories that suggested but did not demand. In "Paying the
Preacher, the Women's Canning Club Brought the Dollars," readers
were told how a rural women's organization proceeded "in a businesslike manner" to buy an up-to-date canning machine. Club members
then could preserve garden goods, sell them, and use the profit to pay
a minister's salary, with "quite a sum left for other purposes." In the
same 1915 magazine issue, a short story emphasized that one could
conduct systematic spring housekeeping while presentably attired in
gingham housedresses, muslin aprons, and dust caps trimmed with
lace. The message, as in a South Dakota Farmer article that introduced "the champion woman butter maker of South Dakota," was
that any woman could do the same.[30]

The new technologies of film and radio also served as educational
tools. In 1915 Farmer's Wife informed readers, "Uncle Sam is experi-
menting with motion pictures," citing USDA productions that var-

ied in subject from young people's corn and canning clubs to seed distribution. The magazine encouraged the use of film in education and lauded any woman who worked to have these movies shown in her community as "a pioneer in progress." Agricultural schools readily accepted "these little films . . . covering every subject which could interest the community." In 1916, for example, South Dakota's agricultural college announced the availability, through its extension service, of USDA films titled *Pure Food* (concerned with pure food legislation) and *Out of the Mud* (a film on road building). Educational films were considered experimental, but the positive impact of movies that encouraged food preservation or helped recruit farm labor during World War I convinced the USDA of their usefulness. During World War I over 500,000 people saw government-made films at extension meetings, and at least 4 million viewed USDA films in public theaters.[31]

Radio attracted a still larger audience. Agricultural colleges investigated its impact, just as their experimental stations tested new seed strains. As early as 1914 college radio stations transmitted weather forecasts to farmers, and programming soon included talks by faculty and USDA experts on scientific farming, household management, health and sanitation, child care, and recipes.[32]

College stations were not alone in targeting a farm audience. Commercial radio also sought a rural following. WIBW, a farm-oriented station owned by Kansas governor and then U.S. Senator Arthur Capper, reported in 1927 that its listeners included over 2 million families in Kansas, Missouri, Nebraska, Oklahoma, and Colorado. Among these millions, the station counted "thousands of progressive women on farms." Daily these women heard the "Women's Forum Hour," with discussions on subjects ranging from proper nutrition to getting more eggs per hen to child care. Women editors of Capper's various farm publications talked about "everything of interest to the home," although not all of the commentators were professionally trained home economists. Author Laura Ingalls Wilder, for example, served for twelve years as home editor for Capper's *Missouri Ruralist* newspaper. Her qualifications for that job, as well as a later assignment as poultry editor for the *St. Louis Star*, were an ability to write and personal familiarity with rural life. In the early years of farm women's education, professionals coexisted with those who based their work on firsthand knowledge.[33]

Just as the USDA recognized the potential for film, it saw the possibilities for radio. For the female audience, the USDA Bureau of Home Economics and Radio Service created Aunt Sammy. Introduced as the female counterpart to Uncle Sam, Aunt Sammy went on the air in October 1926. Played by many women, the radio personality offered recipes, talked about clothing and proper use of home appliances, and reported on the latest fads. By the end of 1927, forty-three radio stations nationally, including WIBW in Kansas, carried the program. Its popularity spawned publication of *Aunt Sammy's Radio Recipes*, revised and expanded by the USDA three times between 1927 and 1931. This program, as well as those created by local stations, entertained and informed. Radio reduced rural isolation, brought information, and designed programming with the farm woman in mind.[34]

Radio's impact was just beginning to be understood. Arthur Capper and others, however, already recognized its potential to educate and influence. Listeners agreed. A young woman preparing for her teaching certificate in 1927 later wrote about her required course in the elements of agriculture, where one day the class was asked the meaning of "scarified." She "dimly remembered hearing the phrase, 'scarified sweet clover'" while listening to the radio station of "Earl May and Henry Field, both well-known seed companies in Shenandoah, Iowa." Based on what she had inadvertently picked up from the radio, she gave the correct answer—seed shells cut to hasten germination. This made her a star pupil, however briefly.[35]

The proliferation of information and education in domestic economy and farm duties suggests an intense interest in reaching farm women. Abundant information from many sources was available. Media outlets, often tied to agricultural colleges, supported the progressive, scientific viewpoint. Whether conveyed through the printed word, radio, film, or college courses, the message to women was the same: Scientific domestic economy had a place in home and rural living. Efforts to reach rural women were well organized and designed to deliver the most up-to-date information in a quest to make farm women educated and, therefore, progressive and modern. As early as the 1900 Lake Placid conference on home economics, Henrietta Goodrich, director of the Boston Domestic Reform League School of Housekeeping, voiced the opinion that home economics was "in line with the great social and industrial forces of the day" and "in the direct line of progress."[36]

Like progress in scientific farming, progress in home economics had many aspects. It could mean improving the way foods were cooked or achieving more economical household management. On the whole, it implied innovative thinking about domesticity and its functions. Certainly, the experts and home economics professionals attempted to transmit a defined viewpoint to farm women, but whether they succeeded is an open question. It would be foolish to suggest that every rural woman received the message of domestic economy. The movement began, after all, by targeting women who had already showed an interest in education by attending farmers' institutes. It also would be rash to assume that those who heard the message wholeheartedly accepted and incorporated all its lessons.

Nevertheless, it is reasonable to argue that participation indicated interest. The thousands who were involved in some form of educational activity, as well as the expansion of college extension programs for women, show that women willingly explored what domestic economy had to offer. That willingness was essential if change and reform were to come for rural women and their communities.

3 A Need for Organization

THE PROGRESSIVE ERA WAS MARKED BY AN obsession for club work and organization. Every reform idea seemed to have a representative group. Activists interested in expanding children's opportunities for recreation formed the Playground Association of America. Women organized to lobby for female suffrage. The Woman's Christian Temperance Union (WCTU) expanded from an antiliquor coalition to one that addressed women's issues in general, including domestic economy. Church and scouting organizations for adolescents and teenagers were popular. Both cities and rural villages had chapters affiliated with many national organizations as well as local temperance, church, library, and literary groups catering to immediate community interests.

In rural America, despite what Roosevelt's Country Life Commission and others said, there was abundant organization. Modern Woodmen of America, the Farmers' Educational and Cooperative Union, and the Society of Equity enjoyed farmer support and membership. State and county associations formed for stock raisers and cattle ranchers, some of whom were women. The Grange encouraged female membership and recognized women with certificates of achievement such as the Degree of Flora. It offered social opportunities, an outlet for education, and an arena for local involvement. Of the or-

65

ganization in her community, one woman observed in a 1915 issue of
Farmer's Wife: "We have a Grange . . . that brings the farmers and
their wives together. . . . We meet at the different farm homes, and I
assure you that this is a stimulant to many farmers to show their neighbors that they can have conveniences in the home and comforts that
were once thought unnecessary." As this woman suggested, group interaction at Grange meetings allowed participants to gauge what others
had in the way of home conveniences. The point was not necessarily
to keep up with the neighbors; but if one farm family added running
water, others might follow because they saw that it was possible.[1]

Numerous groups and clubs had both men and women members,
but women had their own organizations. Some of these were infor-
mal quilting or social clubs. Others, including many in South Dakota, were community or countywide associations for women who
regularly attended farmers' institutes. A number of local women's
groups were affiliated with the WCTU or the National Federation of
Women's Clubs (NFWC). In fact, some NFWC state councils considered segregating rural and town women—just as some refused membership to black women's clubs. It was decided, however, that "the
interests of the homemakers, whether they lived in the city or the
country, were found to be so much alike that the idea of separate
meetings was abandoned." (The federation overlooked the possibility that in sanctioning rural clubs in general, it might be accepting
nonwhite members at a time it refused membership to urban black
clubs.) Some rural clubs were not WTCU or NFWC affiliates but
instead had ties to regional organizations such as the Daughters of
the Confederacy. Additionally, there were two national farm women's
organizations, the National Farm and Garden Association and the
National Congress of Farm Women. The presence of choices adds to
the picture of farm life a dimension not usually considered. Women's
groups and club work often are viewed as only having existed among
urban women with time and money to spend. Rural women, however, had so many opportunities for involvement that a South Da-

kota newspaper declared, "If the average farmer's wife does not actually belong to a woman's club, she no doubt, in most cases, comes within its influence . . . and [has] been benefitted and given an impetus toward progress."[2]

Despite the proliferation of clubs and neighborhood groups that met informally when time allowed, agricultural colleges and the USDA were not content with the level of activity. From their standpoint, many organizations did not focus on domestic economy or channel women's energies in that direction. Therefore, agricultural colleges and the federal government worked to create a network of women's clubs devoted specifically to domestic economy and improvement of rural living. These took the form of home demonstration (or home extension) units.

Encouraged by the work of such women as Martha Van Rensselaer at Cornell University, home demonstration became central to extension programs. Agricultural schools, the American Farm Bureau, and other farm groups hired female agents in home extension. This expanded employment was solidified with passage of the Smith-Lever Act, an important piece of legislation directed at promoting scientific farming and coordination between the USDA and agricultural colleges. The law also held significant consequences for female education. Under the act, each state received $10,000 earmarked for an agricultural college; a portion of these funds had to be used for home extension work. Thus, a basis for permanent programs was established, and many interests devoted to rural women saw great possibilities. Soon after its passage, the "generous new Smith-Lever law" received notice in Farmer's Wife, which began its own campaign to "urgently advocate [employment] of women county agents." Citing success stories of newly hired agents, the magazine implored all rural women to clamor for their own local homemaking advisers. They seemed to need little urging. Said one agent, "people are becoming better acquainted with extension work and know now more of what to expect and how to get it."[3]

Two related types of home extension work were practiced. In the first, agricultural college faculty acted as roving teachers, going out to local communities and presenting talks and lessons to demonstrate a specific way of doing things. In the second, just as men were hired as county scientific farming agents, female home demonstration agents were employed by a county or group of counties that formed a district. Texas, for example, used the district model because of the state's size and widely dispersed population; Kansas, by contrast, followed a county plan. Agents organized and managed women's extension clubs and their programs. The earliest employer of home demonstration agents was the American Farm Bureau, perhaps spurred on by complaints that it was not doing enough for farm women. Wrote one disgruntled female member: "Men contribute to home betterment just as women contribute to farm betterment and both men and women are needed to solve the problems of the farm, the home and the community." It was high time, said the member, that the Farm Bureau "think of farm women and provide them a demonstration agent just as a male agent is provided farmers."[4]

It was also time, many argued, for agricultural colleges to act. Thus, schools expanded programs, increased positions for women faculty, hired college graduates for extension work, and explored the possibility of permanently assigning home demonstration agents to a county or district. In this latter endeavor, organized support came from the Farm Bureau, county agricultural committees, fair associations, and local councils of the National Parent-Teacher Association and National Federation of Women's Clubs. Not every county or region in a state received a home demonstration agent. In fact, that component of extension work did not see significant gains until the 1920s; marked increases followed in the 1930s with the recovery programs of the Great Depression. In Kansas, the first Farm Bureau–sponsored agent was hired in 1914 to serve northeastern Leavenworth County; however, the bureau did not establish a program for women in centrally located Dickinson County until 1925, and no agent was hired until

1929, when eleven county clubs demanded attention. A majority of Kansas counties reflected the national trend and did not have home demonstration agents until the mid-1920s. In part, this was because the Farm Bureau had fixed membership requirements; in sparsely populated Comanche County, Bureau-sponsored extension did not arrive until 1927, when Kansas women were allowed to count members from a neighboring Oklahoma county in their clubs.[5]

Sometimes the availability of agricultural school instructors slowed the hiring of county agents. If colleges were willing to provide visiting teachers, there was less reason to hire an agent. Finney County, Kansas, was typical in its 1921 experience with the Kansas State Agricultural College faculty. In February of that year, the school's extension service sent a Mrs. Allard to spend a day giving lectures and demonstrations in domestic science at the Garden City and Holcomb high schools. Later, Susanna Schnemayer spent four days in Garden City, the county seat, presenting six programs on appliances, furnishings, and "feeding the family for efficiency." Total attendance was 235, and a local hardware-store owner said the meetings increased sales of "certain articles of kitchen equipment" for his store.[6]

Whether county agents or college extension representatives, these home economists were expected to organize women's extension clubs and provide domestic economy lessons. An agent's presence and her role as club organizer changed the dynamics of women's information sharing. Traditionally, women informally exchanged tips on household cleaning, cooking, or health care; often, young women sought advice from older relatives or neighbors. In the framework of home extension clubs, however, the focus changed: The agent was *the* expert. Club discussions centered around what she had to say, not on the knowledge that came from folklore, ethnic customs, or everyday practice. Although agents never entirely supplanted women's casual informational network, they interjected an authoritative voice for modernization.

By mobilizing rural women and introducing domestic economy, experts hoped to fulfill the dream of a fully organized, homogeneous rural society. Ellen Batchelor, who became Kansas State Agricultural College's assistant state leader of home demonstration in 1920, made the point quite clearly: "Our job as Home Economics Extension workers, is to reach the more isolated rural homemaker and help her in solving her more vital problems. . . . It is the distinctly rural homemaker, or the genuine farm homemaker who needs the work most and for whose benefit extension funds are appropriated." Associations for rural women aimed to demonstrate new methods of doing things and to change attitudes; they were supposed to unify women of many backgrounds and encourage them to "give up traditions of the past."[7]

Erasing traditions and old ways of thinking was at the crux of female organization. Urban experts insisted upon it, and professionals in several fields agreed. Agricultural reformers wanted conformity, not individuality. Nevertheless, their plans were thwarted when geography, demographics, and settlement patterns encouraged cultural diversity and tradition. Immigrant groups tended to settle in clusters, creating majority populations of Germans or Swiss or Norwegians in some rural counties. Agrarian blacks in the Plains states usually congregated together in rural districts. When racial or ethnic groups made up a majority of a local population, it was likely that women socialized within their own circles, shared a common background, and often were related through extended family networks. The dominant culture of American society as a whole may have been that of white, American-born Protestants, but in many rural communities the prevailing culture was something else. Despite changes that were reducing agrarian isolation, a measure of insulation persisted, allowing the local majority to retain its traditions. One Russian-German woman, born after her family emigrated in 1912, recalled that it was easy for her to "visualize how it had been in Russia" because things were still done the same way in America. Moreover, interaction occurred between nondominant cultures. When German-Russian immigrants settled on a portion of North Dakota's Standing Rock Indian Reservation, for example, they borrowed from their Sioux neighbors, adapting the latter's foodways, children's games, and use of native plants for home remedies.[8] Domestic economy advocates did not always consider the social structure or fabric of rural areas. If they expected a melting-pot effect across the spectrum of agrarian society, they were disappointed.

In truth, experts did not intend for some groups ever to unify with others. Extension programs and clubs were often segregated by race. Texas home extension, like that in many southern states, was conducted on a "separate but equal" basis. However, blacks were not overlooked in Texas or ignored in other sections of the central Plains. In fact, the domestic economy movement's desire to erase traditional patterns meant that all rural women, no matter their racial or ethnic background, received the same messages. That some drew attention later than others, or were addressed separately, was a result of the period's attitudes and of government and school decisions about where to expend time, energy, and funds.

Many early home extension clubs were created from preexisting organizations. Some of these were quilting groups or church societies, but most were canning clubs. These associations predated home extension, but more organized under the guidance of extension agents. The first home demonstration unit in Kansas was a canning club, as were many of the ones that followed. In Washington County, six home demonstration clubs existed by 1917; all began as canning clubs, with five operating as mother-daughter groups and one including adult women only. In one month during 1919, five home demonstration units organized as canning clubs in western Meade County. In McPherson County, clubs formed after an extension agent gave eleven demonstrations (in which the participants canned over 800 quarts of meat). When the Lucky 13 Club organized in Montgomery County, "canning and sociability was the theme of the club the first year."[9]

It was no wonder that one extension agent believed, "In the minds of many people Home Demonstration Work means canning." Extension agents who dispensed information on this important technology in food preservation were aided by companies with a vested interest in their success. The Ball Company, famous for its jars, published its own canning recipe book. Commercialism aside, women seemed eager to learn about this process. Canning fruits, vegetables, meats, and fish opened up a new world in preservation. It expanded farm diets beyond foods that were seasonally available or could be salted away or dried. Said one Oklahoma woman: "It was so much easier to preserve canned meats than it was to fry them down and store in the cellar. . . . It was a wonderful benefit to people, to be able to preserve things. . . . For many, many years I canned meat—sometimes four or five hundred quarts a year, and an awful lot of vegetables." Quantities preserved were often staggering. In 1924, black women and girls in Texas clubs canned over 224,000 quarts of fruits and vegetables and over 46,000 quarts of meat and fish. Canning, especially of meat, and the butchering that preceded it, were "community affair[s]," remembered a Kansas woman.[10] Women often gathered together in what was an intensive task. As an Indiana woman recalled:

> Mother attended an Extension lesson that taught her how to cold pack fruits and vegetables. They blanched the fruit or vegetables, cooked them and packed them in cans, sealed the lids, put the wash boiler on the stove with a wooden slat false bottom [so cans did not touch boiler bottom], put in the 11 cans (I think mother's boiler held 11 cans), went to the pump outside, pumped water and brought it in to fill the boiler to one inch above the cans. Then we fired the wood stove until we boiled this water for three hours. Sometimes we gathered corn cobs in our aprons to finish firing the stove to keep the water boiling.[11]

The process described here was the new water-bath canning method. Since the late 1800s, women had preserved food through what was known as open-kettle canning. Fruits, tomato juice, whole tomatoes, and relishes were prepared in a kettle over heat and then sealed in jars; pickles kept in a brine also were preserved in sealed jars. The open-kettle method, however, was not workable for many vegetables and was disastrous if tried with meats. When canning techniques using the water-bath method or a pressure-cooker were introduced, variety was added to what could be processed and saved. Other new methods, called cold or hot pack, depending upon temperature, required some preparation beforehand, such as blanching, but they made it possible to preserve just about every foodstuff. Women's magazines routinely explained and promoted canning methods. *Modern Homemaking* called them "a sound and economic policy enabling the housewife to stock ahead when garden and farm products are at surplus production." Meanwhile, *Needlecraft Magazine* stressed the efficiency of women who planned ahead and had the proper and quality utensils at hand. Of course, such advice was meant for town women, too, but the benefit was most important for rural families. Diets no longer turned on seasonal availability. As one Kansas woman recalled, no matter the time of year, she "could always go down to the cellar and bring up a can of this meat" and it would be "just perfect."[12]

Food preservation and home extension received a boost with World War I. Conserving the nation's food supply and preparing to feed war-torn Europe became synonymous with patriotism. Women were told to raise as much produce as possible and can it by the newest methods; absolutely no food was to be wasted. If leftover scraps could not be turned into a delectable dinner, they could be fed to chickens or pigs—regarded by many farm women as their garbage disposals. Declared Mabel Ward, home economics professor in South Dakota: "As women we should realize our grave responsibility as guardians of the nation's food supply. Let us accept this responsibility with an earnestness and intelligence worthy of our allegiance to the flag."[13]

The South Dakota school offered short courses to educate farmers for wartime production. Meanwhile, women received special lessons in nutrition, canning, and other forms of food preservation, such as drying fruits. Support came from the federal Food Production Act, which provided money for specialized canning programs and employment of county home demonstration agents. The latter were developed by USDA employee Gertrude Warren, who was uniquely suited for the job because she was farm-reared and a trained home economist teaching at Columbia University. Imitating federal programs, states organized committees and departments for home-front activities; often, their importance was underscored by names that included the word "emergency." In Kansas, the Department of Emergency Home Demonstration Work expanded club work and extension programs. The state's agricultural college responded by reaching at least ninety homemaker clubs with information on food substitutes for wheat, animal fat, and sugar. At a time when foodstuffs were being diverted from home consumption to feed the army, substitutes were important. Ellen Batchelor, later to join Kansas State's faculty, was hired at $100 per month "to teach women and girls to can meat, fruit and vegetables; to make war breads [using wheat substitutes] and stretch butter." Nationally, rural women's clubs received these lessons, and they added their own projects. Many met to gather blankets or to make clothing for soldiers. The Wild Rose Women's Club of Opheim, Montana, for example, quilted, attended demonstrations on various household topics, and made garments for American troops. Some groups banded with the American Red Cross or Salvation Army to roll bandages or dispense refreshments to troops at depot canteens. The women's club near Clear Lake, Iowa, donated a carload of corn for Belgian relief.[14]

The emergency of wartime brought an almost frantic burst of club organization and extension work, and the number of home demonstration agents dramatically increased. At the time the United States entered the war, home demonstration agents nationally totaled 545. By November 1918, at war's end, the number was 1,724. In 15 southern states, 268 women were employed for wartime extension work among blacks. In Iowa, the number of home economists statewide increased from 1 (operating in a predominantly urban county) to 41 in 1918. Agents, USDA specialists, and agricultural college faculty assigned to war extension work had an immediate impact on rural organization. The effects, however, reverberated long after war ended. Home demonstration units did not disband, and demonstration agents were not fired with the armistice. There is evidence, nonetheless, that hands reaching out to minority groups withdrew in the calm of peace. The pace of black education slackened in some districts, and in New Mexico educational funding for Hispanic women ceased. Overall, however, agents remained in place and provided a nucleus for further organization of women.[15]

War also brought more women, however temporarily, into agriculture. With the creation of the Woman's Land Army, girls and women from cities, towns, and rural areas were mobilized by private organizations, the USDA's emergency extension program, and the National Council of Defense for the purpose of raising food. These women brought in crops and harvested truck gardens and orchards. One California magazine featured women housed at a farm camp near Vacaville. Photographs showed them laughing, happily working in the fields or resting after a day of labor. The women were portrayed as contributing to a national cause, and the article strongly stated that no one was exploited. It was a salient point, as migrant camps already had a rather infamous reputation for worker abuse. As they brought in needed crops and participated in the war effort through club work, women learned lasting lessons in organization.[16]

Near war's end, a South Dakota woman received a National Council of Defense award for developing a "bee culture" that produced over four thousand pounds of honey in one year. The accomplishments of this woman and many like her during the war suggested economic opportunities in peacetime. Women saw possibilities that had been looked at differently before the war. Traditionally, women's groups raised money for local improvements through bazaars, entertainments, and auctions of homemade items. In Kansas, for example, quilting groups held socials to support community programs, and rural church organizations routinely raffled homemade quilts and com-forters to pay ministers' salaries or fund church repairs. Women's groups turned the money they earned over to some worthy cause; for example, a Huntley, Montana, club raised beets and used the proceeds to develop a community park.[17]

These activities did not end with the organizations and ideas that emerged from World War I, but there was a subtle change in thinking about women's labor, with greater emphasis on channeling earning potential to achieve personal gain. USDA and college extension programs considered money-making projects and home industries that allowed women in groups or as individuals to increase their incomes. After all, a 1920 USDA study of almost ten thousand farm homes in western and northern states found that 81 percent of the women were already raising poultry. In terms of business management, they had the raw materials at hand and were familiar with the basic selling and buying practices of small businesses.[18] This was true for rural women in general, but in southern and southwestern states, USDA and state home extension programs concentrated on developing agriculture-related enterprises for black and white women, generally overlooking Hispanics and Native Americans. The federal agency believed that "many thousands of women and girls who are developing the resources of their farms and farm communities, under the guidance of home demonstration agents, have profited much by learning to standardize and market their surplus home-grown and homemade products."[19]

Home industries development was almost exclusive to the South and Southwest. Perhaps the USDA and home demonstration saw the women in these areas as more impoverished and more needy than women elsewhere. Whatever the reasoning, although other regions saw some home industry programs, women across the tier of southern states received the most information and organizational support. In one Alabama county, women shared $1,800 from one month's sales of homemade pine-needle baskets, and in Arkansas a county women's club sold braided and hooked rugs. Neither the experts nor the par-

ticipants saw these activities as salting away pin money or gaining
something by barter or trade. Home industries paid for "betterment
of the living conditions, better and more suitable clothes, education
of children, [and] household expenses while the farm crops pay off
land notes."[20]

Texas extension also reflected an interest in home industries. Businessmen familiar with manufacturing's scientific management approach lent their expertise through home extension programs,
introducing concepts such as quality control, adoption of trade names
to allow quick public identification with a product, and the use of
product labeling. One man helped agents and clubs establish consistent quality standards for string beans, chili, chicken soup, and
sauerkraut. This was extremely important, said one agent, if "club
members are to market profitably their surplus farm products." There
was ample proof that women applied the lessons. A woman in Kaufman
County, Texas, made thirty-five dollars a month by selling homemade
potato chips to local merchants. Another parlayed her neighborhood
sales of butter and milk into a full-fledged dairy farm. Some women
sold goods out of their homes. Others, with their clubs, established
market days or co-operatives. By 1927, 2,736 black Texas women were
involved in home industries, and a number had established co-operative ventures. The same could be said of white women in Hidalgo
County, where the Marmalade Marketing Association formed. The
women incorporated business methods of production and distribution and sold their goods to stores, cafes, and the Missouri Pacific
Railroad; trains running out of Houston routinely carried the marmalade made in Hidalgo County. Food products were central to this new
entrepreneurship, but some women focused on other types of goods.
Mrs. Sam Ellerd, Route 9, of Tyler, Texas, said of her $150-a-year
income from selling homemade cotton and wool hooked rugs: "I began this business as an experiment to see what there was in it . . . and
will say I have had all I can do, without a single complaint from my
customers."[21]

Home extension organized women, taught food preparation, and stressed financial opportunities. Programs also began to suggest that rural communities needed to come together and improve themselves. Rural women's organizations, like philanthropic urban groups, could provide the nucleus for social and cultural uplift. Said a Leavenworth County, Kansas, club participant, "one can learn and improve oneself as well as the surroundings." Experts in social change and reform expected women to be a force in redirecting rural life by improving education, health care, and the economy. However, rural women's clubs did not always act as the professionals intended. Rather than striving for sweeping reforms, the women began with basics, addressing local needs as they saw them. In Anderson County, Kansas, rural women, with help from a home demonstration agent, furnished a restroom in the courthouse basement. This was an essential amenity for country women, whose trip to town could be an all-day affair. The room provided toilet facilities, chairs, beds for small children, and a separate room in which women could prepare and serve lunch to their families. Meanwhile, rural club women in Rusk County, Texas, saw other needs. To encourage local tree planting and landscaping, they pledged to plant at least one fruit or nut tree near their homes; similarly, members of the Big Timber Women's Club in Montana distributed seventy dozen asters for rural planting.[22]

Efforts for local improvement were not isolated events. Women understood the larger issues of agrarian reform, but pragmatically they knew that changes began in small ways. Playing out their collective role as the social conscience, the promoter of culture and beauty, women put their energy into home and community beautification as a form of rural transformation. Few reformers would have chosen this as a step toward change, but they eventually applauded such undertakings.

Rural clubs often had exchanges for swapping and distributing vegetable and flower seeds, and women's magazines published personal requests and trade offers. Through *Modern Homemaking*'s "Flower Exchange" column, for example, Mrs. Ethel Wills, Route 5, of

Carthage, Texas, asked for specific types of geraniums and roses, promising to send in return seeds or cuttings from her own garden.[23] Love of growing things and beautifying one's surroundings began with the individual, but experts and the popular press also saw an opportunity to address both personal and community shortcomings. Increasingly, women were asked to ponder the aesthetics of their homes and neighborhoods. Women already were engaged in such activity, but professionals made it their cause, too, expanding ideas and expectations through the domestic economy movement.

Of specific interest was the farmhouse. Many homes, said the experts, were dreary and run down because rural residents put their energies into constructing and maintaining usable barns and outbuildings, neglecting their dwellings. In some places the house stood like a postage stamp amidst plowed fields; in others there was little to distinguish the yard from the livestock pen or corral. Reporting his observations, one architectural expert described a particular farmhouse as representative of many: "This house was not in any sense a social center, and the brightest perspective for the broken wife and mother was the nearby graveyard on the hill between home and the village post office." USDA professionals concurred that rural families did not have to sacrifice productivity for beauty; they needed to realize that farm and ranch were places of both business and residence. Keeping this in mind, one USDA expert wrote, "it would be ridiculous to adorn the inside of the home and leave its surroundings ugly and repulsive."[24]

It was time for home improvement. If rural families were scientific in their approach to agriculture and domestic science, home and its surroundings should reflect that outlook. Again, the experts and media stepped in to guide. One of the first items on the agenda was the home structure itself. In many publications—both popular and agriculture-based—blueprints, house plans, and articles encouraged renovation of existing buildings or construction of new ones. A California magazine published plans in 1918 for "what may be accomplished in the building of better ranch homes"; the bungalow-style home example featured a stucco-over-brick exterior and included a basement for a heating plant, indoor plumbing, a screened porch, and three bedrooms. Enthused the article:

> Contrast this delightful type of ranch abode with the cheer-less, isolated "shanty" of remote regions throughout the farming areas of the United States, where even today there are hard-working ranch wives without one of the modern conveniences to lighten their daily toil. Fortunate indeed is the rancher's wife who can combine the healthfulness and airy spaciousness of country life with up-to-date inventions that minimize labor.[25]

If a bungalow was not quite what one had in mind, perhaps the "pretty cottage of five rooms" pictured in the *South Dakota Farmer Semi-Monthly* would suffice. This farm publication and others carried house plans and advertisements from suppliers. Arthur Capper's *Household Magazine*, for example, included an article on modernizing kitchens in May 1928. It also offered readers a book of seventy bungalow-style house plans. Popular women's magazines also published housing ideas, with *Ladies Home Journal* offering the largest number. Then, there were mail-order companies that shipped prefabricated homes anywhere the railroads went. Precut Sears, Roebuck and Company homes usually arrived in two boxcars and came complete with cabinets, plumbing fixtures, and (if purchased separately) furniture specifically designed for the chosen house style. The simplest house, classified as a "workingman's cottage," could be constructed in eight hours; the more elaborate homes and precut barns took longer.[26]

Sears was not unique. One of its competitors, the Alladin Company, sold 3,600 houses in 1924; prices ranged from $5,000 for the "villa" design to $2,300 for a more modest cottage. Farm families could choose from an array of ideas and possibilities for modern housing. The repeated message was to move beyond basic shelter. One newspaper in 1920 spoke for many in the central Plains by declaring: "This is the year of the passing of the sod house in Kansas. In years of figuring and worrying to make both ends meet the farmer . . . was content to live in a soddy but now prosperity is here and the sod house has passed with the poverty of former years." In reality, sod houses had not passed from use, but their social acceptance had. Other kinds of shelters also fell into disfavor. Buildings, often built by East European immigrants, that housed both family and livestock under one roof were unwanted; the dugout and homesteader shack were also out of date. By the 1920s, all of these farm dwellings were deemed remnants of a past best put aside.[27]

USDA and agricultural college publications offered their own modern farmhouse designs. One USDA article pictured plans for a "hired-man's" cottage, arguing that if accommodations were attractive, it would be easier to find and keep hired help. Meanwhile, Kansas State Agricultural College bulletins detailed house plans in styles from bungalow to colonial, all designed with farm living in mind. "The average house that is well adapted to city living is wholly inadequate for farm life and its problems," said Kansas State's professor of agricultural architecture. In towns, where men and women had separate areas of work, the man "may seldom see the kitchen . . . [and] has no business there and possibly nothing more than a financial interest in the kitchen so long as it serves its intended purposes." On farms, however, everyone was in and out of the kitchen; it was "the workshop for the women from dawn until dusk" as well as the family's social center. In light of its importance, the kitchen received special attention in the designs. One Kansas State bulletin suggested that the kitchen be placed so that all would have easy access to it from the farmyard and so that the farm wife, as "assistant manager," could maintain visual contact with activities at the barn, henhouse, and so forth.[28]

In addition to focusing on room placements, architectural plans encompassed modern conveniences. Country kitchens required large areas for indoor pumps, sinks, and storage for food and water, and perhaps a cream separator. When these could not be accommodated in the house, outbuildings or an attached lean-to contained them. New plumbing fixtures and electrical appliances did not require as much room, however, and electric and gasoline stoves changed the area needed for heating and cooking systems. Unfortunately, primitive dwellings such as soddies or tar-paper shacks had too little space for anything. Chores such as laundry and dairy processing were done in outbuildings, and during summer months many domestic duties such as cooking and canning were moved outdoors. Houses that included only one or two rooms demanded replacement, not renovation.

To encourage adoption of new house plans and ideas for remodeling, bulletins tried to demonstrate how easily changes could be made. Kansas State's bulletins included "Water Heating in the Home," illustrating indoor versions fueled by coal or gasoline; "Sewage Disposal for Country Homes," dealing with problems that came with indoor plumbing (particularly contamination of water supplies by open sewers); and "The Water Supply of the Farmhouse," addressing a battle already too familiar to farm women: the lime and minerals in spring and well water that affected the taste of water-cooked foods and made it almost impossible to build up a soapy lather to wash clothes or utensils.[29]

Experts did their best to inform, educate, and cajole. However, there was no getting around the simple truth that farm families, no matter how interested in improvements, lagged behind their urban counterparts. In 1919 the University of Missouri's extension service surveyed 645 farm residences and found that 461 had no indoor water supply; in 385 homes, the women carried the water. These results corresponded with those of a 1920 USDA study involving 9,896 farm homes in 33 northern and midwestern states. Water had to be carried in 6,511 households, and women did the carrying in 61 percent of such homes. In addition, 85 percent of the surveyed homes had outdoor toilets, but the study failed to note if there were households with no facilities whatsoever. The University of Missouri, however, asked the question and found, to its horror, that 229 families had no privy—

not even an outhouse. The situation was not unusual. Wrote Anna Sorensen in North Dakota: "In 1904, when my dad built the barn, he finally had enough pieces left over so that they could make an outhouse. And were we happy. We were so proud of that outhouse. One big hole and one little hole, and did we enjoy it."[30]

Experts found it difficult to reconcile expectations with reality. From farm to farm, vast differences existed in amenities and conveniences. In the 1920 USDA study, 79 percent of the homes surveyed used kerosene for lighting. However, in many of the homes where water had to be carried, there were some labor-saving devices. Sewing machines, most often of the foot-treadle variety, were present in 95 percent of the homes; 47 percent had carpet sweepers; and 57 percent had a washing machine powered by hand, with gasoline or kerosene, or, in a few cases, by electricity. Rural people were not ignorant of what was available, but they often could not afford the cost of installing electricity, running water, and the machinery involved. One long-time Kansas rural mail carrier observed that people on his route often had electricity in their barns but none in their homes because that would mean "having to buy all those appliances"; when these items broke, the owner would incur further expenses for repair or replacement. One economist identified such expenses as "one great reason that there are so few conveniences in the country homes."[31]

In 1885 a Kansas newspaper noted that as settlement days and the "age of necessities" passed, farm people "should cultivate a taste for the aesthetical and make our homes beautiful . . . [a]nd create those environments which contribute so much to the enjoyment of life." No doubt the newspaper meant to comment upon a broad improvement of frontier communities. For many women, however, greater enjoyment of life meant something as simple as having better work tools. Wrote Nebraskan Louise Ritter in 1907, "In addition to my washing and sewing machine, I now have a dough kneader [resembling a large flour sifter, prongs turned and worked the dough]. I have been using it for two months and am very satisfied with it."[32]

USDA and agricultural college staff knew that steps toward home improvements and rural beautification would be made slowly. Nevertheless, the drive to update rural dwellings and surroundings continued, and rural women played a large role in this effort. In Dickinson County, Kansas, women asked the Farm Bureau agent for help in landscaping—after all, the area had "some fine country homes." The agent agreed, and a "Better Homes Week" was planned in April 1930. Women planned to visit several farm homes, see what had been done, and hear suggestions from a professor of horticulture sent out by the agricultural college. Unfortunately, rainy weather made country roads impassable, and the group visited only one home. Interest did not end, however. The professor gave additional talks, and women continued to study the subject through club work. Almost seventy years later, one woman recalled club lessons in landscaping, noting that her mother's efforts on the family farm were presented as a demonstration of what could be accomplished.[33]

Across the Plains, rural women worked together to improve surroundings. Oklahoma's agricultural college reported that by 1916 there were 21 counties with home demonstration agents. The college proudly noted that, because of agents' home improvement lessons, 1,592 homes had added door and window screens against flies and mosquitoes; 62 had built outhouses; and 441 had undertaken yard landscaping projects. In 1924 much the same was reported in Texas, where 1,520 homes had added screens and 1,090 "sanitary toilets" had been constructed. Meanwhile, one Montgomery County, Kansas, women's club took the beautification campaign beyond the home and landscaped the grounds of a community church, and women in Motley County, Texas, attempted to do the same at their county courthouse. There, unfortunately, the water used to keep the plants going contained gypsum and soon killed all the vegetation. Undaunted, the women set about raising the money needed to finance the digging of a deep well for a usable water supply.[34]

It might be argued that beautification and the addition of home amenities were not lessons women needed to learn. After all, frontier literature is replete with examples of women who intended to make their new homes, however humble, "homelike." The homelike atmosphere, as historian Elliott West has noted, not only provided comfort but also tangibly expressed a family's values.[35] Rural reform simply took the concept one step further. If a home displayed a family's values—and, intrinsically, a woman's influence—then a community's physical beauty and improvement told a great deal about the women there. Men and women alike accepted the premise that land could be managed for greater farm productivity. Women translated land management to also mean their yards, schoolgrounds, and public places.

Beautification was one way for women to show that they were learning new lessons. A more immediate way was to change their "workshops" for more efficiency. A USDA retrospective report in 1962 noted that farm housing became a formally recognized research area in 1931 with the President's Conference on Home Building and Home Ownership. This event was supported by reports from Maud Wilson at Oregon State College and Evelyn Roberts of Washington State College that established standards for work-surface heights and use of space in farm homes. The conference and reports, however, only validated domestic economy's preexisting interest in improved rural housing.[36]

Beginning in the 1920s, extension programs aimed to remodel the physical layout of homes—particularly kitchen areas. This plan incorporated business strategies of efficiency, including time and motion studies. These ideas redirected women's thinking about how work was performed. A New Mexico woman could say that the addition of running water to her home saved her 260 miles a year in walking from well to kitchen; one might ask how she arrived at that number. Domestic economy lessons encouraged women to keep notebooks on how much time was spent on each chore and actually to count the number of steps taken to perform a task. Such knowledge suggested how effort could be reduced.[37]

Extension agents provided demonstrations for which they had been trained in a number of ways. Wrote a 1927 graduate of South Dakota's land-grant college, "Our Home Planning class included a project where by we were to prepare a notebook on a home place, drawn to scale. Also, each room [in the plan] was accompanied by pictures taken from magazines, catalogs, etc." Cutting pictures from magazines or keeping notebooks may hardly seem adequate training, but the exercises demanded investigation and conceptualization. Out of the classroom, women transmitted information about modern furnishings and room arrangements. They demonstrated their knowledge at club meetings and exhibitions. State and county fairs began to put model farm kitchens on display, with an extension agent in charge. In a Kansas example, an agent helped one club prepare a modern kitchen model for a county fair. Club members took over the duty of giving talks to fair visitors. They spoke to over eighteen hundred women, emphasizing the "advantage of the improved equipment and better arrangement." Women also offered their kitchens for makeovers. Writing in 1928 of one before-and-after story, an agent described the existing kitchen as a "shed" with miscellaneous pieces of furniture pressed into use. One table came from the "husband's folks", who had started housekeeping in 1890. Although it was not unusual for families to have hand-me-down furniture, the modern kitchen could do without them. In this case, however, the woman could not afford new furnishings, so the agent showed how the existing ones could be refurbished or added to at little cost. The furniture was repainted and rearranged so that fewer steps were required between table, stove, and sink; a "utensil cabinet" was constructed from a box that cost only fifty cents. The finished result made this particular farm woman feel that she had taken one more step toward a modern kitchen.[38]

Practical demonstrations occurred across rural America. Lectures and demonstrations for both white and black women's clubs were standard in Texas, where extension leaders decided to generate more interest with "improved kitchen" contests. Women competed at county, district, and state levels in one of two categories; the first included kitchens in which improvements were made for under twenty-five dollars, and the second was for those where costs exceeded that amount. Women were asked to explain how they financed changes. Most raised money by selling dairy goods, poultry, or garden produce; some sold a pig or cow or picked cotton. Extension leaders were encouraged by the number of participating farm-tenant wives, who evidently wanted improvements even though they did not own their homes. Success with kitchen contests led to competitions in improved living rooms, in which women were judged on how well they created a center for family entertainment and conversation. These events drew fewer participants than the kitchen contests, however, because not all farm homes had living room space, and many rural families held to the kitchen as a family center.[39]

Statistical accounting suggests that thousands of women heard and responded to home improvement messages, but a Wyoming woman added a caveat: "There was a club out north that had an all-day meeting, and after luncheon in this woman's home, they reorganized her kitchen. After they had worked all afternoon, she looked it over and said, 'I'd druther have it the way I'd druther have it.' But most people were very much pleased with this sort of help."[40]

Home modernization was supported by many publications. *American Motherhood* provided articles on saving time in the laundry and kitchen, including one that suggested women had much to learn from their daughters, who studied these new methods in college. Then there was the agricultural press. *South Dakota Farmer* articles such as "Economy in the Home: Make Housework Easy" and "Make the Farm Home Modern" emphasized the carefully arranged kitchen, discussing spatial relationships that saved women's "vital energy" by reducing the steps between work spaces. The latter article also took men to task for allowing women to carry water when it was possible to install pumps and drainage systems inside or adjacent to kitchens. There was, said the article, simply no excuse for men to ignore the possibilities for their wives and daughters to better manage time and motion. After all, there was abundant proof that women were trying.[41] Wrote one Kansas woman:

> In the earlier years of my experience at keeping house
> the thought had never occurred to me to make a study of step
> saving and making things in my kitchen as convenient as lay
> within my means, but the Farm Bureau has opened my eyes
> to these things and with the suggestions and kindly patience
> of the home demonstration ladies, I am now accomplishing
> my work with more ease and pleasure than I ever thought
> possible, besides realizing I can be a better wife and mother
> than when worn and jaded by the necessary and unnecessary
> work I was doing.[42]

This woman had the sink, table, and counter measured and adjusted to her height so that "no unnecessary energy is wasted there." A stool was constructed so she could sit at many chores rather than bending over them. Utensils were arranged within easy reach, and kitchen surfaces were either painted or enameled to make cleaning easier. Another aid to a clean kitchen was a floor covered with linoleum. This covering, also placed in living rooms and bedrooms, added a bright touch. It was not, however, just decoration; it was an indicator of modernity. It was more time-efficient because it made cleaning easier, relieving women from having to scrub wood floors or maintain ones of hard-packed earth. Remembered a woman of her family's 1910 housekeeping routine in a western Kansas sod house: "Our soddy had a wood floor, and a piece of linoleum that mother had brought from Abilene [Kansas] covered it adequately." The tone of the woman's reminiscence suggested that the dwelling was not "home" until the linoleum was laid. In the same vein, a North Dakota woman wrote to *Modern Homemaking* magazine: "In my opinion the four things which go the furthest in easing one's housework are: kitchen stove, dish-drainer, bread-mixer, and linoleum." The 1919 University of

Missouri study found 374 farm homes with linoleum. It was a hopeful sign among less encouraging findings (such as the lack of toilet facilities).[43]

Kitchen linoleum was considered when women applied for the title of "Master Farm Homemaker." Sponsored by *Farmer's Wife* magazine beginning in 1927, this program took its inspiration from the "Master Farmer" program begun in 1925 by the Illinois-based *Prairie Farmer*. (By 1935, there were over fourteen hundred Master Farmers nationally, including at least six women). The Master Farm Homemaker designation honored the farm woman for "the way she has adapted herself and her homemaking to conditions; how she is doing her 'job' of homemaking in view of the circumstances under which she is working." To be considered, women had to complete a lengthy set of detailed questions about home and work. How many rooms were in the house? Where were foodstuffs stored? What canning methods were used? What were the lighting facilities? Did the family own a car? Who drove it? Was there a privy? Was it inside or outside? How old were the children? Where did they sleep? The questions assessed women, but they also prompted an examination of work habits, surroundings, and areas for improvement. The answers provided a small survey of farm homes and the women who lived in them. One question asked about linoleum; of 87 applicants, 72 (or 83 percent) had it. Though most simply listed "linoleum," some were specific. Mrs. James Cook near Wakefield, Kansas, had a "printed light blue linoleum"; Mrs. C. D. Pottorff near Dodge City had a "red and green congoleum"; Mrs. Edward Deschner in Harvey County had a "linoleum rug"; and Mrs. Mary R. Hollis, also in Harvey County, answered "Gold Seal Congoleum." This last was a quality product advertised in national women's magazines and sold through mail-order companies. It certainly would have been a point of pride for Mrs. Hollis.[44]

These women represented the thousands who had been reached through extension work. By their participation in the Master Farm Homemaker program, they indicated self-confidence in what they had accomplished. All canned by the newest methods, owned and drove automobiles, and remarked on their own home efficiency methods. They did not share the same amenities, however. Mary Hollis, Mrs. Pottorff, and Mrs. Deschner had electricity, whereas Mrs. Cook relied on kerosene for lighting. They were bound, nevertheless, by an interest in being modern and up to date.[45]

Extension work fostered these feelings and provided a strong base for female organization. Clubs were social outlets, but, as important, they disseminated information relevant to women's daily lives. In the twelve meetings of one Coffey County, Kansas, club in 1926, for example, lessons focused on making cheese and cottage cheese, preparing meat and egg dishes, storing food correctly, creating millinery, and judging manufactured products to get the best quality at the most economical price. The last skill rose in importance as rural women became larger consumers of material goods. Nationally, club lessons covered nutrition, balanced meals, and school lunches. The last emphasized hot school lunches and correct packing for transport. (In one year, 105 women in Anderson County, Texas, "properly" packed 871 lunches.) With tenacity, women also tackled lessons in sewing by machine and hand; constructing mattresses; making dressmaker dummies and altering commercial patterns; refurbishing clothes and hats to imitate the latest styles or for children's hand-me-downs; sprucing up furniture with homemade slipcovers (as one Kansas woman recalled, "Oh, those terrible big flower prints"); and using appliances such as carpet sweepers and coffee percolators. In home nursing lessons, women learned to recognize symptoms and to make a bedpan from a cooking pan, an ice bag from an inner tube, and a bed tray from a wooden crate.[46]

For reinforcement, women competed at county extension meetings, county or state fairs, and expositions. Entrants in a Texas women's biscuit contest were judged for their distinctive abilities in making both sour-milk and baking-powder biscuits; the state champion walked away with a twenty-six-piece set of silverware. Competitions also pitted club against club. Four Leavenworth County, Kansas, clubs in

1918 sent more than five hundred jars of canned fruits, vegetables, and meat to fairs in Topeka, Hutchinson, and Wichita and exhibited the same at a farmers' institute. At a majority of these fairs, only whites competed, but black and Native American women also had opportunities. The Potawatomi Indian Fair near Mayetta, Kansas, limited participation to members of the Potawatomi, Sac and Fox, Iowa, and Kickapoo tribes, all of which had reservations in Kansas. Like other women, Native Americans competed in livestock and farm produce categories, but they also demonstrated their skills in domestic categories ranging from beadwork to canning. Exhibition and competition served as a form of communication for all women, regardless of background.[47]

Competition and club involvement entailed both conformity with and departure from the expected female roles that had become so entrenched during the nineteenth century. The severe separation of male and female spheres during the Victorian period, it may be argued, were played out by farm women when they engaged in domestic improvements and chose to display their skills within a public forum. These activities support the evaluation of such historians as Gayle R. Davis who has written about the female quilt culture and what she outlines as "separate social systems of recognition and evaluation of an individual's achievements." Certainly, women were judged by other women, separate from male evaluation of their contributions or achievements. However, they had avenues for public recognition other than domestic work. At home and in fair competitions they displayed their abilities to raise quality livestock, garden produce, and marketable crops. The domestic economy movement and rural women in general saw the world beyond the walls of the home. Wrote Anne Evans of the USDA, extension programs and club activities aided women in developing "every phase of activity which will mean better home life on the farm, broader and bigger agricultural opportunities for the future, and an ideal rural community life."[48]

This is not to say that the domestic economy movement was without limitations. Some groups, such as quilting or church-based clubs, refused to be pulled into the fold of home extension. Moreover, time- and motion-efficiency tools and labor-saving devices reached a point of diminishing returns. Domestic economists promised that those with efficiently run households would enjoy work weeks of from fifteen to thirty-eight hours (the difference represented unexpected or seasonal chores); nevertheless, a 1928 USDA study determined that farm women worked sixty-three hours a week on average. This finding leads one to wonder if an improvement actually occurred and, if so, what the hours must have been *before* domestic economy stepped in to save women's energy. Earlier, private efficiency studies and federal home economics research funded by the 1925 Purnell Act found that the combined average for housework among urban and rural women was fifty-two hours a week. Studies for 1924–1925 (repeated in 1930–1931) determined that an average work week for farm women was sixty-one hours. College-educated urban women had the lowest time—forty-eight hours—either because they had domestic help or because they worked outside the home and thus spent less time on housework. Despite numerous and varied labor-saving devices, the number of hours required for housework did not decrease between 1925 and 1930. On the surface, then, it would appear that women were led down the garden path when they were told that new material goods and a "right" attitude would reduce their work loads.[49]

Actually, it was not so much that basic lessons failed women; other factors came into play. Analyzing the changing situation in 1919, Mary Bigelow of *Farm, Stock, and Home* magazine concluded that although isolation had once been considered the greatest hardship endured by rural women, the automobile and easier mobility were changing that. Now women faced the prospect of a greater social life; as a result, however, there was more peer pressure to display home-making ideals, particularly for women in extension groups. Women also found that housekeeping actually expanded in renovated or newly built farmhouses. The very structure of modern homes, which had more rooms, increased the area that demanded cleaning, decorating,

and general upkeep. Adoption of new strategies and labor-saving devices might reduce the time spent hauling water or bringing in fuel,
but, as one Kansas woman observed, ideas about cleanliness made
other demands, as did new appliances. A powered wringer washing
machine, for example, required at least as much water as had been
needed to wash and rinse clothes by hand in a tub. Time spent running wet clothes through a wringer hardly differed from time invested
in the earlier mode of laundering. A cream separator saved women
the task of hand-skimming milk, but the machine needed daily cleaning.
It was an onerous job and, if done improperly, produced a glutinous mass
of milk residue that could take hours to remove. As one woman recalled,
"I hated that separator with a purple passion. . . . When we quit milking
and doing our own separating, I used to wake up in the middle of the
night and think, 'Oh, land, I forgot to wash the separator.'"[50]

Nevertheless, women attempted to create more efficient kitchens
and to practice strategies that reduced steps and labor. They generally accepted the goals set down by experts and reformers: scientific
homemaking methods, improved home environments, and increased
economic opportunities. Agriculture itself gained from women's contributions, many argued; rural reform occurred when women involved
themselves in community betterment. One may interpret these expectations as continuing the societal view that women's roles lay in
protecting and enlivening home and social life. However, rural women
were presented with something more—opportunities for individual and
group contributions that belied domestic demands and reached to the
heart of the reshaping of rural America. Many believed that farm women
were the foundation of efforts to modernize and reform agricultural districts and their populations. Before such changes could be accomplished,
the women had to be informed. The domestic economy movement provided an important avenue through which this education could be
achieved. It defined women's interaction with one another and asked
them to consider alternatives in conducting their daily lives. It begged
for change in rural living and promised benefits for all.

4 Better Babies and Rural Health

      A KANSAS WOMAN NAMED BLANCHE BEAL LOWE wrote: "One time when I asked Mama about the picture of Ethel, Ralph, Carl, and Loney, she said the picture was taken in the fall of 1891, a year before I was born. One of the boys in Ralph's room at school had come down with whooping cough, which meant the whole class had been exposed. Right away Mama and Papa took the children to have their pictures taken, 'in case they got whooping cough,' Mama said, 'and we lost one.'" The children did come down with whooping cough, but the family doctor "pulled them through." All, including the sister who would be born in 1892, weathered other childhood illnesses. The Beal family was not just lucky that the children survived; it was somewhat atypical in this respect. As the mother, Anna Beal, said, "They hardly knew a family that hadn't lost one or more of their children to whooping cough or diphtheria."[1] Anna and William Beal, a Kansas couple who tried homesteading, farming and town life, reacted to the possibility of death by photographing their children—just in case. However, they also brought in a competent doctor. Other families did the same, but some, far from town or living in communities without a physician, had to rely on home remedies or the nursing knowledge of neighbors.

Childhood death, infant mortality, and maternal death in child-birth were ever present in both rural and urban environments. Often a feeling of helplessness prevailed. A childhood memory of one Kansas woman was of her baby brother's acute reaction to a spider bite: "Mother brought him out [for us] to kiss him goodbye. He was going to die." The quick help of a neighbor and advice from a doctor by telephone saved the child, but the experience was not unlike that of Hamlin Garland, who watched his daughter cling to life, suffering through the last stages of diphtheria. "My only hope was in the nurse, who refused to give her up. I could not talk or write or think of any other thing. The child's suffering filled my mind with an intolerable ache of apprehension."In some cases, a disease seemed to attack in an instant, and too little was known to fight it off. In others, ignorance or lack of proper medical attention took a life that might have been saved. Even the presence of a physician did not ensure quality care. Wrote one country doctor in disgust: "Many women in this neighborhood died of puerperal fever, chiefly due to one doctor who divided his time between practicing medicine and raising hogs. It was his practice to administer a large dose of ergot in order to hasten labor so he could reach home in time to feed the hogs. He sometimes washed his hands after the completion of labor but never before."[2]

The availability and quality of health care varied widely from one community to another. A University of Nebraska Extension Service circular, for example, simply stated what all knew: "This means that the rural homemaker especially will often need to rely on her own judgment for remedies and care." The collective American mind, however, held to the agrarian image of pure, wholesome country life. This perception placed rural residents in an ironic position. Whereas medical care was often nonexistent, popular culture portrayed farm people as healthy and robust. Many city dwellers accepted this image and dreamed of a country refuge; magazines encouraged these longings with stories and illustrations. Urban charities urged programs that sent destitute children to rural summer homes, providing them a few weeks in a wholesome atmosphere. Country children were presented in the popular press as round creatures with apple cheeks, and young adults were drawn as strapping males or glowing maidens—the boy behind the plow, the milkmaid at her chores. The agrarian press was hardly reluctant to perpetuate these images. *Farmer's Wife* magazine's cover illustrations presented women in blooming health, and county fair posters often featured plump and happy children posed around a garden's bounty. Extreme as some of the romantic examples were, few people disagreed with the belief that the country offered a healthy alternative to urban tenements, the stench of poor neighborhoods, and badly ventilated factories.[3]

Nevertheless, by the 1920s national health care indicators raised concerns. On a positive note, the national death rate from typhoid and diphtheria was cut in half between 1900 and 1913. On the other hand, the nation ranked eleventh in the world in infant mortality rates, and maternal death from puerperal infection was on the rise. The latter was certainly preventable, but experts seemed unable to explain its increase. Perhaps voicing the shortsighted view that "it can't happen here," one rural doctor suggested that puerperal-related deaths were more likely to occur in city lying-in hospitals than in country homes. The important point, however, was that in a nation touting its strides in industry, technology, and science, health care was for many substandard or completely lacking. More specifically, the level of health care in the heart of America, its rural communities, compared unfavorably with that of urban centers, particularly in access to medical aid and in reducing infant mortality.[4]

Social workers and health care professionals for so long had concentrated on improving prenatal, early childhood, and maternal care in cities, particularly in the poorest sections, that rural conditions generally were ignored. Through the last decades of the 1800s reformers, charities, and governments worked to eliminate the blight of the tenements, to establish public health clinics for urban mothers and their children, and to educate a largely immigrant population in child care, nutrition, and first aid. By the 1920s these efforts saw real results, although some improvement was perceptible a decade earlier. Studies in 1915 indicated that 94 out of every 1,000 infants born in rural areas died in the first year; in urban areas the number was 102 out of every 1,000. Although the margin was only 8 children per thousand, the numbers still supported the long-held standard that rural children were more likely to survive their first year of life. From 1915 to 1921, infant mortality rates in rural and urban regions remained close. However, a steady drop in urban mortality was evident, whereas the figures for rural sections remained virtually unchanged, with a slight rise just after World War I (possibly reflecting the national influenza epidemic). Between 1915 and 1921, urban infant mortality rates declined by an average of 24 percent, but in rural areas the drop was only about 15 percent.[5]

These numbers held many implications. Perhaps the most significant pertained to the geographical distribution of health care and preventive medicine. Whereas the worst in urban life was put under a magnifying glass and great strides were made in bringing improvements, rural communities were left alone to grapple with disease and death, pretty much as they had from the time of settlement. If a qualified doctor was nearby, fine; if not, one simply had to make do, as did the South Dakota ranch woman who acted as her own surgeon and saved her life after being bitten by a rattlesnake. Isolation often forced rural women to endure bitter loneliness, but in matters of sickness it could be life-threatening. One Montana mother and her three children, forty miles from the nearest doctor, went for several days without medical attention when they came down with scarlet fever. They survived, but when a five-day-old infant in the same Montana district fell ill with an unidentified sickness, it perished; parents could not reach a doctor because they could not cross a flooded waterway.[6]

Problems of inadequate care and disparities between rural and more populated areas were recognized by many. Reporting on the state of American agriculture in 1918, the secretary of the USDA devoted two pages to rural health and sanitation, noting:

Every means should be adopted to see to it that the benefits of modern medicine accrue more largely to the scattered populations of the rural districts. Formerly the urban communities were characteristically the homes of disease. They possessed all the disadvantages of concentration of population without adequate sanitary safeguards. Now no cities and very few of the larger towns are without substantial equipment in the way of drainage, sewage disposal, and hospitals. They have the services of specialists and of trained nurses. . . . As a consequence, among the inhabitants of the larger communities the ravages of smallpox, typhoid fever, and malaria have been in large measure controlled. The rural districts still have advantages; but a vast deal remains to be done . . . to give the country districts the advantages of modern hospitals, nursing, and specialized medical practice.[7]

Rather surprisingly, the emphasis in agricultural states also focused on public health efforts in growing towns and cities. Dr. Samuel Crumbine, head of the Kansas State Board of Health, became nationally known for his "Don't Spit on the Sidewalk" campaign to stop the spread of tuberculosis and for his fight to abolish shared drinking cups and towels in public places, particularly on passenger trains. For the doctor and his peers in public health, rural life was often an afterthought. Commenting on Kansas's "Swat the Fly" campaign, Dr. Crumbine noted its tremendous impact in getting town residents to add screened windows and doors to their homes. These stopped the spread of disease by stopping the fly. The campaign encouraged the screening of some farm homes and was accompanied by home demonstration lessons in making flyswatters (some used screen material; others were made from leather strips fastened over wire coat hangers). Nevertheless, for Crumbine rural controls were secondary, despite the prevalence of flies carrying filth from barnyard to house, spreading disease. "The number of flies all over the house, and on the baby's face," wrote one doctor, "was limited only by the available standing room."[8]

Crumbine and public health officials in other states were intent upon eradicating communicable diseases, which threatened to reach epidemic proportions in populous areas. To some extent, these officials relied on college extension programs and the USDA to bring about rural improvements. After all, extension bulletins dealt with sanitation matters, and the USDA called for rural communities to form sanitation committees and inform families "that babies can be killed with fly-infected food as well as with an ax [and] that they ought to be willing to work as hard to exterminate the fly as they would to exterminate a gang of murderers." Despite real conditions, the myth of healthy rural life persisted, both in the national mind-set and among rural denizens, who often conceded that problems existed—but not in their particular locale.[9]

Slowly, health care specialists and social workers realized that rural health demanded attention. This they provided, often with the hope that studies and statistics would nudge the federal government to provide funds and set up intervention programs. However, the experts, though experienced in studying urban populations, had preconceived notions about farming regions. Only too familiar with the desperate conditions of some city neighborhoods, they expected to find correlations in the country. No doubt those expectations were sometimes met, but studying an immigrant population on the farm was different from observing the same group in the city. In rural settings, immigrants tended to settle together and to maintain their cultural values and behavior. There was less emphasis on joining the mainstream of American life, and there were fewer arenas in which the acculturation process took place. But urban patterns often shaped social workers' expectations; trained to identify social factors as the cause of a condition rather than as a result, they commonly ignored larger rural issues such as isolation or local group values. A case in point was the Children's Bureau's compilation of infant and maternal mortality surveys conducted in North Carolina, Kansas, Montana, and Wisconsin. Those for Montana and Wisconsin are of particular interest, for they included both American-born and immigrant populations (with an emphasis on the immigrants) and reflected rural realities that sometimes astonished bureau researchers.

The Wisconsin survey, taken during 1914–1915, looked at 453 families in two counties. One was a northern county in the Plover River Valley, where the population was a mix of American-born settlers and German and Polish immigrants. In the other county, situated in the state's southwestern section, the predominant population was American-born, with second-generation Germans, Swedes, and newly arrived Swiss-Germans also present. The study covered both counties but emphasized the northern county's German and Polish families, probably because many were first-generation. In the 1916 Montana study, confined to the western half of one county but including 5,500 square miles, 463 families were surveyed. The majority were American-born, but there were also Russian-German immigrants.[10]

The two studies compiled mortality rates, but they also looked at living conditions and the presence of doctors and midwives. Midwives were given special notice in Wisconsin because they were regarded as "an established institution" among the Germans and Polish, and most were not registered with the state (a law frequently violated). Moreover, as Joan Jensen has noted, midwives may have received special scrutiny because doctors suspected them of performing abortions. Although the Wisconsin researchers did not mention the latter in their report, they were surprised and at some loss to explain the study's results. They found that children in the southern county were on par with national averages for mortality, and babies in the northern county were discovered to have a "considerably better chance of survival than average." In fact, when various ethnic groups in the northern county were separated, the one with the highest infant mortality rate—the Polish—still reflected the national average (one infant in ten dying before its first birthday). The results did not suggest any lack of care peculiar to the Polish. Rather, they reflected a higher pregnancy rate among this group; forty-two women experienced at least ten full-term pregnancies. As one doctor of the time remarked, if a woman "decided she wanted to raise six [children], she would need to bear ten." Additionally, mortality rates for women in childbirth, including the Polish, were well within the national average; they were lower than in Montana, where maternal mortality was twice the national average. In both Wisconsin counties, rural infant and maternal death rates were at the national norm or below. In Montana the rates were higher, but, said the study, they were still lower than "for any city studied by the bureau." In fact, the Montana surveyor was surprised to find most infants and young children "unusually healthy and sturdy."[11]

These positive indicators were somewhat puzzling, in that the majority of women in both studies were not attended by a physician (in Montana, however, 104 of the 463 women left their remote homes before they came to term in order to be delivered by a town doctor). Some women had delivered themselves alone or with their husband's help and had not called in a midwife; although some swore that no midwife was needed because their children were "born in two pains," it was more likely that delivery was quick because these women worked through their first hours of labor and only took to their beds when birth was imminent. Furthermore, most women, regardless of ethnic background, did not confine themselves to bed after delivery for the medical profession's prescribed ten days, although the number that did was higher in Montana than in Wisconsin. Understandably, bed rest often was not an option. Said one Montana woman, "The men expect work done up just as well at that time [just after confinement] as at any other." Almost none of the women enjoyed the luxury of hired help, and neighbors could only pitch in for one or two days before returning to their own families. Thus, women were up and working too soon after delivery, and the researchers were horrified with the extreme examples. One Wisconsin woman never went to bed but "got supper and milked the cow the same evening" of her delivery day; another propped herself up in bed "with her dough board in front of her trying to make biscuits" just hours after giving birth. Showing a bias, investigators expected American-born women to be drastically different from immigrants in postdelivery behavior, but such was not the case: "Even the American mothers had inadequate opportunity for recuperation."[12]

The experts were no less surprised that these women sometimes nursed their children for a longer period than the nine months approved by "most medical authorities." Actually, only about 16 percent of the Wisconsin mothers exclusively suckled their children through the ninth month, but those that did tended to extend the period past the second birthday. The same held true in Montana, where mothers followed the same nursing patterns and were even more reluctant than those in Wisconsin to feed children solid foods before their first birthday. The prolonged nursing time, in fact, contributed to a lower infant death rate because children weaned over a longer period did not experience what one country doctor called "the dread second summer." This was the time when infants, taken from the breast and given cow or goat milk and food from the table, suffered gastrointestinal problems related to the quick spoilage of food in the summer months when poor or no refrigeration was available. There were, of course, canned milk substitutes such as the Borden Company's Eagle Brand Milk, but these products were used more often in urban areas than in the country. Therefore, particularly during summer, rural infants suffered diarrhea, followed by dehydration and sometimes convulsions. "The result," wrote one doctor, "was a frightful mortality rate. Many a weary night have I spent bathing a child whose convulsions were due to an unsuitable diet, only to lose the battle in the end."[13]

A North Dakota woman recalled her own family's experience: "Mother's baby, who was six months old, got very sick with what they called 'summer complaint' at that time. . . . And that was a very sad thing. My mother could never get over it 'cause she couldn't nurse the baby and had no place to keep the milk cool, and she thought the baby got sour milk, possibly."[14] And a one-time farm boy observed that the combination of summer heat, flies, and poor sanitary practices was deadly:

> If you could go back with me and see our cows, or barn, the milk pails and cans, and our lack of facilities for keeping milk cold, you would doubtless have been convinced that no baby could survive such unsanitary milk. It is my belief that I could have survived being fed on milk contaminated with stable filth. It was the cloth strainer which a baby would not compete with by his defense mechanisms. We rinsed the strainer after pouring the morning's milk through it, and hung it up to dry. In summer, fifty or more flies would alight on it within a minute and feed upon the milk residues, speckling it with fly-specks. In the evening, the fresh milk was poured through this fly-excrement-laden cloth. A baby could scarcely ever fail, when fed such contaminated milk, to suffer from diarrheal infection and die.[15]

An unmistakable relationship existed between infant mortality and summer conditions. The 1916 death rate in states that made up the national death-registration area (most of the northern and western states had vital-statistic legislation requiring that deaths be recorded) showed a startling rise in the summer and declined as autumn set in. The number of infant deaths for June was 3,250; July, 7,092; August, 10,284; and September, 7,814. By October the number had declined to 4,252. Certainly, not every recorded death resulted from gastrointestinal problems, but medical officials placed this as probably the second largest cause of death—behind a category that included badly handled deliveries, premature births, birth defects, and stillborns.[16]

Both studies firmly denounced the hard work women performed during pregnancy and soon after delivery. Chores commonly included hauling water, chopping firewood, digging potatoes, and raking hay. One Wisconsin woman reported that, although badly nauseated, she milked five cows, made butter for sale, and cared for garden and chickens until her immediate confinement. The Wisconsin study found that one-half, or 168, of the women in the northern county did some fieldwork during pregnancy. Polish women were most likely to be found outside, cutting stubble or helping in the harvest. Life could be hard, but, asked the women, who would do the work if they did not? Domestic help was at a premium everywhere. One Kansas woman remembered, "we looked far and wide for someone who could come and stay with me." Rural families understood that physical strain both before and after delivery contributed to health problems and caused miscarriages. Women might not die in childbirth, but their physical well-being was jeopardized, especially when multiple pregnancies were the norm. Nevertheless, the work had to be done, and few women thought of prenatal care. Researchers were appalled that less than 1 percent of the Wisconsin women and only about 2 percent of those in Montana received any kind of medical examination or consultation. The experts were quick to assign blame for this state of affairs on the husbands, who, it was said, refused to spend money on a doctor.[17]

Cost was only one consideration, however. Distance also played a part, and, as Sandra Schackel pointed out in her New Mexico study, language barriers presented real problems in communication and slowed the building of trust between health care professionals and non-English-speaking populations. In some cases, male doctors were not called in because rural residents still clung to the age-old belief (also prevalent among Native Americans) that their presence at deliveries violated female modesty.[18]

The Wisconsin and Montana studies, like others conducted by the Children's Bureau, produced a mixed view of rural life. The Wisconsin researchers were extremely critical of what they found, despite the positive relationship between European traditions and lower infant mortality. Perhaps their reluctance to accept this correlation reflected a refusal to give immigrant populations their due. On the other hand, the Montana investigator was more sympathetic, perhaps because she dealt with fewer immigrants and because those she found were, by her description, "literate." Moreover, she was overwhelmed by the western environment, and she felt real admiration for the women who lived with "tremendous, almost incredible distances" and the "[w]ild vastness of earth and sky." Researchers having direct contact with rural women were, however, in the minority. Most reformers and health care professionals were removed from their subjects and sometimes made harsh assessments, citing ignorance as a reason doctors were not consulted more often. As one woman in public nursing put it, the farmer and his wife had "not yet learned to regard childbirth as a serious and important event."[19]

This statement is telling. Many experts—middle to upper class and urban in orientation—viewed rural life from a distance and took stands that supported their own positions and class expectations. A continuing professionalization and specialization within the medical profession ritualized pregnancy and childbirth. Long confinements before delivery, delivery with doctors in attendance, and days of bed rest were the proper way to do things. When rural families could not duplicate these, they were labeled as being too casual in attitude.

In truth, childbirth *was* taken seriously. The Montana survey noted that one-third of prospective mothers tried to obtain prenatal information from books or magazines, and there is no doubt that many farm women faced the prospect with dread. Mary Logan in Kansas had five children, the youngest six years of age, when she found herself again pregnant. She was "none too happy about it at first," and the birth convinced her that this must be her last. "Mrs. Haeger and Mrs. Laidig [neighbors] and Doctor Demay were with me during the ordeal. They tried to soothe me but there were no opiates. . . . [T]he pain was so intense I begged to die. The baby was crossways and had to be turned by hand. Afterwards, I was terribly weak and sick. I had nervous chills for months." Logan certainly was not alone in her experience. Mary Kincaid, writing in 1896, expressed for many the apprehension: "Mamie, I got two hard months before me yet that if I count right, I just dread the time coming. . . . I wish there was no such thing as having babies. I wish I took George Willard's recipt and left the nasty thing alone. I will next time you bet I [will] not have any more if I live through this time which I hope I will. Well, Mamie it is there and it has to come out where it went in. Well might as well laugh as cry it be just the same."[20]

As Mary Kincaid suggested and as Elizabeth Hampsten illustrates in *Read This Only to Yourself*, rural women relied on each other, sought published information on prenatal care, shared materials that surreptitiously referred to contraceptives, and read between the lines of medical journals for clues to both birth control and abortion. "George Willard's recipt" hints at an effective abortive formula; just as medical publications suggested that ingestion of "old fashioned tansy tea, steel filings, and ergot" could induce menses. At a time when city and state anticontraceptive laws prohibited distribution of birth control information (though Margaret Sanger, among others, defied the law and openly discussed the subject), any bit of deductive reading from journals or veiled patent medicine advertisements would do.[21]

In the real world of limited medical knowledge and uneven availability of care, agricultural America could present a horrifying picture. Rather than an idyllic pastoral scene, it could resemble a minefield of hazards waiting to catch the unaware. As if childbirth and the prospect of child death were not enough with which to contend, accidents frequently maimed or killed. Among the graphic stories printed in the *South Dakota Farmer* were those of eight-year-old Belle Fourche, drowned in an irrigation ditch; Leah Pettit, whose "recovery was doubtful" after she was thrown from her horse while herding cattle; another whose prospects were "bright" after she sustained a serious cut when the team she was driving broke and ran, throwing her under a plow; and fifteen-year-old Hazel Cheney, killed when the oil cookstove she was lighting exploded. Some called this the "dark side" of farming. The picture was not one to encourage country living.[22]

City life and work, however, were no more safe or antiseptic, and industrial machinery could be just as dangerous. In fact, many argued that, despite the dangers they faced, farm women were better off than their city counterparts. Argued Florence Ward of the USDA:

Anyone who has experienced the satisfaction of living in the open country knows that the average farm woman is more fortunately placed in many ways than her average city sister. Studies of living and working conditions of city home makers bring to light in many homes not only handicaps in home equipment and conveniences, but an environment detrimental to health, happiness, and development. The varied interests of the farm woman's life, her contact with growing things, her enjoyment of seasonal changes in nature, and her freedom from noise, dust, and confusion is not to be lost sight of in comparing her conditions and opportunities.[23]

Some social scientists in the Children's Bureau may have found Ward too sanguine. In fact, the bureau was often more critical in its assessments of rural life than the USDA, probably because of the two agencies' contrasting makeups. The bureau attracted professional social workers and was headed by Julia Lathrop, who had worked with Jane Addams at Chicago's Hull House. Generally, the staff was urban-centered and intent on huge social reforms. The USDA, too, had staff members trained in sociology, but these were rural sociologists, not urban social workers. The USDA also wanted reforms, but its outlook and language were less strident than those of the Children's Bureau. It projected an attitude of working with, rather than acting on, rural populations.

Both agencies agreed, however, that state and federal educational programs were needed. The bureau meant to educate farm women and to secure federal aid for women in general. Its studies, as well as those conducted by other federal agencies and nongovernmental groups, were meant to arouse support for the Sheppard-Towner bill, which would provide federal money to states for maternal and child health care and education in order to correct deficiencies in rural areas. However, the bureau's health care advocates often showed little understanding of agrarian realities or of the burden women carried as home nurses and doctors. The bureau had to consider the national picture and sought to devise a campaign that applied to both city and rural populations. As a by-product of any such program, farm medicine would be pulled into the twentieth century.

One of the first, and most ambitious, programs was the "better baby" movement. Fostered by the Children's Bureau, the movement had several components. As these filtered down from the national to the county level, the plan took on a life of its own. It met obstacles or acceptance depending on local values, created new avenues for extension education to women, and used contests and clinics to bring about changes in the home. The better baby movement recognized no boundaries; it reflected the belief that science and medical research could improve anything.

When the movement began, more diseases were being controlled by medicines gained from scientific research. Technology was bringing a consistency to manufactured medicines, and eugenics was becoming widely accepted as a field of study. The latter was often debated, but it had supporters. In fact, the Eugenics Research Association felt entitled to ask that the 1920 U.S. Census survey form include questions on ancestry. Tracking the population's ethnic origins was, eugenists argued, of scientific importance. So, too, was the application of science to child health care and child rearing.[24]

In a world that was embracing science and technology, reformers began to look at the child as a biological machine—"the mechanical baby," to use Daniel Beekman's term. Standardization of care—from strict schedules for eating and exercise to continuity in training—could produce nothing less than the perfect child. Many believed that the only reason this result had not been achieved before was a lack of understanding of eugenics, insufficient medical knowledge, and poor education of women in child care. Motherhood, like food preparation, was now treated as a science. It was not by chance that a social worker, writing for *Social Service Review* in 1927, exhorted women to exhibit "maternal efficiency" by providing a sanitary environment, adequate sleep and fresh air, and proper food at regular intervals and in correct quantities. Women's magazines, too, preached efficiency. In June 1930, for example, *Woman's World* included an article on keeping regular schedules so that children responded "repeatedly in the desired way to the same conditions." The magazine promised that if mothers reduced "to a perfect system the 'raising' of Mr. Baby, his habits will all be of the best." The prescription resembled one for industrial efficiency: keep on schedule and properly maintain the machines. The nursery was a factory, with mothers as managers, technicians, and maintenance crews. Maternal love and intuition might have their place, but hard logic and science were the keys to children's emotional and physical development. This departure from the nineteenth century's sentimental view of motherhood reflected the thinking of twentieth-century America.[25]

Although a scientific approach to child rearing was expected to occur mainly in urban middle-class homes, experts believed the idea could transcend class and geographic lines. A popular periodical, *American Motherhood*, published such articles as "What a Farmer's Wife Can Accomplish," and *Farmer's Wife* and other rural publications reinforced the experts. The *South Dakota Farmer* wholeheartedly agreed that women needed education in the "business of motherhood" and supported the Children's Bureau: "For some time Uncle Sam has been paying considerable attention to the improvement of hogs, chickens and livestock, as well as teaching us how to raise pumpkins and potatoes, and it is encouraging to find attention now being turned toward improving the human race."[26]

However, farm women's use of the scientific approach to motherhood—when they accepted it—was often a far cry from what professionals expected. Hannah Bell in North Dakota recalled: "I remember

. . . seeing a deer a short distance from the house and as I wanted to take my rifle and get the deer, and the grass was so high I did not care to leave Oscar who was just at the toddling around age and would possibly follow and get lost, I tied him to a bed post with a rope while I shot and brought home the deer."[27] This was maternal efficiency at work: The possibility for disaster was foreseen; a logical plan of action was decided and acted upon; and the outcome for the family was positive in terms of safety and nutritional needs.

The Children's Bureau, established in 1912 under the U.S. Department of Labor, was a product of the Progressive Era. It reflected society's reverence for scientific investigation; it articulated the concerns of women and children and accepted medicine, psychology, and education as keys to improving and protecting the lives of children. The bureau was primarily concerned with health dangers and exploitation of women and children in the urban environment. Lantern slide shows, pamphlets (some printed in Spanish as well as English), silent movies (some with subtitles for specific immigrant groups), and eventually "talkies" were used to educate urban mothers. These visual aids also found rural audiences through the bureau's traveling exhibits, which were available to clubs and home extension workers.[28]

While printed materials and film reached some rural women, the problem was one of saturation. The Children's Bureau sought a program that was equally effective in rural and urban locales. The result was "better baby weeks," during which all American mothers, farm as well as city dwellers, weighed and measured their children. Professional medicine, through the growing field of pediatrics, had established fixed ranges of "normal" heights and weights for children of specific age groups. Children who fell outside the norms were believed to have early health problems, many of them related to poor nutrition. If children were weighed and measured, physicians and parents knew instantly if something was amiss. When data were collected on a regional and later national basis, experts and agencies concerned with child health could measure and catalog health needs.

In 1915 a systematic plan to organize examination clinics began with the better baby weeks program, which involved club women, extension organizations and agents, doctors, ministers, and businessmen at the local level. Not coincidentally, the clinics encouraged rural communities to further organize. Near Renwick, Iowa, for example, a rural women's club joined two in-town clubs and the state agricultural college to run a better baby clinic. Nationally, clinics operating one or two days a week were set up in rural county seats. Some isolated areas were reached via state health board trucks; the Kansas board borrowed the demonstration train idea and used a railroad car equipped with instructional displays for mothers and examination compartments for children. Parents were urged to bring their children for checkups. Although measurement and standardization were the focus, general medical examinations often were performed. Declaring her community's program a success, the Nemeha County, Kansas, home demonstration agent noted, "One of the physicians in the county reported that as a result of this child welfare work he has had 70 operations from tonsils and adenoids." This reference to tonsil and adenoid examination was not unusual. These problems were considered contributors to poor health and indicators of the more serious—and sometimes life-threatening—inflammation of the mastoid bone behind the ear.[29]

Supplementing clinics were better baby contests held at county and state fairs. Citing a need to "arouse interest in child study," the Interstate Fair at Sioux City, Iowa, held contests for a number of years. In 1920 alone, three hundred babies were "tabulated and examined"; another two hundred were turned away for lack of space and time. The Sioux City contests also included a dimension not found everywhere, mental tests that complied with "the requirements of scientific psychological laboratories." The questions asked on these tests are not clear today, but they probably were the same as those listed on the *Woman's Home Companion* "Better Babies Standard Score Card" used at a number of state and regional fairs. This card explained that mental development could be assessed with a version of the Binet-Simon intelligence test, which was meant to gauge performance of basic tasks at a certain age. For example, a six-month-old was graded on the ability to sit alone, react to unexpected sounds, and reach for and grasp objects. Failure to do so reduced the score and might indicate, among several possibilities, inadequate nutrition. Thus, many fair programs tried to identify relationships between environmental factors, such as improper diet, and child development. Seldom, however, did nutritionists or doctors suggest that low scores might be signs of mental retardation or cerebral palsy.[30]

At the Sioux City fair and the Kansas State Fair, children were entered in specific classes by age. Understandably, standards for a twelve-month-old differed from those for a twenty-six-month-old. The South Dakota competitions considered children up to the age of three, whereas the Kansas fair included four-year-olds. Boys and girls were not judged together, and rural children were separated from town children. Thus, award certificates, provided by *Woman's Home Companion*, went to the best rural boy and girl in an age group, and the same went to the best children from towns with populations of over one thousand. This system suggests a belief in environmental differences. One might conclude that rural children were separated to keep them from winning all the awards—their wholesome country life supposedly having produced glowing health—but the truth was different. Despite rhetoric extolling country living, those in charge of the better baby contests doubted that rural children could compete against their city cousins.[31]

Fair clinics reached down to the county level, where contests made no distinction between city and rural children. The Indian Agricultural Fair on the Potawatomi Reservation in Kansas simply awarded prizes to the best male and female babies under eighteen months, and the Kickapoo Indian Produce Fair in Horton, Kansas, considered its few better baby candidates as a group. The Johnson County, Nebraska, fair also dismissed complex categories and simply offered twenty-five dollars each to the best boy and best girl under the age of two. Meanwhile, clinics appeared at national and international events. The 1915 Panama-Pacific International Exposition in San Francisco featured Children's Bureau exhibits that explained the importance of mother's milk in fighting summer diarrhea and the need for prenatal care. Through glass partitions, fairgoers watched demonstrations of infants and toddlers being weighed and measured.[32]

Activities showed no signs of slowing. In fact, they gained momentum during 1918, designated Children's Year. This proclamation was in part a result of relief efforts for refugee children in war-torn Europe, but the special year paid attention to the needs of American children as well. The Children's Bureau cooperated with the Child Conservation Section of the National Council of Defense to begin a campaign targeting those of the "neglected age"—preschool children. Weighing and measuring clinics continued, but with a new purpose. Identifying health problems and educating parents were considerations, but clinic results forwarded to the Children's Bureau provided raw data for statistical studies. These, in turn, became arguments for the Sheppard-Towner bill.[33]

During the Children's Year, preprinted weighing and measuring cards were distributed nationally. These contained a list of questions on one side; a set of comparative tables for above, below, and average measurements filled the other. Questions mainly related to the examination at hand, but they also asked the child's name, the parents' backgrounds, and whether the birth was registered. This last reflected another issue of national import. Rural population and infant mortality rates could not be properly determined if births went unrecorded. Rural doctors, nurses, and midwives often failed to file birth registrations, though state law required it. Perhaps the question on the card would spur action.[34]

The Children's Year did inspire a frenzy of weighing and measuring clinics. Some of these were open to children up to ten years of age. Others restricted themselves to infants and toddlers. A few confined themselves to children of minority groups. In Riley County, Kansas, for example, the home extension agent took charge of clinics for black children and gave child care lectures to forty-five mothers. The agent reported that fifteen children were examined; the "most perfect" score was 96 percent on the national scale, but "none of the children were up to the standard" of white children for height. Many had bowed legs, prominent abdomens, and defective tonsils. Almost all had perfect teeth. Notwithstanding that over half of the black children's scores were at or above the national average, the agent decided that their defects resulted from eating "too many potatoes too early in infancy" and not having enough milk. Similar clinics took place in U.S. territories. From Honolulu, Hawaii, it was reported that "all classes have been reached, from the child of the millionaire to the tenement." It was, however, difficult to reach some country districts, particularly those on remote islands. Nevertheless, Hawaii's health coordinator was able to return two thousand completed cards to the Children's Bureau.[35]

Total examination in any region was, of course, impossible. It was hoped, for example, that Kansas would record at least 37,000 children, but it only reported on 25 percent of that number. South Dakota and Nebraska reached only about 40 percent of their target levels; North Dakota about 45 percent; Oklahoma barely 15 percent; and Texas only 8 percent. Local reports explained difficulties in reaching children. In Florence, Texas, sixty-three children aged one through ten were weighed and measured; of these, fifty-six were examined by a doctor, who found twenty-six problem tonsil and adenoid cases. Of those who did not see the doctor, the parents of four youngsters "thought physical examination unnecessary." Three other children failed to appear for physical examinations "on account of sickness."[36]

Although the campaign was generally accepted and highly promoted, the numbers suggest the program's limitations. Despite attempts to reach remote areas, not all were visited or organized for local clinics. Because of vague guidelines, some state coordinators developed programs that included adolescents, not just toddlers. The target numbers established by the Children's Bureau for each state also raised questions, as the agency's literature and in-house papers never completely explained how these were determined. How, for example, did it decide that exactly 86,423 Texas children should be examined? It is unlikely that the bureau had precise child population numbers for each state. In all probability, it made guesses based on states' general populations.

Evidently no one questioned the numerical projections, but the program still had detractors. When supervisors of the Children's Year campaign debated what to do with the flood of raw data, a professor from Howard University took them to task: "In the midst of the living truth, statistical facts are mere dead formulas. . . . [W]hen you and your trained staff of statisticians get to Heaven, as of course you will, I trust you will put them to the task of determining how much milk and honey are necessary to maintain an adult saint for ten thousand years. And after you have made your calculation remember that it requires just as much to maintain a black saint as it does to maintain a white one." The professor then suggested that cold statistics overlooked the reality that black children were emerging from a history of slavery in which their predecessors had been exploited merely for their "animal and mechanical powers." To believe that only half a century of freedom had sufficiently overcome "the heavy handicap of these traditions" was not only impractical but racist. This criticism was certainly true if black families, especially those in the South (who were of great interest to the Children's Bureau), were condemned when their children's development did not meet medical standards set by white doctors.[37]

White rural residents had their own doubts. An Iowa program coordinator asked the Children's Bureau to drop clinics in her county and suggested that the bureau replace her if it wanted to carry them through to conclusion. This organizer had encountered little positive response and concluded that in her district, "The families are small, and the children are all given the very best medical attention by their parents." Diplomatically, the Iowa coordinator stated resistance, but other commentators were not so subtle. A Walla Walla, Washington, newspaper editor wondered: "Is not trying to measure and weigh all babies and grade them to a fixed standard like judging Jerseys and Holsteins [cattle] by the same rules? Difference in size does not mean difference in vitality. Many a little man has worked a big one into the grave." The analogy was one that rural residents understood.[38]

Some families complied only because they thought refusal violated federal statutes. Some state and local clinic committees hinted that examinations were required by law. The Children's Bureau let misunderstandings stand unless citizens demanded clarification. When the Indiana Society for Medical Freedom opposed the program, the Children's Bureau attempted to discredit the group as being made up of Christian Scientists, chiropractors, and others outside "the regular medical profession." At least one doctor called the program a "fiasco" because women's committees, sometimes inept and guilty of misinformation, replaced health officials in local organization. Julia Lathrop sent the complaining doctor an icy message: If people misunderstood the program's voluntary nature, that was not the bureau's fault. The end result justified any confusion. Data collected would benefit all.[39]

Despite reservations, rural populations as a whole did not boycott the campaign. Farm families willingly took their children for examination during better baby weeks. They allowed their children to be judged at fairs, just as they would enter their cattle, quilts, or jellies in competition. The Kansas State Fair made just such a comparison: the "entering, examining, and awarding of prizes [consists of] the same basis or principles that are applied to live-stock shows." These were not beauty contests. In at least one instance, farmers placed not only their children but themselves in competition. The Topeka Free Fair, with support from the Kansas State Board of Health, offered "fittest family" prizes and a Grade A rating (a designation usually reserved for farm produce.) Though town families also participated, rural residents were willing to take part in such competitions, which saw each family member tested physically and psychologically. Examinations included the usual weighing and measuring of children. Adults, however, were subjected to laboratory work that included blood and urine tests and a Wassermann test (for syphilis). Mental fitness was determined through a series of procedures overseen by Dr. Karl A. Menninger of Topeka's respected Menninger Clinic.[40]

Those intent upon improving their farms and lives with scientific farming and domestic economy evidently agreed with the Iowa woman who wrote: "The time has come to apply the biologic laws, so carefully worked out through the years on plants and animals, to the next higher order of creation."[41] The number of rural children that appeared in clinics and at fair contests suggest that a segment of the population believed such programs proper and beneficial. The new age of science could improve farm life in many ways. Having healthier, stronger, better babies was just one of many possible outcomes.

Results of the Children's Year activities and better baby campaigns were mixed. The Sheppard-Towner Act was implemented in 1921, with each state granted $5,000 in the first year provided that it designated an agency, usually the state board of health, to work directly with the Children's Bureau in submitting detailed plans for expenditures. The act also created the Federal Board of Maternity and Infant Hygiene, responsible for future better baby programs.

Although the Children's Bureau claimed a resounding victory, long-term effects were less significant. First, some states, perhaps fearful of federal guidelines, chose not to participate. By the end of fiscal year 1923, eight states—Connecticut, Rhode Island, Vermont, Massachusetts, Maine, Louisiana, Kansas, and Illinois—still refused federal funds. More significant, when they did come into the fold, no great drops occurred in maternal or infant mortality rates. In fact, by 1927, three states—Kansas, Massachusetts, and Virginia—reported rising mortality figures; Maine, New Hampshire, Kentucky, Nebraska, and California showed no noticeable reductions. Although the work of historian Sandra Schackel demonstrates the legislation's positive influence in midwife education and health care reform for Hispanics and Native Americans in New Mexico, the Children's Bureau's claims that Sheppard-Towner brought great national changes were not supported by the agency's own statistics. There was never any concerted attempt to explain why certain areas did not see reductions, particularly strange given that some of the states involved (such as Kansas and Massachusetts) were regarded as being among the most progressive in health care and preventive medicine. One of the answers could be found in Nebraska, where the Sheppard-Towner Act was accepted in 1923 but repudiated in 1925 when the state legislature refused to fund rural nursing programs and restricted monies spent to Omaha's city limits. In much the same way that it responded to complaints over weighing and measuring clinics, the Children's Bureau chose to ignore the negatives and to continue educational programs on child care and development.[42]

If federal legislation did not accomplish all that had been expected, at least awareness was heightened. This effect reverberated throughout rural education and extension work. In some cases, small remnants of the campaign left long-lasting impressions. For example, the Children's Bureau encouraged education officials and women's clubs to see that children were routinely weighed and measured at school and the results recorded on grade cards. After one countywide home extension meeting in Texas, an agent reported that "82 women became interested in having the school children weighed and measured." Rural women's clubs purchased scales for local schools, and some states mandated periodic recording of student height and weight. The latter, argued some, was really in states' best interest to ensure the development of educated, productive citizens. Wrote a Kansas professor, "We are gradually discovering that most of our dunces should be sent to the surgeon rather than the schoolroom pedestal. Most of them have adenoids or defective teeth or weak eyes. When the physical needs are given attention, they are as capable of rapid mental growth

as any child." Sometimes teachers added their own touches to encourage good health habits. One Kansas woman recalled that during
her school days a certain teacher gave gold stars to students who met
the height and weight norms at each recording time; remembering
those prized stars, the woman added that she was always underweight
and never received more than a blue star as an incentive to do better.
Periodic reporting and compulsory examinations, purchases of scales,
and individual teacher efforts were all results of the better baby movement. Each demonstrated that rural folk were responding.[43]

On a broader scale, study in child health and development became part of the home economics curriculum. Edna N. White of Ohio
State University, a prolific writer on child development and adult education, influenced the introduction of motherhood lessons in home economics classes. Emulating the work of White and the better baby
movement, colleges began instruction related to child rearing and care.[44]

In 1925, Kansas State Agricultural College's home economics students began an investigation of nutrition and health, using elementary school children as a study group. The children's eating habits
were evaluated, and each child was weighed and measured according
to the standards "used so extensively by child health workers." Earlier, in 1919, South Dakota's agricultural college had introduced a
"practice cottage," or home management house. There, along with
practical experience in running a household, students received "laboratory practice in the most important duty which ever falls to her
lot"—motherhood. To provide this experience, the college took toddlers from a state institution. One of the first students to complete
the program recalled: "The Practice Cottage was a new and daring
experiment in home management training. It included the care of a
child. The townspeople were aghast at the thought of allowing six
flighty girls to be responsible for a child, even under the supervision
of Dean Edith Pierson, who resided there." The plan, however, was
soon accepted, and between 1921 and 1939 ten "home management
babies" were the center of attention. What happened to these chil-

dren later was not recorded, but most likely they were returned to the institution from which they had been "borrowed." South Dakota was not alone in using such methods. Iowa State College had as many as four children at a time in its home management houses. When studies examined the development of these children against those of about the same age in infant boarding homes and an orphanage, it was decided that, although the home management children were "somewhat inferior in language development and adaptative behavior," they showed "superior" physical and emotional health. This was considered a result of their having been raised in an environment where child care and health were treated as a science.[45]

The lessons gleaned from better baby clinics and applied in practice homes eventually reached extension programs and women's clubs. Club meetings routinely discussed food preparation, varied diets, and nutrition. The latter received increased notice because recently discovered vitamin groups were linked to food content and diet. Wrote a surveyor of women's groups: "The study of foods at club meetings raises the standard of family health and tends to remove physical defects caused by malnutrition. The woman's club is often the only channel open to the married woman through which to continue the study of such subjects."[46]

With the lessons came concerted efforts to increase consumption of some foods. Marion County, Kansas, saw a nutrition campaign in 1920 that promoted wider intake of milk among children. An extension agent provided lessons on milk's value and, with a nurse, visited 125 schools to weigh and measure children. The agent later reported that of the 3,704 children examined, 69 percent were underweight. She also encountered some resistance from mothers who believed their children's diets already included enough dairy products. Like most agent reports, this one did not mention the county's ethnic or cultural makeup, although it certainly could have (the area boasted a large Mennonite population). Almost a decade later, in 1930, the same scenes were played out in Dickinson County, Kansas, where a

nutrition campaign promoted greater consumption of milk and vegetables other than potatoes. No mention of ethnic background was
made, although there were families descended from German immigrants. The agent simply concentrated on her countywide survey and
the physical examinations, conducted with the county nurse. Of 3,228
children, more than 2,000 (or about 62 percent) were said to have
"defects." Most were attributed to diet. As a result, extension clubs
joined to sponsor a dairy day at the county seat. Tents were set up on
a main street. Children received free milk, and a carnival atmosphere
prevailed. Meanwhile, clubs conducted nutrition lessons. Said one
woman: "I always thought that milk was good for children and occasionally when I thought of it I gave them some but now since our
lesson I never forget to put a glass at every place. Nothing is ever said
but the glasses are empty at the close of the meal." Such activities
planted the rather novel idea that living on the land and enjoying its
produce did not ensure a good diet or healthy children.[47]

At the USDA, nutrition science developed steadily, from the early
work of Ellen Richards to that of Helen Atwater in the 1920s. Their
findings were passed on to peers and filtered down to extension clubs.
By the mid-1920s the USDA applauded itself and the home extension movement for increasing nutrition awareness, deterring women
from frying too many foods, and introducing menus that were expanded from "meat-bread-potato" fare to include more fruits and vegetables. Again, one has to wonder how women applied lessons in
preparing a "buffet luncheon" to feeding a threshing crew. It also must
be asked how women raised fruits and vegetables in poor soils or un-
favorable climates. Food lessons resulted in more flavorfully cooked
vegetables and probably created more variety. Nevertheless, meals
still reflected available and economical choices. Writing of her family, one woman recalled: "When I think of the food of my childhood,
I never think of it as lacking variety—a tribute to my mother's ingenuity. The two categories of food that were lacking on the prairies
were fruits and vegetables. . . . But the North Dakota soil seems to be

able to produce potatoes under any conditions." Of the meals served during Montana's threshing days of the early 1900s, one man remembered that "all farm women had the same ideas" about feeding hungry work crews: "[All] could look forward to having a few servings of 'delicious' fried chicken on each job." Women meshed practicality with the new lessons of nutrition. As they learned more about food preparation, they seemed willing to enhance diets and adopt methods that did not "cook out" nutritional quality.[48]

Some may argue that the intrusion of social workers, researchers, and health care professionals was just another example of elitists forcing their ideas upon an unwilling population. Yet it must be asked what would have happened if rural residents had been ignored. Should infant mortality rates or maternal health problems have been left to solve themselves? For farm residents the problem of having too few doctors and medical facilities was not easily resolved, but they found they could do certain things to improve their chances for better health. There was a feeling of gaining some control. Putting screens on doors and windows, weighing and measuring children, or changing dietary habits may seem elementary steps, but their popularity speaks volumes about the rural population's readiness to make changes in pursuit of better health and an improved quality of life. The Children's Bureau's better baby campaign provided some measure of medical access and education. Home extension agents and clubs became involved with health-related issues, and the USDA reinforced the campaign with its own nutrition and health care projects. As a result, women were active participants in government and local programs. They continued to shoulder much of the responsibility for keeping families healthy and for nursing them when sickness came, but the new information they received from a number of sources gave them confidence to react and intercede.

Cherokee County, Kansas, farm families pose with their automobiles while attending a farm extension meeting. (Cooperative Extension Service Historical Files, University Archives, Kansas State University)

A home demonstration lesson in altering commercial patterns, 1920.
(Cooperative Extension Service Historical Files, University Archives,
Kansas State University)

Poultry fed the family and served as a source of income. A home extension agent (left) and two farm women clean chickens in assembly-line fashion. (Cooperative Extension Service Historical Files, University Archives, Kansas State University)

Home industry canning lessons for Texas club women emphasized preserving canned goods in tins for sale to stores. (Cushing Memorial Library and Archives, Texas A & M University)

A "Strength Conservation" fair exhibit displayed labor-saving devices, including a four-section clothes washer, a barrel set inside a cart for hauling garbage, a homemade fireless cooker, and an organized storage cabinet. (Cooperative Extension Service Historical Files, University Archives, Kansas State University)

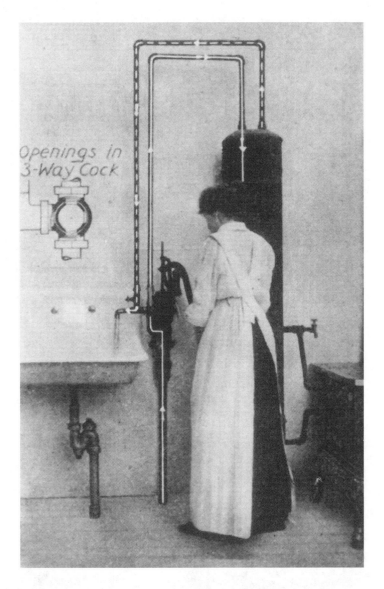

Openings in
3-Way Cock

College and USDA bulletins illustrated home improvements.
In this plan for "a hot-and-cold water scheme," cold water came from an
indoor hand pump; hot water came from a gasoline-heated water tank.
(The Farmhouse Improved Kansas State Agricultural Bulletin, May 1, 1917).

Exercise time at a vacation camp for farm women, 1926.
(Cooperative Extension Service Historical Files, University Archives,
Kansas State University)

Kickapoo Fair baby contest, Horton, Kansas, 1917.
(Kansas Collection, Spencer Research Library, University of Kansas
Libraries)

Students being weighed and measured at a country school in Marion County, Kansas, 1920. (Cooperative Extension Service Historical Files, University Archives, Kansas State University)

To create more local interest Wheat Special demonstration trains promoted Wheat Queen contests. Vada Watson (with wheat bouquet), a Kansas Wheat Queen of the 1920s, and Harper County, Kansas, Wheat Queen hopefuls. (Kansas State Historical Society)

To attend high school, Freda Irvin English boarded in town during the week. On weekends she returned by train to the family farm. (Author's family photograph)

Although Hoxie High School in western Kansas could not offer its students model classrooms, three sewing machines were available. (Kansas Collection, Spencer Research Library, University of Kansas Libraries)

A sewing class at Oklahoma's Chilocco Indian School, 1904.
Some students posed with embroidery or hand sewing. One student sat
at a sewing machine while the girl next to her created beadwork on a
loom. (Kansas Collection, Spencer Research Library, University of
Kansas Libraries)

Cherokee County, Texas, club girls refurbishing old furniture for new use. (Cushing Memorial Library and Archives, Texas A & M University)

McLennan County, Texas, club girls display rugs made from dyed gunny sacks. (Cushing Memorial Library and Archives, Texas A & M University)

Dressed in her 4-H uniform, a girl demonstrates a cooking lesson for members of her club. (Cooperative Extension Service Historical Files, University Archives, Kansas State University)

This "Food Selection and Meal Planning" chart was one of a series produced in 1921 by the U. S. Department of Agriculture in an effort to educate women in providing nutritious family meals. (Photo 16-G-214-1-S-140C, National Archives)

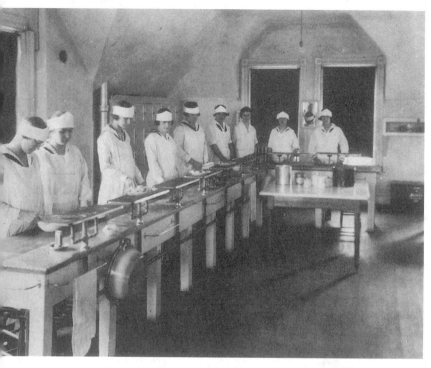

A food/nutrition class at South Dakota State University in the late
1920s. (Photo used courtesy of South Dakota State University Archives
and Special Collections)

5 "I Wouldn't Leave the Farm, Girls"

INTERTWINED WITH THE BETTER BABY MOVE-ment's interest in children's mental and physical development was a growing concern with the quality and content of education. Theodore Roosevelt's Country Life Commission had blamed faulty rural educa-tion for a number of agricultural ills. Heightened sensitivity to young people and their special needs led to increased scrutiny of country schools, teachers, and curricula. A complex web of issues were involved, but one thing was certain: When attention turned to education, the reformist urge was perhaps most visible and calculating in efforts to reshape agri-cultural life. It was a critical time for rural advancement, and reformers took an uncompromising approach. Many discussions of change occurred within rural districts, but outside experts were particularly quick to assign farm women a role in revamping their neighborhood schools.

Concern for improved education signaled a deeper desire to stem the rural-to-urban migration. The rural population decline reported in the 1920 census only confirmed what many observers already knew: Families were moving off the land. When land prices were high, many farmers sold out. Mechanization reduced the need for some hired la-bor, and young people were attracted to towns by higher wages and shorter work hours. Some families moved to the nearest town or city but remained landowners, traveling out to do the work or renting their 141 farm to a tenant for a share of the profit. These town (or "suitcase") farmers ceased to be rural residents in that they no longer exemplified agrarian values and ideals by living on the land. In fact, many rural villages and towns were disappearing as farm families bypassed them for larger communities. Looking back on the changes, a Nebraska newspaper editor observed that with the coming of the automobile and the proliferation of paved roads, rural centers once full of promise dwindled to nothing or to skeleton trading posts. It was simply the way of things, decided the editor: "People are just as happy as in former years but have learned the sad lesson that each improvement in any line kills some other line. One gains, another loses. Just the great game of life."[1]

Few concerned with rural migration cared to be so philosophical. Most commentators mourned those lost to towns, and slight shifts within agriculture were ominous signs for the future. Areas not actually losing population saw little growth, barely holding their own. Absentee landownership rose. Tenant farmers, who as early as 1900 constituted one-third of the nation's farm operators, found it more difficult to become landowners, and many farmers who owned marginal hardscrabble operations gave them up to become migrant workers or day laborers in the area. Added to this group were town residents who traveled each day to toil in outlying truck farms. Though little noticed, women and adolescent boys and girls were among those who daily left their city neighborhoods to work the truck farms. Also among transitory workers were pre-Depression white farmers who gave up their holdings and made their way into California's migrant camps. What became a landslide of migrant workers in the 1930s was already a perceptible trickle after World War I. Noting this phenomenon, one California magazine in 1920 pictured the women in these camps as happy with their work. They were, said the magazine, "real people . . . willing to forgo pretty (and expensive) clothes for overalls and breeches." If "pretty Mrs. Witten" and her family could leave their nonproductive farm to work for someone else, other women and their families could do the same. They would, after all, still be connected to the land.[2]

Clouding the picture of just who and what constituted the rural population was a small, fluttering back-to-the-land movement. The new suburbs, their growth spurred by train and streetcar transportation, further confused the issue. This trend was encouraged by the popular notion that the city was evil and the country good, and by people's desire to have a few acres upon which to raise chickens or plant an orchard. The movement was real, but it was not strong or concerted. The USDA found no comfort in it, concluding that the movement did not embody the "single-minded purpose [of promoting] agriculture for agriculture's sake." With this a number agreed. A publicity agent for the Atchison, Topeka & Santa Fe Railroad called city people who did not know the "difference between a stalk of corn and a gooseberry bush" exceedingly "foolish" for moving to the country. The Children's Bureau concurred, although it was more concerned with the rural-to-urban shift as a "startling exodus of millions of farmers." Undoubtedly the bureau felt these farmers-turned-urbanites added to city overcrowding, unemployment, and needs for charitable assistance.[3]

Anxieties were expressed and solutions offered by a variety of sources. *South Dakota Farmer Semi-Monthly* magazine noted as early as 1915, "an ever-deepening feeling that life must be made more worth living, if the country is to retain its present population." The situation seemed more threatening after World War I, as not all war-displaced families and young rural men returning from service went back to the farm. Leaders such as Arthur Capper in Kansas looked for ways to return men to agriculture because a "steady drift to the cities is unhealthy for all concerned."[4]

Some believed the population shift would slow if women's lives became more comfortable. Florence Ward thought women were the greatest factor in keeping families on the farm. Sociologist Dwight Sanderson agreed, citing women as the force that kept the family in place. There were surely examples to illustrate women's influence in this regard. F. G. Stilgebouer wrote that his decision in 1903 to quit farming in Nebraska, move to town, and take up banking was partly made by his wife: "Rosa, never very strong and being very ambitious, just simply worked too hard on the farm, there being at the time a lot of hard work in the primitive way." Hamlin Garland cited the "intolerable burden" of running a farm household to persuade his parents to return to a Wisconsin village; he was sure the move rescued his mother from "a premature grave on the barren Dakota plain." For the Beal family in Kansas, isolation was the main reason to move from homestead to town: "While living on the farm, Mama had been on the fringe of things. In Wichita, she was in the middle of things. . . . [T]he whole family . . . [was] part of a real church with a regular preacher, a good graded Sunday school, young people's groups, and women's societies."[5]

Married women moved off farms and ranches with their families, but there was also a growing exodus of single women. Ward noted USDA statistics that showed young women leaving rural districts in larger numbers than young men. The figures were so startling in some areas that one sociologist believed 1920 census enumerators must have made a terrible error. He could not accept that "in the brief span of a decade," American agriculture lost over 11 percent of its younger workers, over half of whom were female. Census takers, however, had committed no grave mistake. The Census Bureau's numbers corroborated data collected by the Women's Bureau under the U.S. Department of Labor. Subsequent surveys indicated a continuing drop in population. Between 1920 and 1930, the Women's Bureau calculated that women working as farm laborers—as migrants, on truck farms, on plantations, or in sharecropping—declined by more than 156,000. The numbers reflected, among other factors, the flight of rural black women, who were part of the southern migration to northern cities; the loss of young women on midwestern farms, who were drawn to places such as Chicago or Kansas City; and the departure of women who had homesteaded alone as a speculative venture, then sold their holdings. Women also left because they would never inherit the land upon which they lived or because they could only find education and careers somewhere else.[6]

William McKeever, a prolific writer on agrarian topics, ignored the broader economic and social implications and blamed female migration on families that took their children for granted and over-worked them: "There are too many farmers and stock raisers who take great pride in their sleek, fat porkers and well-groomed horses, while their wives and daughters look neglected and jaded and care worn. . . . These ruralists often seem to be exploiting their wives and boys and girls in the interest of the live stock and the farm products." McKeever advised parents to give their daughters more consideration and time to "bring out the many qualities of refinement that are la-tent within her being." It also would encourage girls to remain where they were. The Children's Bureau concurred. This in itself was sur-prising, as the bureau found so much to reform in rural America. It worked to end child labor in agriculture and decried the fact that girls as young as ten drove hay stackers and raked hay during harvest. Nevertheless, the bureau was sometimes lured into romanticism. Cred-iting country life with rich values deserving of appreciation, a bureau researcher was moved to write that "the charm and mystery of the prairie [was] a part of the inheritance of its sons and daughters."[7]

It was difficult to believe that farm girls willingly gave up their agricultural heritage. If it was a question of earning money, there were opportunities at home. Many wondered why any girl would look for work in town when she could have an income from raising poultry or selling eggs or honey.[8] The answer, some decided, was not that farm women were overworked but that they sought excitement. With this in mind, a South Dakota paper in 1916 published a little ditty that included a stanza just for young women:

I wouldn't leave the farm, girls,
It's much the safest place,
Where you can have your fun, girls,
And will not have to face
Temptations in the town, girls,
Which often wreck young lives;
Our fine young farmers need you
For sweet, pure country wives.[9]

Certainly not every young woman left, and those who remained often fulfilled the reformist ideal by seeking to become modern in appearance, outlook, and education. One of the more poignant examples was the participation of Kansas girls in promoting demonstration trains. When the Atchison, Topeka & Santa Fe Railroad ran its Wheat Specials during the 1920s, company officials and agricultural college staff decided that more folks would turn out for the trains if "young ladies of the community" competed in county "Wheat Queen" contests. These, in turn, led to state competitions. Vada Watson, a Kansas Wheat Queen in the 1920s, was a promotional feature of the demonstration trains. She rode the trains (with a chaperon), spoke to crowds on her father's wheat-farming techniques, posed for railroad publicity pictures, and met with local contestants in county competitions. She was, said a Santa Fe publicist, "a delightfully charming girl with a smile that has made her known from coast to coast."[10]

By 1930, competition was firmly structured. County victors advanced to state competition, where the winner received a $125 scholarship to Kansas State Agricultural College. State contestants were judged on essays about the importance of wheat and its marketing and distribution in their respective counties. Although the essays usually compared in quality and content with high school theme papers, the point was to champion scientific farming and sound business principles in the farm economy. In competition the young women also provided scrapbooks containing photographs of themselves, their families, and their farms. Sometimes a contestant included snapshots of herself with friends, on family outings or vacations (suggesting that hers was not a stay-at-home household), at school, or with the family automobile (proof of modernity). A striking dichotomy emerges from these photographs. Always there were pictures of the girls on the farm; dressed in overalls or jeans, they milked cows or stood on a hay rack or in a vegetable garden. But in other photographs the teenagers displayed their best clothes and hairdos; the dresses were no different than those worn by young women of the same age living in town.

Some contestants even attempted to copy the style of some Hollywood star. Placed side by side, the images made a great impact. Here was the New Woman, the Outdoor Girl, living in two worlds. She was part of the farm environment, but she was also familiar with the larger society and its outward trappings of popular culture.[11]

Actually, it is little wonder that these farm girls appeared as fashionably modern as their town counterparts. They knew what was in style through film, direct contact with town life, popular magazines, and catalogs. Any number of publications carried clothing advertisements and patterns, and some offered beauty tips. A *People's Home Journal* article in 1929, for example, discussed "Make-Up in Moderation," noting that it was no longer "considered disreputable to 'powder and paint' . . . [but] lavish make-up doesn't go." Moreover, when girls studied home economics in school, their textbooks cautioned against "dresses of extreme style" and suggested clothing choices appropriate to the occasion, offering such platitudes as: "Remember that a well dressed girl or woman is never conspicuous."[12]

Instruction also came through club activities. One Kansas woman recalled that her home extension group had lessons not only on dressmaking but also on how to dress, including the kinds of stockings and jewelry to be worn. At first, the woman said, members were a little insulted that anyone thought they needed such lessons. Nonetheless, they followed the lessons, and eventually one could not tell farm and city women apart by what they wore. Home extension groups in Texas took a slightly different approach. They conducted "appropriate dress" contests in conjunction with sewing lessons. Intended to "raise the standard of dress . . . [and] increase interest in good taste and the problem involved in the making of clothing," these competitions were open to white teenagers. Similar events were conducted at Prairie View A & M, a black college, but the latter contests required participants to compete in a timed exercise: In two and a half hours, they had to sew up a dress from yard goods. The young women were judged not only on whether they completed the garment but also on how suitable the finished product was for school wear. It was assumed that the young women already knew what constituted "proper dress."[13]

Just as women were taught to update their homes, they and their daughters learned to modernize themselves in appearance. Whether this knowledge would keep young women on the farms was debatable. Experts took the view that the hope for rural survival rested with early education and its power to influence the next generation of farmers and farm wives. To this end, reformers looked to the country school, asking what they could teach about the value of farm living, the importance of agriculture to the national economy, and the roles of boys and girls in bringing about a bright future for rural America. Country schools also required upgrading to keep families from moving to town in search of better education for their children. Retta Burns, a fourteen-year-old Kansan, wrote that her parents sold their farm and looked for a home where better educational opportunities existed. Such personal testimony was supported by statistics. For example, in a 1916 survey of seventy-five Morgan County, Missouri, school districts, fifty-six reported that one or more families had moved to town within the previous two years. The evidence pointed to a lack of confidence in rural schools. The Children's Bureau agreed, asking if "the country boy or girl is actually getting a square deal" and if rural migration was not based in part on "the farmer's conviction that his children are not getting a real chance."[14]

Many farm parents expected their children to surpass them in education. Gilbert Fite said of his parents in South Dakota: "While they did not have a lot of formal education, they were both very literate. They liked literature, they read a good deal and it was just assumed that their children would go to college and go further educationally than they had gone." One North Dakota woman wrote that her mother was determined that her children attend high school, despite the fact that "higher education was frowned on" in her community: "Most of the parents took the position that it served only to spoil young people and, even more dangerous, it lured them away from farm life." The mother could ignore neighborhood objections but not those of her husband. Nevertheless, she convinced him that his thinking was old-fashioned. Said the daughter who benefited from her mother's stand, "This was the right approach to take with my father because he loved 'progress,' and once he had been persuaded that educating his children was progress, he was all for it." There was also the Kansas woman who remembered that her college-educated mother was regarded by the local community as having rather "high" ideals in wanting educational opportunities for her daughters. Despite such attitudes, many rural children looked forward to education beyond grade school level. Such expectations may have prompted *Harper's* magazine to observe in 1900 that "in another decade or so" farm women with high school and even college degrees would be the norm, not the exception.[15]

Today country schools may represent a pleasant image of bygone Americana, producing from their student ranks some of the country's best and brightest leaders. In 1919, however, the USDA viewed such institutions differently, classifying more than 200,000 as "one-room schools of pioneer type, which, at their best, meet but poorly the needs of modern agricultural communities." The agency urged that rural education be built around agriculture and home economics. The former would instill a "scientific attitude" toward farming; the latter would be "vital to [girls'] interest and welfare." If reorganization in country schools did not occur, warned the USDA, there would be dire consequences: "Unless the nation has a body of enlightened and ambitious farmers, keeping their own farms from generation to generation, agriculture can not flourish and the nation can not prosper."[16]

The federal agency only mirrored long-standing concerns. In 1896 the Committee of Twelve was created by the new breed of professional educators who believed public education need redirection. In formulating goals, the committee decried the state of rural schools, calling them inefficient and poorly directed by communities that knew nothing about modern educational theories and methods. From the committee's perspective, rural residents were incapable of knowing what was best for their children—only professionals could decide that. Many ruralists would have debated the educators' opinion of themselves, but it was generally agreed that improvements were needed. In 1912 the Kansas State Board of Agriculture proclaimed that "the time is ripe for a reorganization of our present educational system." It called for more consolidated school districts and "more county high schools affording first-class advantages for the energetic boys and girls on the farms." Throughout the early 1900s, farm publications provided ideas for reforming education to encompass the rural experience. The *South Dakota Farmer,* as one illustration, addressed education's role in keeping boys and girls on the farm. Some of its articles were harangues for instruction in the "scientific possibilities of rural life . . . worthy of the best intellects." Others attempted to influence by offering examples. One article glowingly reported on twelve Oklahoma school superintendents who were "live wires," making sure teachers offered instruction in the principles of agriculture, health, sanitation, and home conveniences.[17]

Although some voices questioned the use of schools as a "propaganda" machine for farm life, hardly anyone cared to make the fine distinction between improving education and indoctrinating youngsters with agrarian pride. In many ways, rural schools and their supporters attempted to meet the challenge of reform. In 1924 *Farmer's Wife* magazine promised the Children's Bureau that its next big campaign would focus on rural education. The magazine had earlier addressed the subject in a 1915 article, "School and Home," that encouraged school contests revolving around seed-corn testing. Not only was the subject relevant, but contests made learning enjoyable. The same article also focused on one Wisconsin teacher's accomplishments: "Miss Grace Wyman, a rural teacher, found district, school and schoolhouse down at the heel and out at the elbow. She interested the parents, succeeded in getting the schoolhouse remodeled, [and] introduced domestic science. . . . This cleared the way for a still wider work." In its tradition of suggesting changes by example, *Farmer's*

Wife dealt with rural education reform in all its aspects, from revising courses to modernizing the physical environment.[18]

Colleges looked at curriculum and preparing teachers, but they also considered improvement of physical facilities. Just as architectural plans were created for the modern farm home, they were drawn as well for the model school building. The design developed at the Kirksville, Missouri, teacher's college, for example, called for a rural school with a gymnasium, indoor plumbing and furnace heating, and a greenhouse where students could experiment with plant bulbs and cuttings during winter months. The plan included a provision for getting students to school—a covered wagon traveling an established route. This last feature was hardly revolutionary; some rural districts already used horse- or mule-drawn wagons, and by the mid-1920s many had motorized buses or trucks for student transportation. There were also horse-drawn and, later, motorized traveling libraries that visited schools. Not surprisingly, new trends were promoted by American industry, which had much to gain in sales to school districts. Numerous publications, including *The American School and University*, a guidebook for superintendents and school boards, provided a look at ideas for model schools. Diagrams, photographs, and articles illustrated innovative designs, new modes of transportation, correct classroom lighting, furniture, and plans for designing and outfitting modern home economics departments. The last entailed everything from efficiently arranged work spaces to durable utensils to Frigidaire refrigerators.[19]

Meanwhile, colleges looked at other forms and uses of modern technology. They were especially interested in classroom instruction by radio. Kansas State Agricultural College in 1925 offered the "Rural School" program, broadcasting for half an hour every school day. Teachers and students could tune in for short musical and calisthenics lessons, a five-minute "inspirational talk" on nature, biology, or current events, and a three-minute lecture that changed with each day—Monday was devoted to poultry, Tuesday to crops, Wednesday to dairy, Thursday to horticulture, and Friday to livestock. For those teachers unsure of their elements of agriculture, the program was a boon to fulfilling the requirement for agriculture-related material. Kansas certainly was not alone in this endeavor. By 1929 most state agricultural colleges offered such broadcasts through their extension services; programs in Iowa, Ohio, and Connecticut were touted as being especially good.[20]

Every aspect of rural education received consideration, but the primary intent remained to encourage boys and girls to understand and appreciate the world in which they lived. The goal was to get girls, like their mothers who practiced domestic economy, to regard homemaking not as "work" but as a science, an outlet for intellectual development and creativity. To accomplish this, reformers focused on curriculum and sought the direct involvement of rural educators. In 1906 Myrtle B. Farmer, school superintendent in Brule County, South Dakota, announced the introduction of lessons in "home and outdoor life upon the farm." Gardening, basic cooking skills, poultry raising, and sewing were added to traditional subjects. The superintendent was not alone; support for such initiatives came from many sources. State boards of education required teachers to pass certification tests that included agriculture-related questions, and textbook publishers responded by producing appropriate materials. For example, Macmillan came out with a Rural Series that included *The Principles of Plant Culture* (1916), "the best elementary text available" according to the *Wisconsin Library Bulletin*. Would-be teachers prepared themselves for certification by studying such works, as well as Henry Jackson Waters's *The Essentials of Agriculture* (1915) and *Essentials of the New Agriculture* (1924). These publications also tried to instill a sense of the importance placed on relevant education. Waters's 1915 publication observed, "Agriculture, wherever well taught, has proved a source of strength to the school." His second book underlined the purpose of helping "those who are to live in the country to acquire a wholesome respect for their calling—a deep and abiding love for rural life."[21]

This could be accomplished with applied lessons at home and school, and more enterprising instructors agreed. One teacher later wrote: "In one of my last rural schools, I conceived the idea of using the most outstanding farms and farmers as models for my nature-study lessons." The reference to nature study was by no means a casual one. Many educators and USDA specialists argued that nature study in primary grades laid the groundwork for later interest in agriculture. Hundreds of country districts offered such lessons, often in the form of practical hands-on activities. Students raised gardens on school grounds or engaged in farm-related projects with their parents. In 1912 the Nebraska State Board of Agriculture initiated a program to encourage farmers to test seed corn for higher yields. The plan had little impact until the board involved students and teachers in field tests and corn-judging competitions in which boys and girls teamed with their fathers. Of course, instruction was not always so structured. At Prairie View School in Gage County, Nebraska, the teacher taught sewing during recess and at the noon hour. In 1909 she helped an eighth-grade student, Tena Duis, enter her work in the "everyday" dress competition at the National Corn Exposition in Omaha. The dress, of blue gingham with white cross-stitching, won first prize. Tena received a sewing machine.[22]

Fairs and contests became a popular way to interest children and teenagers in agriculture and farm domesticity. The promise of prizes encouraged participation. The Women Farmers Club of Missouri, for example, offered the female winner of the corn-cultivation competition a twenty-five-dollar scholarship to the state agricultural college. In Nebraska, the Johnson County Fair made small cash awards to the rural students who created the best displays of farm products. It also gave individual prizes in an "educational" category that included children's drawings of model farms or farmhouses, posters of Nebraska produce or livestock, and collections of grains and grasses. The opportunity to enter projects, said Johnson County Fair managers, "should appeal to boys and girls on the farm." Additionally, students

working together for a prize were encouraged to pursue further agricultural studies and received lessons in cooperation. Local contests
only drew participants from the limited population nearby, but larger
ones sometimes segregated along racial lines. In Texas, Girls' Yeast
Bread Contest finalists (Anglo females only) traveled to the state
contest at Texas A & M, a trip that for many was the first outside
their home area. Meanwhile, black females were encouraged to prepare exhibits and enter contests at the Gulf Coast Colored Fair. Evidently, neither white nor black organizers questioned this separation.
From their viewpoint, opportunities offered to minorities underlined
the serious commitment given to education through competition.[23]

Localized efforts suggest an interest in relating education for country youngsters to their surroundings and daily lives. As in other rural
reform projects, however, experts wanted tight organization and specific instruction. For farm girls this meant a concentration on lessons
in home economics, particularly at the high school level. This effort
became more feasible as rural school districts consolidated and as more
college-trained home economics teachers became available. Also,
more young women were reached as a rising number attended high
school, often boarding with families in town or renting rooms. One
woman, for example, spoke of her experience and that of her sister:
"We rented a room, and we cooked our own meals, went home on
weekends on the train. . . . It was very common for them [students] to
have a room, and do their own housekeeping." Increasing mobility
and access to education created additional possibilities for domestic
science instruction. Home economist Juanita Shepperd wrote that
school consolidation presented a perfect opportunity for the introduction of home economics, and she cited progressive examples in
which "girl graduates return to their homes and use there their school-
gained knowledge." Schools incorporating this curriculum added their
voices. When the Creston, Iowa, high school yearbook for 1916 pictured the school's home economics class, the caption imitated the
language of the experts: "The girl who possesses a good knowledge of

any of the Domestic Arts has a most valuable means of making herself useful to others, of economizing her own or another's income, or
of defending herself against adversity."[24]

Perhaps even more than words, photographs of girls engaged in
domestic economy education illustrate the point of the movement.
The Creston, Iowa, home economics students, in carefully starched
pinafore-like aprons, conveyed the appearance of nurses or laboratory technicians. Girls in home extension clubs wore the same sort of
uniform, but with the addition of headgear resembling a nurse's or
nanny's cap. Girls competing in the Texas Girls' Yeast Bread Contest
of 1924 posed in white outfits that included head coverings and aprons.
The same was true of black participants in Texas programs. Club girls
in Cherokee County, wearing antiseptic-looking caps and aprons,
posed with furniture being repaired and painted for home use. A
McLennan County, Texas, group was photographed with homemade
hooked rugs created out of dyed gunnysacks. This last group was not
as uniformly attired as those in other photographs—one or two wore
caps, and not all had aprons—but all the members bore the distinctive look of being prepared for the job at hand. These girls, posed
with their projects or pictured in a home economics classroom, offered visual confirmation that they had been influenced by the scientific approach to homemaking duties. Transforming the humble
gunnysack into a useful, decorative home item echoed the notion
that something could be made from nothing. As important, the regi-
mented dress code reinforced the idea that the girls were performing
their work in a laboratory—the home.[25]

By 1917 approximately 20 percent of the nation's public schools
offered some type of home economics course. Although most were
town or city schools, some rural schools provided such instruction.
Courses usually covered cooking, canning, breadmaking, dressmaking, and millinery work. These were regarded as essential foundations
to good homemaking and possibilities for later employment. Experts,
however, remained dissatisfied and demanded expansion of the cur-

riculum. At the same time, home economists reminded their peers that practical studies should be accompanied by "the development of desirable personality traits" and efforts to change habits. That this last goal echoed the tenets of home extension was understandable. After all, high school home economics courses mirrored extension education and the expectations of professionals.[26]

Kansas State Agricultural College conducted a 1924 survey to determine what subjects the 375 Kansas high schools that taught home economics covered. The researchers found much to fault. One problem, said the college, was the limited time spent on the subject. Not enough hours were devoted to pursuing concrete goals, let alone subjective ones of changing habits and traits. Intensive learning in the "food laboratory" required class time of about two hours, not recitation periods of forty minutes; students hardly could prepare an entire meal in the shorter span. Also of concern was the lack of credentials among some who taught the subject. With a note of self-interest in seeing more young women enrolled in college home economics studies, the Kansas State investigators insisted that no woman should be teaching "a subject which she has never studied. . . . A desire for immediate gain often leads a teacher to attempt the impossible." The largest issue, however, was course content.[27]

> The subject matter covered was almost wholly "cooking and sewing," to quote the replies. The manifold possibilities of the field of home economics are scarcely touched. There are innumerable ways to relate the high school course to the management of the home, the needs of the people in the home, and the function of the home in the community. This cannot be accomplished by teaching "cooking and sewing."[28]

The Kansas report overlooked the many reasons for limited course work. Some high schools were still two- or three-year schools, not four-year institutions. Many rural schools lacked ideal home economics classroom facilities. Moreover, school districts not conforming to the federal vocational education act lacked money for facilities and additional teachers. And expanding curriculum and educational opportunities in other academic areas lured young women away from home economics. By the 1920s many high schools, including rural ones, offered specific courses of study; domestic science vied with "normal school" training for would-be teachers and with "commercial" courses for those hoping to find office work or enter business school. At the same time, college preparatory courses emphasized liberal arts and languages (this despite Shepperd's demand that home economics replace Latin as a course for young women).

Potential domestic science students also were lost when they dropped out of school. This trend was proven by a number of studies, one of which was conducted in 1930 in a rural North Carolina county. Of the fifty-eight girls interviewed, all white, twenty-six had attended high school. Four had graduated. Of those not completing school, nine left because heavy demands at home made it impossible to complete class work; three withdrew because their poverty was a cause of humiliation; and five left because of "social isolation" (for two in this group, isolation resulted from pregnancy out of wedlock). Of the remainder, "a few girls thought they had all the schooling they needed." Though recorded in North Carolina, the study results easily could have come from any of the Plains states. No matter the location, educators denied that "the two years of home economics education taken during the high school period are all sufficient."[29]

Considering the very real barriers to gaining an education, a little bit was better than none at all. This was certainly the position of Oklahoma's Maude Calvert; it was part of the reason she authored *First Course in Home Making*, intended as a reference guide for those unable to complete formal education. The volume addressed an abundant number of subjects, detailing the basics of budget keeping, cooking, home nursing, and child care. It also explained how to lay linoleum and then to maintain it with a yearly coat of varnish that kept colors from wearing. For continued at-home learning, Calvert suggested compiling a personal library from publications of the USDA, state extension services, Chicago's American School of Home Economics, and special academies such as the Fannie Farmer Boston Cooking School.[30]

Like Calvert, public and school libraries encouraged women to create personal collections that included more than cookbooks. A library bulletin published in Wisconsin and distributed in several western states listed worthwhile publications. A 1918 issue, for example, suggested that young women request "Waste of Meat in the Home" from the New York State College of Agriculture at Ithaca, "Meat and Meat Substitutes" from Ohio State University, and "Use of Milk as Food" from the USDA. Meanwhile, *Farmer's Wife*, through its "Your Own Library" column, provided listings of current government publications. Of the USDA bulletin "Care of Food in the Home," the magazine happily suggested: "When daughter Mary has read this Bulletin in the light of her own fine, bright personality, it is not difficult to imagine to what wholesome food John and the future little Marys and Johns will be treated." The magazine enthused that there was more material available "than the best informed women among us can fully realize."[31]

Unfortunately, actual situations rarely met such high expectations. Rural girls had to be exposed to domestic economy instruction before they could follow suggestions from textbooks or special bulletins. And the much-heralded Smith-Hughes Act, which regarded home economics as vocational education, sometimes confused plans for female instruction. To receive funds that paid a portion of teachers' salaries, states had to develop programs for both high schools and vocational institutes. These plans then had to be submitted for approval to the Federal Board of Vocational Education, along with a guarantee that a state agency was ready to disperse funds. Of her experiences, one home economist wrote: "We found many educators were interested and wanted the aid, but not all were able to conform to the requirements, and some believed the type of home economics they were giving was the same as that to be set up by this law." In addition, the federal law adversely influenced society's view of home economics instruction. As a "vocational" subject, it was stigmatized as education for the lower classes and disadvantaged, not a discipline that could open up any number of work opportunities and lead to home betterment for girls of all socioeconomic groups.[32]

Nevertheless, home economics professionals chose to ignore any labels that segregated potential students by social or economic class. States attempted to comply with federal requirements, and country schools continued to teach some form of domestic science. Offerings were uneven, but, despite what many said, rural schools often attempted to teach more than cooking and sewing. For example, in 1920 domestic science students at Keats Rural High School in Riley County, Kansas, studied furnishings and room design for the "ideal home"; "cost and efficiency [was the] chief item considered." An "advanced" home economics class at the Unionville, Missouri, high school took another approach and used individuals as study subjects in a food and nutrition course. One girl wrote of her subject, an eight-year-old named "Perky" who was seventeen pounds underweight: "I made out daily diets for his lunches which included a pint of milk, fresh fruits, meat or a meat substitute, soups, and plenty of vegetables, both fresh and cooked." The class prepared Perky's meals and saw him gain ten pounds. For the students this case served as ample proof that "the development of the child physically, mentally, and morally, is one of the big responsibilities of the home maker." Group activities were supplemented with individual studies. One girl undertook a wardrobe project and became "capable of making nearly all of my own clothes and of helping my friends and family in the selection of theirs. I am no longer afraid to tackle a problem no matter how complicated it is." Another teenager studied the caloric and nutritional requirements of her younger sisters. When she found essential vitamins and iron lacking in their diets, "I solved the problem by making out menus that included the right amount." Clearly, course work in its best forms went beyond lectures and memorization of material. It involved basic principles of domestic economy and emphasized a scientific approach to solving homemaking problems.[33]

Desire to teach the various lessons of home economics was no less great in the nation's Indian schools. When the domestic economy movement began targeting rural women, boarding schools and missions for Native American children already had a long history of providing instruction in agriculture and the basics of housekeeping. Meant to assimilate Native Americans into white culture and to provide vocational training, these schools by the 1890s also reflected the movement's push for domestic education and rural improvement. Congress began providing funds for such education in 1891, when the commissioner of Indian Affairs was authorized to use $2,500 to employ "suitable persons as matrons to teach Indian girls in housekeeping." The commissioner also hired part-time assistant field matrons, some of whom were missionaries, to instruct adult women on reservations. They were to teach home management and beautification as well as child care and generally show Native American women how to be American farm wives. The program was important in the process of assimilation. As Clarice Snoddy, a teacher at both Carlisle Indian Industrial School in Pennsylvania and Haskell Institute in Kansas, observed: "Soon after the education of the Indian youth was begun in earnest by the Federal Government it was seen by far sighted friends that Indian *home life* must be changed and improved to assure any real progress." After all, for the lessons of domestic economy to have any lasting impact, girls exposed to the subject in school should avoid being confused by the way of life at home.[34]

At home, changes already were at work. When the "rudiments of modern scientific farming and stock raising" were introduced on reservations, women began to receive training in domestic economy. This form of domesticity often contradicted traditional patterns, but Native Americans in the Plains states were not new to interaction with Euro-Americans or to the assimilation taught in Indian schools.

Reservation life and white education had forced a duality of living in which tribal groups attempted to retain their identity while responding to the dominant culture. In terms of domestic economy this duality was demonstrated in a number of ways. One good example was the Indian agricultural fair, described by a Potawatomi official as "run by the Indians for the advancement of the Indians and as a medium of contact with white people." At these events, fine beadwork and handmade traditional clothing were displayed and judged alongside what the Potawatomi described as "citizen" (white) clothes. Potawatomi, Sac and Fox, Iowa, and Kickapoo women at reservation fairs in Kansas routinely displayed quilting, some of it in traditional patterns but most reflecting designs found in popular pattern-design books of the time period. At these fairs, women also exhibited canned goods—fruits, preserves, vegetables, pickles, and chili sauce. It was a point of pride, said one Potawatomi, that "our Indian women have now learned to can fruit and vegetables quite as well as the women in the white homes." Though these women took from the domestic economy movement pieces of information and adopted sewing designs and food preservation methods, they retained their own skills, traditions, and cultural knowledge.[35]

For daughters in Indian schools, lessons were intensive and, like those on reservations, aimed at assimilation. The Pierre, South Dakota, Indian school reported that students from the fifth through ninth grades were drilled in proper "topics for table conversation" and given "instruction to practical home problems which the girls will soon have to face." Girls learned to make clothes, sanitary napkins, tea towels, and table linens; they received instruction in hand sewing and in operating sewing machines, and they accomplished tasks with simple home appliances. Not coincidentally, the trainees' labor kept the schools' kitchens and laundries operational. Speaking of laundry duties, a report from the Fort Totten, North Dakota, school warmly observed, "It is a pleasant sight to see the large detail of girls, each at her own ironing board, intent on doing her own work in creditable manner." For people such as Clarice Snoddy, these scenes were a happy indication that adaptation was "rapidly taking place." The Bureau of Indian Affairs sought to confirm this assessment by noting that a representative of the Singer Sewing Machine Company had applied for a license to sell at the Omaha Indian Agency; evidently, the salesman expected to have customers.[36]

Domestic science instruction for native Americans brought its conflicts. Speaking at the Lake Mohonk Conference of reformers in 1914, Winnebago leader and educator Henry Roe Cloud criticized the Bureau of Indian Affairs for emphasizing vocational education. He and others saw domestic science as a second-class form of education that deprived students of the academic instruction needed in the pursuit of higher learning. For Roe Cloud, home economics was not an avenue through which opportunities for college or new careers were opened for native American women. In this he probably was correct. Native American women trained as home economists might find employment with the Bureau of Indian Affairs, but in a segregated society it was unlikely that they would find work in a popular magazine's test kitchen or with a white-owned manufacturing company. Whites also complained, but certainly not from the same viewpoint. Field matrons at the Kiowa-Comanche Agency criticized Indian families that refused to live in single-family homes and instead moved out to camp near one another. One matron claimed such settlement patterns hindered her work, damaged agricultural development, and had a "bad effect" on the children.[37]

For those sent away to school and then returned to reservation life, education brought heightened generational separation. Because native cultures relied heavily upon intergenerational relationships, the result was often disastrous. Snoddy, in a fine display of white, middle-class values, offered a prime example: "An old Indian mother was asked about some of the things of the old Indian life, and with painful heart answered in substance, 'Why seek to keep the old things. Let us lose everything that is ours—Our children no longer understand us, nor we them. If change we must, let us quickly lose everything of the past, then at least we may be happy in our homes.'" Oblivious to the meaning of loss or white education's role in causing it, Snoddy turned the statement into an anthem of joy. She called the woman "revolutionary and progressive" for seeing that the old must go, and the quicker the better. Rural women everywhere were encouraged to stay where they were while bringing into their lives modern ideas; the message was no different for Native Americans, as well as other minority and immigrant groups.[38]

There was compliance with and support for these reforms, but resistance also surfaced. A country teacher woefully expressed his inability to inspire students or their parents: "I tried at every turn to show that city life, with all its apparent glamour, was no guarantee against either want or toil. . . . I learned regretfully that it would require a far greater force than a young rural schoolteacher could possibly exert to stem the unrest that was developing among those farmers who could see only their long hours of toil instead of their opportunities." And rural educators sometimes met obstacles beyond opposition to changes in curriculum; at times education's very importance was questioned. Some families thought their children should be working at home, and many school boards were composed of individuals who themselves had little common school experience. As one man recalled, "It used to be quite a battle, there were people interested in education and those that figured it was a waste of time. [One man] on the school board at that time . . . believed only in the virtues of work." Despite lofty plans to educate and indoctrinate youngsters, the job could not be done if children were out of school. Terms often revolved around seasonal work and remained short, barely meeting the durations required by state statutes; in Kansas, for example, a law passed in 1903 called for five-month terms, and no changes were made for twenty years, when the minimum became eight months. Some parents kept their children at home, seeing no value in education; others were simply too far from any organized school to attend. Of her sparse opportunities, one Nebraska woman remembered: "I grew up on quite an isolated ranch. I didn't have any playmates. . . . We didn't have any school until I was ten years old, so in those early years we were pretty much on our own."[39]

Despite such obstacles to education, rural women took up the cause of domestic science. Often with help from agricultural colleges or USDA professionals, they worked to see that their schools and daughters were involved. Rural women's participation mirrored the societal viewpoint of their gender; as protectors of home and the gentle hands that civilized the frontier, they would be expected to interest themselves in education because it directly affected their children. This expected role may have been true, but women also sought to introduce the domestic economy movement and to reform schools to serve the rural population.

Women became most involved through existing clubs and home extension work. As early as 1908 the Household Economics Committee of the National Federation of Women's Clubs worked "largely toward the introduction of domestic science and art into the public school curriculum." On the local level, the Ladies Literary League in Dickinson County, Kansas, lobbied in 1912 for domestic science courses in a county high school. In Missouri the Pettis County Homemakers Club, with over two hundred members, was responsible for extending domestic science into ten rural schools. Farther west, women's rural groups near Grand Junction, Colorado, raised money to support home economics education in one country school. In Montana, women's clubs sent girls to state meetings devoted to home economics and agriculture. Meanwhile, Texas home demonstration clubs bought sewing machines, stoves, and kitchen equipment for high school home economics classes and gave scholarships to girls attending short courses at Texas A & M College. For women already familiar with the domestic economy movement, it was important that young rural women have access to information pertinent to their lives.[40]

It also became important that girls studying domestic economy be further organized. This led to the creation of home economics clubs.

Wrote one teacher involved in these activities: "The value of the club to the school is manifold. It is educational in that it gives an opportunity for motivating and enriching classroom work. It also offers a medium through which its members receive training in citizenship and civic affairs by giving girls varied opportunities for training in parliamentary procedure, for organizing work, and for developing initiative and leadership." A student selected to write a small article for the *Journal of Home Economics* about her club's activities enthused: "Our club work helps to bring us closer together. We work in unison for a common cause—the betterment of our lives through home economics."[41]

As the number of high schools offering the subject increased during the 1920s, the movement for auxiliary school clubs gained support. By 1932 the American Home Economics Association reported that four-fifths of its more than one thousand student-group affiliates were high school clubs. Kansas had twenty-five high school organizations, and the national association noted specific student club activities in Arkansas, Indiana, Louisiana, Maine, Michigan, Mississippi, Missouri, Tennessee, and Wyoming. These extracurricular groups generally applied classroom lessons to include the immediate community. Along the way, clubs taught decision making and responsibility. Some used in-class nutrition training to supervise the planning of menus and preparation of hot lunches for underprivileged children; others focused on organizational training and budget management by raising funds for community improvement projects.[42]

Most often these student groups were simply called the "Home Economics Club," but some gave themselves other names, such as the Future Homemakers, the Vocational Home Economics Club, and the Royal Order of Homemakers. Clubs generally followed the rituals of a sorority, with initiations and club pins. The American Home Economics Association noted that Oregon's state organization of student clubs had a particularly good manual on initiations, detailing a candlelight service. Kansas offered a helpful bulletin on conducting a solemn pin-award ceremony. In some clubs, girls received pins at initiation; in others they were awarded only after specific activities were accomplished. Some clubs met during the school day, but most convened after hours. This meeting time created "difficult problems in rural communities," where girls were needed at home or had some distance to travel between home and school. Nevertheless, country girls participated in these organizations, which intended to make home economics "a vital, cultural element in the girls' experience."[43]

Given the number of local clubs and state organizations, it is not surprising that a national association emerged to encompass school club formation and activities: the Future Homemakers of America (FHA). Although not established until 1945, the FHA reflected the ongoing movement to provide home economics instruction in schools—public and private, urban and rural—and the continuing interest in structuring school-related activities. By the time the national group was organized, thousands of school clubs already existed and were ready to join a nationwide network. FHA's goals matched those expressed in other areas of domestic education for women: opportunities for personal development; preparation for life; promotion of domestic science for homemakers and its importance in related occupations; and the strengthening of the family unit.[44]

In the nineteenth century, a general attitude prevailed that females were born with natural instincts for motherhood and homemaking; these inherent qualities simply were reinforced by instruction from other females or printed materials. With the rise of progressive ideas and the science of domesticity, this attitude diminished. Any instincts a woman might have for domesticity, it was now thought, did not emerge naturally. Only structured education would instill the attitude and skills needed to maintain home and family. Efficiency and the scientific approach were learned traits, not inherited female qualities. Reformers expressed a blind confidence that instruction would prepare farm girls for their future roles, bind them to their home communities, and make them the next generation of leaders in rural progress.

It is of little surprise that reality fell short of such high expectations. Young women who studied domestic science may have been better prepared for married life, but education and club activities changed their goals: Much as college studies in home economics opened possibilities for female graduates, high school education interested many girls in careers. Recalled one woman of herself and her classmates: "They just took that for granted, I think, that they would get married. But I think everybody was more or less anxious to get some sort of work. . . . I was anxious to do something, have some sort of a job and make my own way." Staying near home was of secondary importance to securing gainful employment and finding her way in the world. In 1931 Arthur Capper's *Household Magazine* compared the past to the present: "In the early 1900s the United States was still largely an agricultural country. Most young people had been born on farms or in small towns. The young girl had fewer ambitions because there was far less probability of their being achieved." In the intervening years, however, mobility, mass communication, and education had raised the farm girl's horizons, not only in career possibilities but also in opportunities for individual development of her talents and interests.[45]

Perhaps experts placed too much faith in school reform. Some ruralists resisted the addition of farm-related subjects because they wanted their youngsters to learn the "three Rs," not subjects they could learn at home by helping in the fields or kitchen. In addition, some rural families feared, and rightly so, that increased education would draw children away from home rather than keep them there. Rural women must have faced the prospects of education with mixed feelings. Acknowledging that education could demonstrate the necessity of farm life for national prosperity, women supported reform. Nevertheless, women also must have seen that their daughters might leave them. There were opportunities for schooling and careers away from agriculture. Young women had the chance to emulate the New Woman who left farm or small town behind to follow her dreams in the urban world.

Although agricultural and domestic economy education was touted as a way to keep children on the farm, young people continued to seek other forms of living and working. Cultural resistance at Indian schools and on reservations thwarted white reformist goals, and a steady black migration to the cities signified that adverse social and economic conditions could not be offset by contests, clubs, or school studies. One writer has suggested that programs could not overcome an ingrained black response to the "plantation factor"; another has stated in even stronger terms that plans generally failed because they were based on "an attractive white supremacy notion that had little to do with black progress or economic reality." Both conclusions have merit within the broad agricultural picture. However, the possibility must be considered that black families encouraged female participation in domestic science education because it provided professional training for careers in teaching or home extension, offering an escape from the trap of unskilled labor.[46]

Reform in rural schools, particularly the addition of agriculture and domestic science, was intended to better align rural education with urban opportunities. It also was designed to keep young men and women where they were—on the farm. The results were more positive in some areas than in others; in the realm of domestic economy, instruction was both a savior and a drawback. It provided young women with positive lessons and knowledge that aided in running a household and maintaining home life. However, it also brought cultural and generational clashes between those who resisted and those who accepted reforms. As dramatically, education suggested to young women of all backgrounds alternatives to rural life. The blame for failing to keep young women "down on the farm" cannot rest on the shoulders of domestic education—too many other factors contributed to the continuing decline in the rural population. As a force within education and agrarian reform, however, the domestic economy movement brought unanticipated changes in ideas and attitudes.

6 When the Best Is Better

WHILE RURAL EDUCATION WAS BEING REDI-
rected, another institution evolved to instruct and hold a generation
on the land: clubs related to farm life. Sociologists and rural experts
preached the need for cooperation and organization. If the plan sometimes failed among adults, then it could be augmented through mobi-
lization of young people. They, in turn, would influence grown-ups to
adopt scientific farming and domestic economy. Club activities outside school would benefit youngsters and bring changes in education.
Some optimistically declared that signs were hopeful. Said rural sociologist Dwight Sanderson, "No movement has done more to redirect
and give dynamic to the rural school than has the club work; nor has any
movement done more to train leadership among the coming generation
on the farms." Sometimes self-serving in his statements, Sanderson was
nevertheless a good observer. There were many boys' and girls' clubs tied
to schools, state organizations, and government programs.[1]

Many early youth clubs were organized by individuals prominent
in agriculture. Among the first programs was that of William B. Otwell
of Carlinville, Illinois, who in 1898 began farmers' institutes and corn
production contests for boys. Each year the contests were bigger, the
prizes larger, and interest more widespread. The program emphasized
male participation, but girls also took part. By 1912 young people in 169

thirty-two states were involved, and the Rock Island Railroad's farm magazine claimed Otwell was "engaged in the 'stay-on-the-land movement,' not the 'back-to-the-farm movement'"; his energies were directed at "boys and girls who were born on the farms [and who] are finding them better places to live and realizing the great opportunities they have, not only financially, but socially as well."[2]

Otwell's work was repeated many times over, from New York to Oregon. In Iowa, Rural Youth clubs were established in 1904. These were supported by numerous educators and by Henry C. Wallace, who organized contests for boys and girls through his publication, *Wallace's Farmer*. The Nebraska Boys' Agricultural Association and Nebraska Girls' Domestic Science Association were created as outgrowths of corn, sewing, and cooking projects established by E. C. Bishop. Later, Texas boys and girls joined Agricultural Community clubs, with total enrollment exceeding six thousand by 1924. Youth organizations were established in many states, and numerous adults interested in farm life gave their time to clubs. Among the more influential was Kansas senator and media magnate Arthur Capper.[3]

Through his far-reaching farm publication and radio empire Capper promoted contests and club work. Inspired by a 1906 Kansas State Agricultural College corn contest for boys, Capper sponsored a Boys' and Girls' Corn Raising Contest in 1907. By 1911 such contests had developed into organized corn clubs in Oklahoma, Nebraska, Kansas, and Missouri. Capper also urged young people in Oklahoma to enter corn contests sponsored by Senator Thomas P. Gore. Capper's organizations went by several names. In Missouri they were known as Missouri Ruralist Corn Clubs, named for Capper's farm publication in that state. In Kansas, however, the groups were known simply as Capper Clubs. Soon other projects were added. Capper Pig Clubs for boys were established in 1915, and in 1917 Capper Poultry Clubs for girls were added. At first Capper deliberately limited club sizes so he could loan money to members to begin their projects. By the 1920s club membership had become less exclusionary, and the loans stopped.

Youngsters learned to go to local banks for financing. It was a healthy lesson in the real world of farm economics and business; club members established bank accounts, kept ledgers, and learned to sell in an open market. One woman, pleased with her daughter's experience, noted: "She also has learned a lot about bookkeeping and makes out all her own reports." The importance of record keeping was attested to by another Kansan who joined Capper poultry and gardening clubs. For this woman, projects were secondary to the record keeping lessons that served youngsters for the rest of their lives, whether they were managing farm accounts or keeping tax or Social Security information. By the end of the 1920s, Capper's programs were in decline, replaced by the national 4-H Club organization. Capper was not displeased; he encouraged the new clubs by sponsoring the Capper-Ketchum Act of 1928, which gave federal aid to 4-H through college extension work.[4]

Although most youth clubs were sponsored by men, these organizations would not have gained in popularity had it not been for women's influence. Rural women, particularly those in home extension clubs, encouraged their children to participate. Others did not wait for the club movement to come to them but, on their own initiative, organized girls in their rural neighborhoods. Such was the case for one Lyon County, Kansas, farm woman "of no more leisure or means than her neighbors" who established a club that taught baking, sewing, and mending.[5] Women became active partners by serving as volunteer leaders, especially when 4-H became the preeminent national club organization for rural young people.

In its formative years, 4-H went by several names: Boys' and Girls' Clubs, Junior Extension, or Girls' Home Demonstration. The movement was connected with extension programs of agricultural colleges and the American Farm Bureau. 4-H aimed to give young people "an intelligent point of view and a favorable attitude toward the business of farming and home making by encouraging property ownership and a feeling of partnership in the farm business." The organization's emblem was a four-leaf clover, its motto, "To Make the Best Better." The four H's stood for head, heart, hands, and health, and the club pledge incorporated all: "I pledge my head to clearer thinking, my heart to greater loyalty, my hands to larger service, and my health to better living for my club, my community, and my country." Home demonstration agents were expected to organize local 4-H groups, although male and female leaders usually divided their duties based on a given club's emphasis. Male agents oversaw livestock and grain clubs; female agents directed those focused on poultry, gardening, and domestic subjects.[6]

Clubs began with as few as five members, and local leaders often came from home extension units. As the organization matured, young people who showed particular promise and success in club work became "junior leaders." Clubs usually stressed a specific topic rather than encompassing several at once; there were sewing clubs and canning clubs, corn clubs and cotton clubs, poultry clubs and calf clubs. Often, subject was dictated by location and local economy. In southern states 4-H cotton clubs were organized in 1909, but in midwestern states corn clubs dominated. More specialized crops also received attention. In Kansas, where sorghum cane production rose dramatically in the first decades of the twentieth century, sorghum clubs were popular.[7]

No matter a club's focus, fundamental lessons concentrated on principles of production and business methods. In addition, 4-H promoted citizenship and cooperation; meetings followed rules of order, and each group elected its own officers. And the clubs emphasized the idea of demonstrating what one had learned. It was especially important that young people gain experience in basic finance and learn to keep records of their projects, allowing comparisons between methods that brought improvements and those that did not. The approach was scientific, both for farm produce and livestock clubs and for home-oriented ones. In sewing groups, for instance, girls learned to purchase durable fabrics, to employ cutting and pattern techniques that reduced waste of material and thread, and to show what they had learned through club and public presentations. From extension agents, local leaders, and special agricultural bulletins such as the "Sewing Handbook for Club Girls," club members learned the modern, efficient approach. Lessons were reinforced when county and state fair competitions brought prize money, but fair participation introduced something more: leadership and self-confidence. Club organizers believed these activities strengthened rural youngsters' abilities to meet a challenge and brought them a feeling of self-worth. At the Nebraska State Fair of 1920, the best teams from among almost four hundred clubs gave public demonstrations in canning and cooking. Standing before an audience required confidence and poise; "proud mothers and fathers beamed with joy." At the Sioux City fair of the same year, club representatives from Nebraska, Kansas, Minnesota, Iowa, Wisconsin, and South and North Dakota competed in breadmaking, millinery, and sewing.[8]

For those who failed to keep records, carefully maintain projects, or demonstrate what they had learned, the situation was quite different. Youngsters could find themselves out of their club. This happened to certain club members in Riley County, Kansas, where the home demonstration agent organized a poultry and garden group for black youngsters. Soon after meetings began, she dismissed three of the eleven members for failing to keep records. Then, of course, there was the problem of club members eating their projects—hens and garden produce—before judging took place. Exasperated, the white agent admitted that the club's success was marginal and decided, "The children, although over ten years of age, are not as intelligent as ordinary children, and altho willing, have not always carried out instructions." The agent's analysis smacks of racism and overlooks her own shortcomings in working with these children. Another Kansas demonstration agent, employed in Lyon County, had no such problems organizing and maintaining interest in sewing and gardening clubs for Mexican children who had recently migrated with their parents to the United States. No doubt personality and zeal played a part in local acceptance of club organiz-

ers. One Sedgwick County, Kansas, farm agent termed his female counterpart "dictatorial."[9]

Despite small, local setbacks, the club movement thrived. Clubs
were often designated boys' or girls' groups, but females were not prohibited from crop or livestock clubs. Girls took part in pig and calf
contests at the 1920 South Dakota State Fair, and in Montgomery
County, Kansas, more than two hundred boys and girls planted an
acre each of kafir corn. The best results, some of them from girls, were
displayed at a farmers' institute. Girls' participation was not unusual,
as they, like boys, were exposed to agriculture lessons at school. They
sometimes went on to study agriculture in high school and college
and often worked alongside parents on the farm. Though young
women joined home economics clubs at school, it was not unheard of
for them to join agricultural organizations as well. They were, in fact,
allowed membership in the national vocational organization, Future
Farmers of America. However, after considerable debate the group
decided in 1933 to exclude women, and at least one state chapter
(that of Massachusetts) was threatened with expulsion if it continued to admit young women.[10]

Although 4-H clubs were less exclusionary, segregation based on
race was common. Texas clubs were clearly divided along racial lines
by the state's extension office. Race, ethnicity, and gender did not,
however, determine participation in topical clubs. Nationally, boys
and girls between the ages of ten and eighteen enrolled in poultry,
dairy, livestock, and gardening groups. Girls made up the largest number of those interested in poultry and gardening, and many enjoyed
financial and personal rewards. A Wyoming woman later wrote that
when she married in 1926, she proudly brought to her household "50
purebred Rhode Island chickens, the results of a 4-H project when I
was 13." Another woman, who as a girl participated in an Oklahoma
tomato club, remembered that she planted an acre of tomatoes with
the help of her father, then canned the produce for sale: "Daddy bought
labels with my name on them, and I sold them in the stores."[11]

Canning clubs offered to young girls the same benefits they provided to adults: They demonstrated the latest methods in food preservation and provided a way to earn money. The first tomato-canning clubs for girls were organized in 1910 and 1911 in the South. The emphasis on home industries for women in the South and Southwest also influenced 4-H programs in those regions. Girls were introduced to canning as a money-making project, and participants sold their products under the 4-H label as a sign of quality. Those who did well, such as the girl who made $132 by canning and selling 5,300 pounds of tomatoes, were held up as examples to be emulated. By World War I canning clubs had gained popularity in the Plains states, where they were expected to encourage rural youngsters and their families to try all sorts of new ideas. Experts must have beamed when reports indicated that this intent was being fulfilled. Wrote one young woman: "Do you know I think that all our folks have changed. Everybody is interested in doing things. We have done more things for the comfort of the home, fixing of the house, preparing for the winter this year than ever before." Club organizers cited such experiences as proof of club work's influence upon members, their parents, and their communities.[12]

Club projects for girls mirrored home extension lessons and subjects covered in school home economics classes. Though some clubs focused on canning, other money-making ideas surfaced; in Victoria County, Texas, for example, one girl earned twenty-one dollars in a year by making hats for neighbors. Meanwhile, many clubs emphasized home improvement projects. Young women refurbished their bedrooms with linoleum floor coverings, homemade curtains or bedspreads, and refinished furniture; others beautified yards with plantings of trees or flowers. Often girls faced adverse conditions. An organizer in Texas found that young women could not simply remake their bedrooms because most had to share the space with siblings or slept in a "room which is used as a living room for the entire family." Yard improvement was no easy matter, either. In 1924 "excessive droughts in many sections" of Texas made it nearly impossible to keep plants alive.

During that year in Potter County, eighteen girls braved the elements and set out "grass, flowers, and shrubs according to a landscape plan." Though they doubted their chances for success in that "section of the state [the Panhandle] where planting is rather a difficult problem," leaders were pleased with the effort. Writing of yearly results for 1924, a Texas leader saw 4-H as serving an important function: "Girl club members are making splendid local leaders. . . . Club organizations have given the girls an opportunity to strengthen their ability as organizers—both of themselves and of other people."[13]

Just as World War I accelerated growth in rural women's groups, it encouraged 4-H activity. Extension agents involved in club organization numbered only 143 nationally in April 1917. By November 1918, wartime emergency had increased the total to 762, and this figure did not include USDA specialists and agricultural school faculty assigned to help in club extension work. Clubs formed during this period reflected many of the same home-front concerns of women's organizations: Conserving food, cooking with food substitutes, and making syrup from sugar beets were emphasized. Some 4-H groups, known as Liberty Clubs, made over old clothes as a conservation measure or volunteered for the Red Cross. Clubs continued to expand after the war; in 1920 the USDA enthusiastically reported that national 4-H membership stood at about 216,000; in 33 northern and western states, over 30,000 girls were in sewing clubs alone. For the USDA this was a wonderful sign that club participants would "soon constitute a considerable portion of the adult rural citizenship of the country and be a controlling influence in American farm life."[14]

As important, clubs affiliated themselves with schools, just as Dwight Sanderson predicted they would. Several of the country's Indian schools had 4-H clubs, and in public schools, classroom lessons overlapped with the club movement with such textbooks as *Food Problems* (1918), a discussion of conservation and cooperation for the common good. Rural schoolhouses often served as meeting places, and teachers sometimes worked with demonstration agents to orga-

nize local groups. In Kansas school superintendents and teachers cooperated with the state agricultural college, local agents, and Farm
Bureau to encourage 4-H participation. With such interaction, it was
only reasonable that schools would be uplifted by an infusion of new
ideas brought with club organization.[15]

Like other rural reformers, club leaders used film, radio, and demonstration trains to spread their message. As early as 1915, the USDA
produced and distributed movies that outlined steps for organizing
local clubs. By the mid-1920s college extension services added 4-H
talks to rural school and farm radio programming, and special dem-
onstration-train lecturers gave tips on improving 4-H projects and
attracting more members. Some trains added 4-H competition win-
ners to their on-board groups. For example, the 1928 Atchison, Topeka & Santa Fe's Lime Special included among its attractions Marie
Atrim, the national 4-H Club champion in health. Her presence was
intended as an inspiration for others.[16]

Rural clubs also addressed the Progressive Era demand that children have access to organized play and recreation, just as urban youngsters did. Urban reformers such as Jane Addams and Jacob Riis were
part of the Playground Association of America, founded in 1906 to
push for parks and playgrounds in city neighborhoods. Presidents
Roosevelt and Taft both supported these efforts. Organized games,
neighborhood parks, and playgrounds provided urban youngsters with
a positive environment that progressives and their allies in the field
of psychology believed reduced juvenile delinquency and taught individuals to subordinate their own wants to those of the group. It was
only natural that such urban reforms should be applied to rural life.
This process was supported by a number of agricultural interests, including the USDA, which in 1923 concluded: "As the country has developed, the necessity of doing in a general way for the country what city
planning has done for the city has become increasingly apparent."[17]

Despite the popular belief that rural children enjoyed a wholesome environment, some social workers were consumed with ferret-

ing out signs of juvenile delinquency as proof that country youngsters needed organized play to keep them out of trouble. In fact, when one investigator failed to find "general waywardness" in rural New York state, she threw out legal definitions for delinquency and resorted to her own. She deemed delinquent children who poked animals with hay forks; those who exhibited shocking "sex delinquencies" by writing indecent messages on bathroom walls or on notes passed at school; and about six youngsters under eight years of age discovered "playing doctor." A sociologist sent to find juvenile delinquency in North and South Dakota also found little to report. Without ample evidence of delinquency, the New York and Dakota researchers could only conclude that, although on the surface rural life seemed fine, exhaustive study "yielded up a quota of 'bad' children of various grades."[18]

Child development experts took a different path in arguing for rural recreation. They were primarily concerned not with stamping out juvenile delinquency but with ensuring personal growth. These experts argued that when farm youngsters had no time to play, development of important mental, social, and physical skills was arrested. The Children's Bureau in 1927 noted, "Educators and others have taught an appreciation of the significance of the play element in a symmetrically developed child." Just as medical science established height and weight norms for healthy boys and girls, "a committee of experts" from the Playground Association of America set standards for "leisure-time activities of the child." These provided another way to determine if youngsters were physically fit; for example, twelve-year-old boys should be able to complete the sixty-yard dash in just over eight seconds. Thus, rural children were expected to meet yet another set of criteria in order to approximate the lives of their town counterparts.[19]

Spontaneous fun, such as running and jumping willy-nilly at school recess or taking a quick dip at the local swimming hole on a summer's day, was to be supplanted with planned recreation. Specific time was to be set aside for what Dwight Sanderson called "proper kinds of play." For Sanderson there was no question that "proper" play was directed by experts; "improper" play was created by the youngsters themselves. Sociologists and reformers often ignored the organized activities already present in rural communities, such as sports teams, town or school bands, glee clubs, and social events that revolved around community, school, or church. Farmers' institutes sometimes included motion pictures, musical performances, and readings or recitations as "amusements" for those attending. Farm families gathered around radios or drove to town for entertainment, and roving picture shows, theatrical companies, and local chautauquas provided additional sources of diversion. Nevertheless, some recreation authorities refused to accept these as viable types of organized recreation. They agreed with Children's Bureau leisure-time studies, which placed many activities in a "nonrecreational" category. These included visits between neighbors, "just playing" in woods and fields, or "rocking on the porch." Child development experts continued to argue for organized recreation and school "play days" on which students and parents would engage in structured activities. With parents involved, it was hoped that "the farmer, who does not himself feel the need for very much play, and sees the pressing need of farm work [would realize] the danger of allowing himself to exploit his children for his own profit and their injury."[20]

It was also essential that everyone realize the schoolteacher's function as a trained recreation leader and the school district's responsibility to provide school play equipment. Rural neighborhoods were encouraged to establish their own parks, just as some had constructed community buildings. The USDA offered several examples worthy of imitation, including the efforts of farmers around Niagara, North Dakota, who constructed a park containing play equipment and picnic facilities. Other rural communities carved similar facilities out of country landscapes. To urban-based reformers, so much open space was begging to be developed for some useful purpose, and they encouraged a push for parks and community recreation areas.[21]

Urban commentators were not alone in advocating such programs. Many agricultural areas tried to follow the plan. Three years after the National Recreation Association of America began working with Texas A & M College in 1929, it boasted 354 affiliated communities in Texas. Many Texas settlements initiated their own forms of structured recreation. In Shamrock, for example, a crowd "filled the street for three hours" despite a blasting sandstorm while rural clubs presented skits and "stunts." No one left before the husband-calling contest, in which each entrant stepped to the stage and, using her loudest voice and her own technique, summoned her spouse as if he were in the field and she wanted him in for supper; the winner, Mrs. China Flat, received the enviable prize of an eighteen-quart pressure cooker.[22]

Extension agents, agricultural colleges, rural sociologists, and USDA specialists influenced local recreation. In Kansas, for example, the agricultural college, in its 1915 study of rural problems, said of recreation:

> This is a phase of community life which will "go wrong"
> if permitted to go by itself. The central body interested in
> community welfare will see to it that the people meet and
> discuss the recreational conditions in the neighborhood. . . .
> It may be that playground apparatus is needed at the school
> grounds. It may be that the greatest need is play supervision.
> If the social life of the young people is in jeopardy, in many
> cases the developing of chorus singing, training in folk songs,
> pageants, plays, etc., will produce a healthful social life.
> Attention should be given to the recreation of adults. Men
> and women who play together, easily work together, and they
> remain young.[23]

The list of needed improvements was long and included not only physical changes, such as addition of playground apparatus, but also an alteration in thinking. Rural clubs reacted and joined in the fashion for organized recreation. In the minds of experts, it was far easier to introduce activities in club meetings than to incite an entire population to "play." Arguing for recreation in an especially sentimental turn, one USDA writer observed: "Enduring hardships first pioneers in an area had little time for the finer things in life, but now [1922] the barren prairies of the fathers have become the fertile fields . . . for the children, who, relieved of the stern necessities of mere bodily existence, find time to satisfy the longings of the soul." To meet whatever those longings might be, one of the 4-H "Principles of Club Work" included a mandate that clubs provide social and recreational activities.[24]

As might be expected, local interpretation brought homegrown varieties. When the Children's Bureau investigator searching for juvenile delinquency in North and South Dakota found little to record, she turned to signs of recreation. These were few and far between, said she, but there was a county extension agent who traveled around with a movie projector showing USDA films; one, detailing the intricacies of cleaning out a henhouse, drew "tremendous applause." But, the author was quick to note, "in some sections remote from railroads children as old as 14 years of age had never seen a motion picture." This last, written in a can-you-believe-it tone, illustrates how reformers sometimes reported events to serve their own purposes. At a time when commentators were already worrying over movies' influence on the nation's mores, this social worker chose to see the lack of films as proof that country children were starved for entertainment. Of course, she was not alone. Passive recreation such as film viewing was recommended by Sanderson; the USDA, however, supported films as a form of education but highly favored community sings for recreation. This perspective may explain the importance 4-H placed on group singing of tunes such as "Dreaming, 4-H Club Song for Girls" (1927) and "A Song of Health, For 4-H Clubs" (1929), as well as old standards, patriotic melodies, and spirituals.[25]

Films and choral groups were prominent, although these were popular in many communities without reformers' influence. Added to the recreation list was physical education instruction. In town and city schools, physical education was a part of the school day, and mothers were told, "In the funny old times when violent exercise was considered 'unladylike,' and helplessness was more admired than health, physical education was looked upon as a daring innovation—especially where girls were concerned." It was time for the "efficient mother. . . to recognize play, and later, recreation, as definite branches of education."[26] Urban reformers wanted supervised physical education classes in which exercise was adult-directed and had no relationship to farm labor.

Club leaders went along with this aim. The Riley County, Kansas, agent who found so little success with poultry and gardening work enjoyed more positive results when she organized swimming classes for black girls in club work; the lessons took place at a local swimming hole in a nearby creek. In Texas and Colorado, club members who did well were rewarded with a week of camp (Texas camps were segregated). Camp activities included nature hikes and group sings around a campfire. The 4-H organization ran its own camps; usually traced to West Virginia roots, these held wide appeal. In Clarinda, Iowa, the extension department of the state's agricultural college held a boys' farm camp; its counterpart for girls, named the Camp of the Golden Maids, concentrated on lessons in cooking, sewing, household economics, and nature study. In Kansas, the 4-H Roundup began in the 1920s. Young men and women, acting as county delegates from around the state, came together for recreation and educational programs. Beginning in 1926, a national 4-H camp hosted selected representatives, usually two boys and two girls from each state.[27]

Along with organized camps for youngsters, there were similar activities for mothers. Sponsors considered these essential interruptions to the daily routine of farm women's lives. A continuing concern was that women worked too many hours, leaving little time for recreation. In 1914 over two thousand women responded to a USDA questionnaire in which complaints centered upon work, lack of appreciation, and a scarcity of leisure hours. Wrote a woman from

Texas, "Many farm women don't get off their own premises more than a dozen times a year. The fathers get so accustomed to the mothers staying at home, they seem to forget that they might enjoy a little rest and recreation and really feel that she must stay at home 'to keep the ranch going'. . . . And the mother gets so accustomed to it, she, too, seems to forget she is human."[28]

Two or three camps a year were held for Texas women in various sections of the state. Said a leader in 1924: "Many of the women in that part of Texas [Wichita County] work in the fields and have little opportunity to visit and play with their nearby neighbors and seldom know the women in the far-away part of the county." For the few women able to attend, vacation camps provided some repose, but even there little idle time was allowed. Swimming, craft, and exercise periods were interspersed with healthy doses of household management and child care lessons. In New Mexico, farm women's camp organizers expected attendees to return home and teach others, but Kansas extension agents involved in a Reno County camp in 1925 simply wanted women to have a break in "the every day work-a-day life to which all were accustomed." Of South Dakota's first mothers' camp, held in the Black Hills in 1926, it was noted that agents received "a fair indication of what they could do to help the homemaker." That was true, and vacation days provided a modest but positive recreational outlet for women. Nevertheless, organizers usually ignored how difficult it was for women to prepare their families for their temporary absence and to counter the resistance they sometimes met from their husbands. As one Kansas woman recalled, men did not usually mind if their wives were at club meetings, but they were less supportive of time away to "play."[29]

The same was true, but to a lesser degree, of structured leisure for youngsters. Although farm families generally accepted playtime and camps for children, some refused to allow participation. When a female member of a Grange lodge near Santa Rosa, California, tried unsuccessfully to start a play club, she blamed her failure on the "miserable" conditions of local schools and the community's demand that children stick with a "rigid round of chores." The woman found those youngsters who did attend club activities prone to "rude and violent" games; they seemed little interested in "a kite contest, a bug catching competition and an athletic contest all with prizes." The woman, who once had worked with the urban poor, drew only one conclusion: "Our bright clever intelligent boys and girls are leaving the country to the slow and stupid. . . . The ingenuity, invention and resource called forth by a pioneer life have no counterpart in modern country life." She believed that the best families had fled, leaving her with an undesirable pool of children. She certainly seemed unable to impose her own vision of play on the local population.[30]

Among the many attempts to organize and restructure rural living, the play movement was accepted when attached to boys' and girls' clubs. It encountered more resistance, however, when tied to education. Alonza See, a staunch conservative who fought progressive ideals in general, saw the proposed reforms as interfering with children's natural behavior. In a book, simply titled *Schools*, he admonished reformers: "Children teach us how to play; we cannot teach them. . . . Those in charge of schools have printed at public expense a long list of various kinds of play which they have manufactured." Many in rural education concurred. In country districts, where the value of education per se was still debated and administrators balked at expanding school terms, it was ludicrous to expect overwhelming support for organized play, the hiring of teachers trained in recreation, or the purchase of playground equipment. Certainly, teachers engaged children in games during recess, and many schools had basic items such as seesaws or swing sets. Commercial vendors such as the A. G. Spalding corporation offered potential rural clients an array of options, from playground gear designed for country schools to jungle gyms approved by "expert play leaders and physical educators."[31]

For many rural districts, however, buying equipment aimed at physical development and hiring teachers with special training were out of the question. In fact, as Mary Cordier noted in her study of schoolwomen, rural districts found it was one thing to have a schoolhouse and quite another to keep it up. The cost of maintenance alone often precluded the acquisition of "extras" such as play equipment. Additionally, into the 1920s states wrestled with the problem of untrained and inexperienced teachers in country schools. Said a nineteen-year-old Kansan of her first teaching assignment in 1917, "The children brought the family feuds to school, and recess and noon periods were anything but relaxation and play. . . . There were often wounds to treat and tempers to calm. I kept first aid supplies for the one; for the tempers, I'm afraid I had no cure." Frustration on the part of struggling teachers and the districts that employed them was echoed many times over. The situation actually worsened during and immediately after World War I, when rural districts faced increased teacher shortages. To provide those badly needed instructors, states such as Kansas relaxed requirements for teacher certification. To expect educators to provide expert play direction when some were unable to "conduct an efficient school" was beyond the realm of possibilities. Additionally, graduates of state teacher colleges did not always interpret "organized" activity in accordance with what authoritative pronouncements had in mind. A college-trained instructor in Kansas recalled that in her country schools, "structured recreation" meant fifteen minutes of songs followed by a prayer. Families approved, and although one school board member remarked, "If you have that [prayer], you're not doing it for me," he did not object to his children's participation. Group activities took place based on local values.[32]

Many continued to argue that children were in school to learn the content of books, not to socialize or develop body strength. Physical work on the farm, combined with social activity involving church, extended family, or neighbors, could meet recreational needs. Rural residents, including women who accepted other kinds of organization, were somewhat suspicious of the formalized recreation movement. It was seen as an extension of federal hopes, particularly within agencies such as the Children's Bureau, to control child labor on the family farm.

In fact, although the Children's Bureau concentrated on child labor abuses in manufacturing and mines, it did want to control labor in agriculture. Just as the better baby movement supported federal funding for health programs, the bureau compiled evidence on child labor in the hop yards and apple orchards of Oregon's Willamette Valley and in California's orange groves and truck gardens. One magazine article in the agency's collection included the photo caption, "Japanese youngsters born on the ranch. They have helped harvest prunes ever since they could pick one." The oldest child pictured could not have been over eight years of age. Also collected were complaints from Texas of girls between the ages of ten and fifteen who worked in cotton fields with their mothers for seventy cents per hundred pounds picked.[33]

Children's Bureau researchers spent considerable time studying child labor in the sugar beet fields of Michigan, Colorado, Wisconsin, Nebraska, and Kansas. They found that, although Nebraska and Wisconsin had "progressive" child labor laws regulating sugar beet farming, children as young as five years old were engaged in dangerous work. They also discovered a wide variety of nationalities—Germans, Russian-Germans, Mexicans, Greeks, Polish, Italians, Japanese, and American-born workers. This diversity clearly negated assumptions that any group was more prone than another to allow women and children to engage in this work. Two investigators for the National Child Labor Committee noted this diversity as true in Nebraska. They also reported that, although primitive living conditions made effective housework difficult, many women managed to keep what they had immaculate. Children's Bureau reports were much the same for those working the beet fields near Garden City, Kansas. Contrary to its expectations, the bureau found families that tried to keep their children in school and others that hated to have their children work but were so economically strapped that there was no alternative. The stress of just getting by was reflected in the children: "Little girls of Russian parentage were especially pathetic because of their small, poorly nourished bodies. . . . Mexican and German children were of stronger physique and the Mexican children looked far better nourished." The bureau could do little about such conditions. Despite indications that some parents tried to protect and educate their children and that many women worked to create a good home environment with meager resources, the bureau generally blamed rural residents for lacking "right habits of thinking."[34]

Despite sometimes horrendous conditions and evidence that these children often received little education or medical attention, the Children's Bureau could not avoid the reality that most minors worked with their parents. That fact presented one obstacle to a national labor law for farm youngsters. Romanticization of rural life was another, and experts were just as prone as any fiction writer or agricultural publication to glorify farm living. O. F. Cook, a professor of eugenics, extolled the virtues of a rural childhood: "Not to be raised on a farm is a cruel privation. . . . [C]hildren need farm conditions." Meanwhile, William McKeever argued that agricultural work discouraged juvenile delinquency—"Soil Culture is but a part of Soul Culture; Character Comes with Growing Cabbages." In another publication, McKeever enthused: "That the farm home is an ideal place in which to build up the lives of growing boys and girls has become almost a trite saying." Such aphorisms were believed to be true. The Children's Bureau could muster no counterarguments, particularly when from time to time it, too, idealized rural life.[35]

Nor could the bureau adequately meet resistance from the Grange and the American Farm Bureau, which saw child labor legislation as disastrous for the family farm. Survival of this institution depended upon labor provided by family members, especially when hired domestic and farm labor became more scarce and there were fewer workers who might fill the void if youngsters did not work. The Children's

Bureau relented, terming fears that boys and girls would be prevented from doing home chores "utterly unfounded." When Capper Farm Publications refused to print the bureau's arguments, a researcher pleaded, "We are anxious that farm men and women will understand the child-labor situation and will be sympathetic. . . . There *is* an agricultural child-labor problem. It can probably be [better] met through the improvement of the schools and of the school attendance than through child-labor legislation." Farm interests were not assured. Debate continued into the 1930s, but no real national controls were instituted until 1938, when the National Industrial Recovery and Fair Labor Standards acts were passed. Until then, as the Children's Bureau expected, regulation in the amount of hours spent in farm work and the kind of work performed came only when state boards of charity, welfare associations, and departments of education enforced labor and compulsory school attendance laws.[36]

Another dark side of agriculture was explored for reform, but the immediate results were far from satisfactory. Child labor in agriculture was complex. If legislation effectively corrected abuses, it also limited the extent to which children could work legitimately on the family farm. Thus, they would be cut off from the lessons of agriculture and home living—something that could not be tolerated by those who wanted children to learn about and contribute to agriculture. Certainly, viewpoints clashed. Ruralists saw youngsters' work as productive, something that contributed to the building of personal character, but social reformers saw it as abuse. The labor question was not easily sorted out. Experts, however, took solace in their accomplishments. They had brought the message of scientific farming and domestic economy to those who were in school, participating in boys' and girls' clubs and taking their place among the next generation to stay on the land. Reformers were able to demonstrate tangible evidence of their work and of agricultural interests that rallied to the cause of rural education. Time and again they expressed the sentiment given in 1915: "What these clubs will do in interesting the young people in agriculture and in home life on the farm, and what they will accomplish in promoting education that is worthwhile, is difficult to overestimate."[37]

It was nearly impossible to measure whether clubs and their ties to rural education actually kept the next generation on the farm, although some claimed as much. In 1916 a publicity tract from the Atchison, Topeka & Santa Fe Railroad informed readers: "In thirty communities in six states in which organized effort is made to check the drift of young people to the cities the number leaving the farm in 1915 was 20 per cent less than the number reported in 1914." According to the railroad's publicist, "The needs of young folks have been met." Local leaders concurred. Wright County, Iowa, school officials reported that within a two-year span of progressive home economics and agricultural education students had changed their attitudes from wanting "nothing to do with farming" to a desire to stay. It was never shown, however, whether these boys and girls acted on their intentions.[38]

Like those who placed their faith in agriculture-domestic training to hold young people on the land, those who based their hopes on clubs and play movements were disappointed. Ultimately, how well rural programs brought communities together or kept the farm population in place became impossible to gauge: By the 1930s, the Great Depression had forced the population off the land or into the migratory ranks once occupied by the "pretty Mrs. Witten." However, the measure of these programs and their fundamental aims cannot simply focus on their inability to stem rural to urban migration or to redirect a whole population.

The club movement was something new for rural youngsters. It offered an educational opportunity, but, as important, it provided time for socialization and recreation. It built self-confidence when participants did well, and it enabled young people to build their skills in tangible, measurable ways. Although the recreation movement's presumption of urban problems in a rural world was perhaps skewed, farm and ranch families considered the worth of planned play for themselves and their children. In this, the problem of implementation was a lack not so much of interest but of time. Farm chores, as part of the business of agriculture, were sure to have priority over "play." Yet families accepted the club movement, and farm women played a role by encouraging their children and others in the community to participate. Through involvement, women placed themselves in leadership roles when they served as club directors and organizers. Before the Depression years of the 1930s, the domestic economy movement made a distinct imprint upon rural life. It alone did not reduce isolation or transform farm homes, communities, or schools. But in concert with other influences that acted upon agriculture, it brought a message that was realized in club organization, education, and community activism.

Conclusion

IN 1933, MARY R. BEARD REFLECTED UPON THE
reeling U.S. economy, the decline of the Roman Empire, and the
beginning of Nazism. In her musings, she stopped to consider woman's
place in social and economic history. Her ideas expressed a decided
viewpoint and were heavily shaped by an immediate set of economic
events. Nonetheless, Beard never veered in her writings from arguing
that in the course of history women were a force rather than passing
footnotes. Her analysis of women in general could apply to rural
women in particular:

> No less dynamic in history than woman as force is woman's
> conception of herself and her role in the processes of culture
> and civilization, for, as many writers correctly insist, ideas are
> also forces in social evolution. As thinker and student, woman,
> like every thinker and student, borrows with more or less
> understanding from the heritage of thought in which she finds
> herself; thus she may accept ready-made views of her personality
> and the world as she now accepts ready-made clothing in the
> stores. Or aware of her functional emotions, she may challenge,
> break, or transform borrowed conceptions, in the alembic of her
> intuition, with respect to the basic realities of life.[1]

Rural women were the subjects of discussions that attempted to decide who they were, how they lived, and what they needed to add quality of their lives. They were the focus of study and interest among rural sociologists and reformers, social workers, health care advocates, agricultural and home economics experts, and agencies of the U.S. government. Many "ready-made views" were thrust upon rural women, and sometimes they accepted these definitions. More important, the women were not passive receptors of these views or ideas meant to reshape their lives. Women molded the many plans of experts and their accompanying advice into usable options for meeting their own "basic realities of life." They were both thinkers and students, conscious of their place in agrarian culture and economics.

With their agendas for rural reform and improvement of farm life, professionals and experts often relied on definitions that stereotyped the farm population. It was, after all, a basic sociological approach to divide a study population into groups exhibiting common, identifiable characteristics, and the outward appearance and setting of rural life invited certain responses and expectations. Nevertheless, the rural population remained an enigma. Commentators and researchers offered opinions, and studies tried to isolate problems and characterize the people who faced them. Some concluded that problems were based on the lack of material goods and modern conveniences. Others attributed problems to a number of factors--quality of education, availability of medical care, insulation from the outside world, or cultural traditions. Few experts, including those in black agricultural schools, identified racism or failure to meet dominant-culture expectations as rural problems. At that time, Americanization and acculturation were so strongly a part of the national mind-set that sameness, not diversity, was celebrated. It generally was assumed that the melting pot was at work. Blacks, Hispanics, Native Americans, and immigrant groups were not ignored wholesale by those preaching scientific farming and domestic economy, so racial and ethnic inequalities were seldom raised as problems in rural reform.

In these discussions of problems and solutions, women received far less negative characterization than males, who, when they failed to fall in with scientific farming ideals, were pictured as obstinate and backward. Somehow, experts believed that when women of any ethnic or racial background learned about new ways of doing things, they adopted them. Thus, country women were credited with possessing a progressive outlook that would ultimately improve and uplift themselves, their families, and their neighborhoods. By extension, all of agrarian society profited.

Reform encompassed numerous areas, but the place of women in farm economics was never far from discussions for general improvement. Writing for the American Academy of Political and Social Sciences in the early 1930s, Mary Meeks Atkeson looked at economic roles in rural life and decided that "most of the prosperity of American agriculture has rested squarely upon the backs of the women and children who worked without pay." Modernity, Atkeson agreed, meant acquiring new conveniences, adopting time and motion schedules, and understanding scientific principles that applied to farm life. The point, however, was that women's contributions and standing in agriculture demanded notice; it took partnership to make the farm survive and prosper. Although women might call themselves "homemakers," they served as managers in the business of farming. They often kept the books and helped decide how income was saved or spent. The Children's Bureau investigator sent to Montana wrote that because women shared the burdens of farm life with men, they also deserved at least half the credit for successes: "Indeed, it was largely the money she earned by the sale of butter which made possible the installation of the windmill and other improvements." Rural women were, to quote historian Laurie Mercier, "economic linchpins" whose industry and financial contributions brought material comforts, farm necessities, and economic gain. Farm publications understood this and were quick to feature women whose profit-making enterprises excelled over other farm operations. One such article, "Baker Quits

Hogs When His Wife's Turkeys Win in Profit Race," noted that the woman's "turkey money" was putting three children through college.[2]

This is not to say that every woman enjoyed equal status within her own family or local community. As Atkeson and others suggested, women often were taken for granted. Men dominated land ownership and controlled most of the income. However, a thread ran throughout discussions and rural families' own statements: the belief that, because home and family were intricately tied with the workplace, male-female relationships in rural districts had qualities absent in urban areas. Lines of labor blurred, with couples "working in harness"—side by side, heading for the same goal—just as plow horses worked together to get the job done. Urban professionals might find it difficult to understand the down-home comparison, but the same idea sprang from their writings. The social unit of family, so worrisome to urban reformers, seemed to have a fabric all its own in farm life. In 1922, F. H. Newell of the U.S. Land Reclamation Service, wrote that farming could be regarded strictly as a money-making occupation. In a business sense, it was reasonable for unprofitable areas to be abandoned and unskilled farmers to be forced into another line of work. Newell, however, could not advocate social Darwinism's "survival of the fittest" paradigm because he saw farming as something more than just an occupation. It was "a mode of life--one which is primarily for the production of man rather than of money." Caroline B. Sherman, of the USDA, agreed: "[The] farm and farm home constitute one economic unit. . . a cooperative enterprise in which is found a blend of work and home atmosphere which is not inherent in any other business." Henry Wallace, in his 1915 *Letters to the Farm Folk*, also saw business and family as inseparable: "[Farm life] is really a family life, combining home and business, and in which self-interest binds the family into a unit."[3]

Sociologists added similar observations. Said one home economics magazine, "Sociologists tell us that the only family that has an ideal setting is the farm family." Dwight Sanderson concurred. Although he argued that most homes still could stand improvement, "nowhere are conditions so favorable for the enjoyment of all that is most precious in family life as in the better American farm homes." The reason was simple. Unlike the urban white, middle-class household, in which the male left home to conduct business, the farm household saw men nearby. Rural men often worked with sisters, mothers, wives, or children. The same home economics journal that cited sociologists' thinking went on to add: "Farm men have a rare privilege—they are with their children as they grow up. . . . Probably no farmer says to his wife, 'Mary, look what your child is doing.'" The implication was that just as women were involved in farm operations, men were engaged in child rearing.[4]

Each commentator stressed that the blend of work and social relationships formed a partnership within the rural family. Close proximity of home to business made these families special and placed women in roles and relationships that were different from those of their counterparts in the urban world, although the urban environment itself was changing. In the post-Victorian decades, and especially after World War I, family patterns and roles changed. This change was reflected in a number of ways: the popular images of the New Woman and Outdoor Girl; the worry about the family as a sustained social entity; and recognition of what sociologists later labeled the "companionate" family, in which the parents, though partners with each other, relinquished to experts some control over their children. Wrote a sociologist studying middle- and upper-class urban families in 1923: "This change of ideal from the man as single head of the family to the equal partnership of man and woman--must inevitably involve difficult problems of personal and social adjustment before it is fully worked out in general practice."[5]

In "general practice," rural women were already familiar with partnership structures. Rural families, though based on a cooperative outlook in which all members were supposed to work for farm and family survival, also exhibited elements of the companionate model. Certainly, both women and observers of the agricultural scene had something to say about the social and economic unit of family and the blend of home and occupation. In these discussions, however, the commentators were not always impartial reporters. Some went overboard with praise for the rural family, glorifying rural male-female relationships with the simple hope that if women saw themselves and what they did in a glowing light, they would not leave the farm.

Still, amid hyperbole and agrarian boosterism, there were elements of truth. The very nature of farm as home and business created relationships different from those in urban life, and women regarded their role as one of partnership. The relationship was not without bumps and problems, but women did not expect a problem-free existence. Said one: "I married a farmer and, oh, it was rough. I've helped my husband saw wood rather than for him to hire someone and have to pay them back. And I'd help in the hay—I didn't mind it. I was used to it, for I helped my dad like that. But I had always said when I was growing up that I'd never marry a farmer. But you get ambitious, and when you work together it works out pretty good." This woman's marriage was not a one-sided arrangement; in the home, her husband helped with the children. Another woman who had the same experience recalled: "I would help him [husband] in the field all day long, and then we'd come in at night and we'd get supper, put the babies to bed—a lot of times he gave the children their baths and put on their little pajamas and put them to bed, while I was doing something he couldn't do. . . and he never would go to bed and leave me up ironing."[6]

Men and women working together exemplified the business perspective, the conception of family as a corporation. The domestic economy movement did not claim that it would result in an equal partnership between men and women, but it did promise to make women more able managers and larger economic contributors. The members of the family corporation would be better off in health, education, and outlook if women successfully managed the home. One of the basic attitudes domestic economy advocates wished to convey, and one to which women responded, was that woman's place in agriculture was multifaceted and important.

> The mother of the farm . . . has the opportunity to use all
> her business ability in assisting her husband. She is a partner.
> She must feed the men and in times of a shortage of help,
> assist in the field. Many times she helps manage the dairy
> herd and almost invariably she has complete charge of the
> poultry. Her husband discusses with her any improvements
> to be made, the purchase of a new tractor, land that is to be
> rented, and the crops that are to be put in. She is a necessary
> factor in the running of the farm. . . . Her active mind is
> necessary in the farm program. She is not only a mother but
> a business partner.[7]

Coming from a home economics journal, this statement could be dismissed as more of the same idealization of farm life and woman's place. Yet when women added their voices, they often agreed. *Farmer's Wife* magazine provided a forum through which women discussed themselves and their circumstances. They were especially vocal in 1915, when the publication asked if rural women were really nothing more than "beasts of burden." A small number responded in the affirmative. They had few material conveniences to lighten their work, almost no leisure time, and little male support. Others wrote that although their mothers had been overworked and neglected, they themselves were better off. Said one woman, "My mother was situated like that till we children could earn money. Such a condition could no more be possible in our home today than that I should starve while my husband was well fed."[8] More emphatic and representative of responses were women who saw themselves as partners. One letter stated:

> We moved to our farm twelve years ago. Its tumbledown
> buildings, brush fences and unsightly places made us both
> determine to do all we could to make it a home to love and

be proud of. I can assure you it was no easy task but we worked on the equal partnership plan. . . . The first few years we both realized that better barns and out buildings were necessary and I willingly contented myself in the old house. Together we planned all things. Our barns were hardly completed before my husband began to study plans and specifications for a model farm home which was left entirely in my charge as he always said that as I must spend most of the time therein I should be the one consulted rather than he. In this I did not agree and again all things were planned and discussed together.[9]

Another woman explained that she lived on a 440-acre farm, did all of her own housework, raised chickens, and cooked for up to six hired men during harvest, upholding her end of the bargain. She had access to a banking account, and she spent money for what she thought necessary. On a rather defiant note she concluded, "As for the oil stove, fireless cooker and the like, I always buy what I want in that line and I would like to see the man that would keep me from it if I did my share of the housework." Summarizing what this woman and others said in one way or another, one observer concluded: "The lot of the farmer's wife is what she makes of it."[10]

Advocates of domestic economy and its offshoots believed that farm women received skills and education that enabled them to make a great deal of their lives. Though it can be argued that the domestic economy movement was intrusive, there is little doubt that women welcomed it. They attended farmers' institutes and college classes, joined extension clubs, participated in better baby clinics, and worked for rural improvements—all of their own free will. The government offered no financial enticements, such as loans. Agricultural schools and extension programs had no leverage with which to force women and rural youngsters into clubs. The only incentive was the promise of improving existing circumstances through the education domestic economy offered. Women voluntarily involved themselves and their families because they wanted change. The movement offered to ease and enhance their lives, and it gave them a chance to demonstrate their concrete contributions by engaging in home industries, modernizing their homes, and changing work strategies.

In *Promise to the Land*, Joan Jensen wrote, "Farm women not only planned and managed, but they also maintained. They often did this by subordinating their interests to the unity of the farm family. . . . They asked only for success of the farm family in reproducing itself, of passing the farm on to the next generation."[11] An essential desire of the domestic economy movement was to keep the rural population on the land. However, the movement did not ask women to subordinate their interests—it assumed that farm women's interests lay in preserving the rural world. To the extent that this was true, the movement actually asked them to expand their interests and expectations. If a woman was not focused on family and community but sought a career instead, then the movement held little relevance—except for the variety of domestic science careers it offered. Indeed, an important message of the movement was that women did not have to subordinate themselves to a harsh farm environment. Just as businessmen could control industry and males could overcome problems in farm production, women could gain control. With training and different ways of thinking, they could actively bring about change.

A whole spectrum of professionals and specialists recited the expert view of rural life, repeating lists of expectations, processes, and outcomes. In the final analysis, however, the women chose what was important to them and their immediate surroundings. Common ground was established between what experts offered and what women found useful. Some resisted attempts to change traditions and cultural patterns, but those who ignored the movement failed to keep it from affecting the whole of rural life. In fact, the movement's staying power can be found in today's agrarian world. Home extension and 4-H clubs remain mainstays of farm communities (4-H is now also found in urban areas), and domestic education continues, providing lessons reflecting current concerns and technology--recycling, microwave cooking, or home computers. There are still Master Farmer and Master Homemaker programs. Conferences for farm women continue to discuss rural education, health, and time management. Rural communities still struggle with a scarcity of doctors and medical facilities.

Clearly, many of the problems identified by Progressives and reform experts in the years before the Great Depression have not gone away. Agricultural economics and a shrinking rural population base continue to pose threats to farmers' survival and quality of living. Despite their promises, the scientific farming and domestic economy movements did not solve all of agriculture's problems; science and technology did not create a perfect world. Nevertheless, at the time these movements were introduced and gained acceptance, agrarian society was willing to explore their lessons. Women found much in the domestic economy movement to accept. A woman might not have indoor plumbing or electricity, but she found that she could do things to modernize her home, ensure better health and nutrition for her family, and beautify her home and community.

In the first decades of the 1900s, agriculture was shaped by many forces. Science, technology, mechanization, and the involvement of experts played their roles. Not to be overlooked in these decades of change, these years of "revolution," were the evolving social attitudes about women's roles and the mark made by the domestic economy movement. The New Woman image and domesticity may seem contradictory. They do, however, share commonalities. The New Woman was a sign of post-Victorian America; the domestic economy movement signaled reform and change for rural women. Both were about social and economic transformations. What the domestic economy movement stood for and the ways in which women followed and used it for their benefit must be considered when addressing the complexity of farm women's lives during the early twentieth century.

Notes

Introduction

1. *The American Domestic Cyclopaedia* (New York: F. M. Lupton, 1890), iii–iv.
2. Lawrence W. Levine, *Highbrow/Lowbrow: The Emergence of Cultural Hierarchy in America* (Cambridge: Harvard University Press, 1988), 195.
3. Paula M. Nelson, "Women and the American West, A Review Essay," *Annals of Iowa* 50 (Fall 1989/Winter 1990): 272.
4. Joan M. Jensen, "Crossing Ethnic Barriers in the Southwest: Women's Agricultural Extension Education, 1914–1940," *Agricultural History* 60 (Spring 1986): 180; "Home Demonstration Work Among Negroes in Texas for 1932," in "Annual Report of Extension Work in Texas, 1932," 681, Archives, Texas A & M University, College Station, Tex. (hereinafter cited as Archives, Texas A & M).

Chapter 1

1. John Milton Cooper, Jr., *Pivotal Decades: The United States, 1900–1920* (New York: W. W. Norton & Co., 1990). See also Thomas J. Schlereth, *Victorian America: Transformations in Everyday Life, 1876–1915* (New York: HarperCollins Publishers, 1991), especially the introduction.
2. Lois Rudnick, "The New Woman," in *1915, The Cultural Moment*, eds. Adele Heller and Lois Rudnick (New Brunswick, N.J.: Rutgers University Press, 1991), 70–73; Cooper, *Pivotal Decades*, 204; Maureen Honey, ed., *Breaking the Ties that Bind: Popular Sto-*

ries of the New Woman, 1915–1930 (Norman: University of Oklahoma Press, 1992), 10–11, 162–91; Katherine Douglas, "Trail's End: The Story of a Girl's Experiences in Her Log Cabin on the Plains," *Farmer's Wife: A Woman's Farm Journal* 17 (April 1915): 312; Kate W. Searcy, "The Loafer of the Paladora: The Story of a Girl's Pluck and Courage," *Northwest Magazine and the Corn Belt: An Illustrated Monthly* 21 (April 1903): 15–16. See also Rosalind Rosenberg, *Beyond Separate Spheres: Intellectual Roots of Modern Feminism* (New Haven: Yale University Press, 1982), especially chapter 3, "The New Psychology and the New Woman."

3. Elizabeth Hampsten, *Read This Only to Yourself: The Private Writings of Midwestern Women, 1880–1910* (Bloomington: University of Indiana Press, 1982), 46–47; *South Dakota Farmer*, Sioux Falls, S. D., March 23, 1906, p. 7.

4. *Kansas City Star*, November 13, 1890, Agriculture Clippings file, Library, Kansas State Historical Society, Topeka (hereinafter cited as KSHS); Mrs. A. B. Cross to A. P. Miller, September 15, 1899, and July 1901, and Ida S. Cross to A. P. Miller, June 14, 1910, Anna M. Cooley Correspondence, 1891–1925, Manuscripts, KSHS; *South Dakota Farmer*, February 8, 1917, p. 11.

5. Carl N. Degler, *At Odds: Women and Family in America from the Revolution to the Present* (New York: Oxford University Press, 1980), 405, 409.

6. Ibid., 408–9.

7. Hampsten, *Read This Only to Yourself*, 229; Master Farm Homemaker Work Sheet, 1928–1929, for Mrs. Faith C. Dodge, Master Farm Homemaker Work Sheets file, Cooperative Extension Service file, box 10, University Archives, Kansas State University, Manhattan (hereinafter cited as Archives, KSU); Tom English Memoir, 2, Archives, Sangamon State University, Springfield, Ill. (hereinafter cited as Archives, SSU).

8. W. Jett Lauck, "Japanese Farmers in Texas," *Texas Magazine* 6 (September 1912): 358; Eleanor Arnold, ed., *Voices of American Homemakers* (National Extension Homemakers Council, ca. 1986), 277.

9. Dorothy Williams Burke, "Women at Work on Chicago Truck Farms," *Social Service Review* 1 (June 1927): 194, 199; Paula M. Nelson, *After the West Was Won: Homesteaders and Town-Builders in Western South Dakota, 1900–1917* (Iowa City: University of Iowa Press, 1986), 54, 56; Sandra L. Myers, *Westering Women*

and the Frontier Experience, 1800–1915 (Albuquerque: University of New Mexico Press, 1982), 238–39; Josphine Boltz, "I Remember," 8, typescript manuscript, Lane County Historical Society, Dighton, Kans.

10. Glenda Riley, The Female Frontier: A Comparative View of Women on the Prairie and Plains (Lawrence: University Press of Kansas, 1988) and Deborah Fink, Open Country, Iowa: Rural Women, Tradition and Change (Albany: State University of New York Press, 1986) and Agrarian Women: Wives & Mothers in Rural Nebraska, 1880–1940 (Chapel Hill: University of North Carolina Press, 1992) rely on urban Victorian dictates; Riley concludes that gender's strict expectations applied to all women regardless of region or culture.

11. Darlene M. Ritter, ed., The Letters of Louise Ritter from 1893–1925: A Swiss-German Immigrant Woman to Antelope County, Nebraska (Fremont, Neb.: Siegenthaler-Ritter Publications, 1980), 93; Nelson, After the West Was Won, 159–60; Dorothy Schwieder and Deborah Fink, "Plains Woman: Rural Life in the 1930s," Great Plains Quarterly 8 (Spring 1988): 79–88; Freda Irvin English Memoir, 13, Archives, SSU.

12. Deborah J. Hoskins, "Brought, Bought, and Borrowed: Material Culture on the Oklahoma Farming Frontier, 1889–1907," in At Home on the Range: Essays on the History of Western Social and Domestic Life, ed. John R. Wunder (Wesport, Conn.: Greenwood Press, 1985), 124; Sentinel, Harper, Kans., November 28, 1889, p. 2; Ritter, Letters of Louise Ritter, 151.

13. Hampsten, Read This Only to Yourself, 30–31.

14. Arnold, Voices, 9.

15. Gladys Vail, "Kansas Kitchens," Home Economics News 6 (April 1919): 26; South Dakota Farmer, June 4, 1915, p. 9.

16. Gordon West, "Electricity," Kansas Farmer: 100 Years of Kansas Agriculture, Commemorative Issue, 1861–1961, Topeka, Kans., January 21, 1961, p. 24; South Dakota Farmer, August 24, 1906, p. 11.

17. Ted Holt, interview with author, Hoyt, Kans., November 8, 1991.

18. Des Moines Register & Leader, quoted in South Dakota Farmer, July 18, 1902, p. 1; South Dakota Farmer, August 6, 1906, p. 11.

19. Dodge City [Kans.] Times, May 10, 1879, p. 5; Gilbert C. Fite, The Farmers' Frontier, 1865–1900 (New York: Holt, Rinehart and Winston, 1966), 129–31.

20. Martin Ridge, ed., *Frederick Jackson Turner: Wisconsin's Historian of the Frontier* (Madison: The State Historical Society of Wisconsin, 1986), 7. See also Jeffrey B. Roet, "Agricultural Settlement on the Dry Farming Frontier, 1900–1920," (Ph.D. diss., Northwestern University, Chicago, 1982).

21. Alvin T. Steinel, "The Modern Circuit Rider and His Mission on Behalf of the Gospel of Better Agriculture," *Southwest Trail* 32 (December 1912): 3.

22. "Agricultural Colleges in the United States," in *United States Department of Agriculture Yearbook, 1920* (Washington, D.C.: Government Printing Office, 1921), Appendix, 505–7; Allen W. Jones, "The South's First Black Farm Agents," *Agricultural History* 50 (October 1976): 636–38.

23. Earle D. Ross, *Iowa Agriculture: An Historical Survey* (Iowa City: State Historical Society of Iowa, 1951), 126; Roy V. Scott, *The Reluctant Farmer: The Rise of Agricultural Extension to 1914* (Urbana: University of Illinois Press, 1970), 280–81; Barton W. Currie, "The Backbone of America," *Country Gentleman* 80 (April 24, 1915): 771; *Farmer and Breeder*, Sioux Falls, S. D., December 15, 1920, p. 15.

24. "Human Interest Stories," in "Annual Report of Extension Work in Texas, 1928," 700, Archives, Texas A & M; *South Dakota Farmer*, February 23, 1906, p. 10, March 2, 1906, p. 2, May 17, 1907, p. 8; Thomas Wessel and Marilyn Wessel, *4-H: An American Idea, A History of 4-H* (Chevy Chase, Md.: National 4-H Council, 1982), 31. See also Alan I. Marcus, *Agricultural Science and the Quest for Legitimacy* (Ames: Iowa State University Press, 1985).

25. Ross, *Iowa Agriculture*, 125; Scott, *The Reluctant Farmer*, 120, 179–83; "A Poultry and Hog Special" (April 1913) and "The Cow, Sow, and Hen Specials" (May 1924), clippings, Santa Fe Collection, Manuscripts, KSHS; Earl H. Teagarden and Robert L. Johnson, comps., *Extending the University to the People: Kansas Cooperative Extension Service, 1914–1989*, 4 vols. (Manhattan: Kansas State University, 1989), 1: 29, 48–49.

26. John Hamilton, "The Farmers' Institutes in the United States, 1910," in *Annual Report of the Office of Experiment Stations, 1910* (Washington, D.C.: Government Printing Office, 1911), 388; Scott, *The Reluctant Farmer*, 176; *South Dakota Farmer*, July 18, 1902, p. 8; M. E. Pennington, et al., "The Egg and Poultry Dem-

onstration Car Work in Reducing Our $50,000,000 Waste in Eggs," in *Yearbook of the United States Department of Agriculture, 1914* (Washington, D.C.: Government Printing Office, 1914), 363–65.

27. Roet, "Agricultural Settlement on the Dry Farming Frontier," 269, 297–98; Clayton S. Ellsworth, "Theodore Roosevelt's Country Life Commission," *Agricultural History* 34 (October 1960): 172.

28. Dwight Sanderson, "The Teaching of Rural Sociology: Particularly in the Land-Grant Colleges and Universities," *American Journal of Sociology* 22 (January 1917): 435, 438–39, 445.

29. Daniel D. Holt, *A Time of Contrasts: Progress, Prosperity, and the Great Depression, 1900–1940* (Topeka: Historic Preservation Department, Kansas State Historical Society, 1990), 33; Teagarden and Johnson, *Extending the University,* 4: 110.

30. Harold Ellis Jones and Herbert S. Conrad, "Rural Preferences in Motion Pictures," *Journal of Social Psychology* 1 (February 1930): 419–23; "The Small Town Woman's Reactions to Metropolitan Fads and Habits," *Woman's World* (August 1930): 3. For a 1920 sociological study conducted to determine assimilation, see Brian Q. Cannon, "Immigrants in American Agriculture," *Agricultural History* 65 (Winter 1991): 19.

31. Ellsworth, "Roosevelt's Country Life Commission," 163; *South Dakota Farmer,* August 14, 1908, p. 4.

32. Ellsworth, "Roosevelt's Country Life Commission," 165; Olaf F. Johnson and Thomas B. Jones, "The Unpublished Data From Roosevelt's Commission on Country Life," *Agricultural History* 50 (October 1976): 586, 591; Cooper, *Pivotal Decades,* 59, 210, 270; Dwight Sanderson, *The Farmer and His Community* (New York: Harcourt, Brace and Co., 1922), 154; Roy W. Meyer, *The Middle Western Farm Novel in the Twentieth Century* (Lincoln: University of Nebraska Press, 1965), 10.

33. L. L. Bernard, "A Theory of Rural Attitudes," *American Journal of Sociology* 22 (March 1917): 630–49; Walter Burr, "Community Welfare in Kansas," Kansas State Agricultural College, Extension Service, Bulletin No. 44 (January 1924), 3, 26.

34. W. C. Nason, "Uses of Rural Community Buildings," U.S. Department of Agriculture, Farmers' Bulletin No. 1274 (July 1922), 2; T. N. Carver, "The Organization of a Rural Community," in *Yearbook of the United States Department of Agriculture, 1914,* 93–129, 134–35.

35. Larson and Jones, "Unpublished Data From Roosevelt's Country Life Commission," 586, 590; Ellsworth, "Roosevelt's Country Life Commission," 165.
36. Ellsworth, "Roosevelt's Country Life Commission," 163, 166–68.
37. "Committee on Country Life [1918]," and "National Country Life Conference, November 1918," Rural Child Welfare file, Central file, box 140, Children's Bureau, Record Group 102, National Archives and Records Administration, Washington, D.C. (hereinafter cited as CB, RG 102, NA); "Sixth Annual Conference, American Country Life Association, November 8–11, 1923," meeting program, and "Meeting of the National Council of Agencies Engaged in Rural Social Work," agenda, 1924, Country and Rural file, Central file, box 161, CB, RG 102, NA; A. R. Mann, "Social Responsibilites of the Rural Community," Rural Community Conference, Cornell Farmer's Week, Cornell Extension Bulletin 39 (1919), 1.
38. Robert G. Athearn, *High Country Empire, The High Plains and Rockies* (New York: McGraw-Hill Book Company, Inc., 1960), 297–301; *South Dakota Farmer*, February 23, 1906, p. 5; William L. Bowers, "Country-Life Reform, 1900–1920: A Neglected Aspect of Progressive Era History," *Agricultural History* 45 (July 1971): 215.
39. Donald C. Horton and E. Fenton Shepard, "Federal Aid to Agriculture Since World War I," *Agricultural History* 19 (April 1945): 115–16.
40. "Kansas of To-day," *American Monthly Review of Reviews* 26 (September 1902): 359–60; Sara J. Keckeisen, "Cottonwood Ranch: John Fenton Pratt and the English Ranching Experience in Sheridan County, Kansas," *Kansas History: A Journal of the Central Plains* 14 (Spring 1991): 41–42; "Report of the Secretary," *Yearbook of the United States Department of Agriculture, 1909* (Washington, D.C.: Government Printing Office, 1910), 9.
41. W. C. Nason, "Uses of Rural Community Buildings," U.S. Department of Agriculture, Farmers' Bulletin No. 1274 (July 1922), 5, 15–16; I. M. Spasoff and H. S. Beardsley, "Farmers' Telephone Companies: Organization, Financing and Management," U.S. Department of Agriculture, Farmers' Bulletin No. 1245 (December 1922), 3–4; *Farmer and Breeder*, December 1, 1920, p. 24; Mann, "Social Responsibilities," 1; Kellee Green, "The Fourteenth Numbering of the People: The 1920 Federal Census," *Prologue: Quar-*

terly of the National Archives 23 (Summer 1991): 138–39; "How 'Ya Gonna Keep 'Em Down on the Farm (After They've Seen Paree)," words by Joe Young and Sam M. Lewis, music by Walter Donaldson, 1918.

42. Sanderson, The Farmer and His Community, 23.

43. D. Jerome Tweton, "The Golden Age of Agriculture, 1897–1917," North Dakota History 37 (Winter 1970): 41–55; Robert W. Richmond, Kansas: A Land of Contrasts, 1st ed. (St. Charles, Mo.: Forum Press, 1974), 194; South Dakota Farmer, June 21, 1907, p. 15.

44. William L. Cavert, "The Technological Revolution in Agriculture, 1910–1955," Agricultural History 30 (January 1956): 18; Ellsworth, "Roosevelt's Country Life Commission," 155; Mary Sydney Branch, Women and Wealth: A Study of the Economic Status of American Women (Chicago: University of Chicago Press, 1934), 52–54.

45. L. C. Everard, "Science Seeks the Farmer," in U.S. Department of Agriculture Yearbook, 1920, 109.

46. Avis M. Woolrich and Mildred S. Howard, "The House on the Farm," in After a Hundred Years: The Yearbook of Agriculture, 1962 (Washington, D.C.: Government Printing Office, 1963), 660.

47. Florence E. Ward, "The Farm Woman's Problems," U.S. Department of Agriculture, Circular 148 (November 1920), 15.

Chapter 2

1. Olive Capper Diary, 1895, pp. 53, 79, Manuscripts, KSHS.

2. "Program of Projects as Outlined by Miss Edna Groves, Supervisor of Home Economics," Pierre Indian School, file 812, box 36, and Bert R. Betz, ed., "Annual of the Fort Totten Indian Industrial School, 1909–1910," 19, file 820.3, Fort Totten Agency, Bureau of Indian Affairs, Record Group 36, National Archives, Central Plains Region, Kansas City, Mo. (hereinafter cited as BIA, RG 36, NA–Central Plains); Jessie Hoover, "Home Economics in the Agricultural College," Journal of Home Economics 4 (April 1912): 151; Lulu Craig, "History of Nicodemus Colony," 38, Lulu Craig Papers, file 3, Kansas Collection, Spencer Library, University of Kansas, Lawrence, Kans. (herinafter cited as Kansas Collection, KU); "Nicodemus," 1910, Negro clippings file, Library, KSHS; Glenna Matthews, "Just a Housewife": The Rise and Fall of Domesticity in America (New York: Oxford University Press, 1987), 148–49; Susan Strasser, Never Done: A History of

American Housework (New York: Pantheon Books, 1982), 41, 191, 203–5; Barbara Ehrenreich and Deirdre English, *For Her Own Good: 150 Years of the Experts' Advice to Women* (Garden City, N.Y.: Anchor Press/Doubleday, 1978), 155–60; *Chicago Examiner*, quoted in *South Dakota Farmer*, March 27, 1908, p. 6, May 29, 1914, p. 6; Julie A. Matthaei, *An Economic History of Women in America* (New York: Schocken Books, 1982), 157–67, 176–84.

3. Ellen Batchelor, "History of Home Economics Extension," 1, History of Home Economics Extension file, box 3, Archives, KSU; Scott, *The Reluctant Farmer*, 119.

4. *South Dakota Farmer*, February 29, 1906, p. 9, January 25, 1907, p. 1.

5. *South Dakota Farmer*, January 10, 1908, p. 10; Scott, *The Reluctant Farmer*, 118; *Royal Baking Powder Cookbook* (Royal Baking Powder, ca. 1927), 44–45; Margaret Sexton, interview with author, Abilene, Kans., October 12, 1991.

6. Hamilton, "The Farmers' Institutes in the United States, 1910," 387, 392; *South Dakota Farmer*, March 27, 1914, p. 3; Teagarden and Johnson, *Extending the University*, 4: 101; F. G. Moorhead, "Teaching a State to Cook," *Collier's* 46 (January 21, 1911): 21; Scott, *The Reluctant Farmer*, 121.

7. Hamilton Cravens, "Establishing the Science of Nutrition at the USDA: Ellen Swallow Richards and Her Allies," *Agricultural History* 64 (Spring 1990): 122–23; "Ellen Henrietta Swallow Richards," *Dictionary of American Biography*, vol. 15 (New York: Charles Scribner's Sons, 1935), 553–54; "Home Economics Association Meeting," *Home Economics News* 3 (August 1926): 15.

8. Nellie S. Kedzie, "Domestic Science," in *Report of the Kansas State Board of Agriculture* (Topeka: Hamilton Printing Co., 1895), 200.

9. Alfred D. Chandler, Jr., *The Visible Hand: The Managerial Revolution in American Business* (Cambridge: Belknap Press of Harvard University Press, 1977), 272–73, 277–76, 282, 285; Ida M. Tarbell, et al., *Women at Work* (New York: New York Career Tours, 1939), 82.

10. *Farmer and Breeder*, October 1, 1920, p. 16.

11. *South Dakota Farmer*, April 17, 1908, p. 6, April 16, 1915, p. 2, November 12, 1915, p. 9, February 22, 1918, p. 6; Ward, "Farm Woman's Problems," 14; "The Farm Kitchen on a Business Basis," *Farmer and Breeder*, March 15, 1921, p. 15.

12. Ehrenreich and English, *For Her Own Good*, 147; Lydia Ray Balderston, *Lippincott's Home Manual of Housewifery* (New York: Lippincott, 1919; reprinted, 1924); Christine Frederick, *Household Engingeering: Scientific Management in the Home* (Chicago: American School of Home Economics, 1920); Matthaei, *An Economic History of Women in America*, 159.

13. Grayson B. McNair, "Illumination for Farm and Town Homes," Kansas State Agricultural College, Engineering Experiment Station, Bulletin No. 1 (December 14), 11; R. G. Kloeffler, "Electric Cooking Appliances," Kansas State Agricultural College, Engineering Experiment Station, Bulletin 1 (December 1, 1917), 69; Mrs. Frances Runholt, oral history transcript, 14–15, Southwest Minnesota Historical Center, Southwest State University, Marshall, Minn.

14. A. M. Daniels, "Electric Light and Power in the Farm Home," in *Yearbook of the United States Department of Agriculture, 1919* (Washington, D.C.: Government Printing Office, 1920), 223.

15. W. A. McKeever, "A Better Crop of Boys and Girls," in *Seventeenth Biennial Report of the Kansas State Board of Agriculture* (Topeka: Kansas State Board of Agriculture, 1911), 573; *South Dakota Farmer*, September 23, 1904, p. 6, February 8, 1917, p. 11, October 24, 1919, p. 6.

16. Strasser, *Never Done*, 42; Arnold, *Voices*, 181–82.

17. Edna B. Day, "While She Waits," in *Eighteenth Biennial Report of the Kansas State Board of Agriculture* (Topeka: Kansas Department of Agriculture, 1913), 750–56; Maude Richman Calvert, *First Course in Home Making* (Atlanta: Turner E. Smith Co., 1924), 2; *South Dakota Farmer*, September 11, 1914, p. 16; A. Grace Johnson, "Does Home Economics Pay?" *Journal of Home Economics* 25 (August–September 1933): 583; "Fifty Years of Home Economics Education at K.S.A.C.," *Home Economics News* 1 (April 1925): 4; Elliott West, *Growing Up with the Country: Childhood on the Far Western Frontier* (Albuquerque: University of New Mexico Press, 1989), 57–61.

18. *South Dakota Farmer*, November 30, 1905, p. 1, March 27, 1914, p. 3, February 23, 1917, p. 11; Hoover, "Home Economics in the Agricultural College," 152.

19. Strasser, *Never Done*, 203; "Fifty Years of Home Economics at K.S.A.C.," 4; "A Hundred Years: Home Economics at South Dakota State University," unpublished manuscript, 7–8, College

of Home Economics, South Dakota State University, Brookings, S.D. (hereinafter cited as "A Hundred Years"); *Nebraska Blue Book for 1899 and 1900* (Lincoln: State Journal Co., 1900), 312; Addison E. Sheldon, ed., *Nebraska Blue Book and Historical Register* (Lincoln: State Journal Co., 1915), 259, 256.

20. Strasser, *Never Done*, 203; Juanita L. Shepperd, "The Possibilities of a Home-Maker's Course," *Journal of Home Economics* 4 (April 1912): 147.

21. "A Hundred Years," 8–9, 27, 32; *South Dakota Farmer*, September 3, 1915, p. 6.

22. Calvert, *First Course in Home Making*, 4–5; Blanche Ingersoll, "Opportunities for Home Economics Graduates," *Home Economics News* 1 (April 1925): 8–9, 31; "Housekeeping," *Modern Priscilla* 34 (January 1921): 29.

23. Calvert, *First Course in Home Making*, 3–5; Ingersoll, "Opportunities for Home Economics Graduates," 9.

24. Sallie F. Hill, "Result of General Activities—District No. 8," in "Annual Report of Extension Work in Texas, 1928," 738; and "Personnel," in "Annual Report of Extension Work in Texas, 1932," 683; Archives, Texas A & M; "Conie C. Foote," *Topeka Capital-Journal*, Topeka, Kans., March 16, 1992, p. 2-C; "A Hundred Years," 56.

25. "Washing Overalls Made Easy," *Farmer and Breeder*, March 1, 1921, p. 11; "The Homemaker," *American Needlewoman* (October 1925): 28; "The Homemaker," *Modern Homemaking* (September 1927): 18; "Washing," *The American Domestic Cyclopaedia*, 474. Cleaning tips recommending the use of lye, gasoline, or kerosene suggest the toxic and potentially hazardous nature of materials that women kept in the home and routinely employed. Dangerous effects for women and their families were recognized only by occasional warnings to keep supplies out of the reach of children.

26. "Selecting Kitchen Utensils," *Modern Priscilla* 34 (January 1921): 29; Elizabeth C. Condit, "Dishwashing," *People's Home Journal* 44 (April 1929): 14–15; Nina Simmonds Estill, "The Vital Effect of Diet on Health," *Woman's World* (August 1930): 19.

27. Annie R. Gregory, *Woman's Favorite Cookbook* (Chicago: Monarch Book Co., 1906), 7; *South Dakota Farmer*, January 31, 1908, p. 6, July 3, 1908, p. 5, August 7, 1908, p. 15; "Clothing," in "Annual Report of Extension Work in Texas, 1932," 299, Archives, Texas A & M.

28. Hoover, "Home Economics in the Agricultural Colleges," 155; Kenneth J. Matheson, "Making and Using Cottage Cheese in

the Home," U.S. Department of Agriculture, Farmers' Bulletin No. 1451 (May 1925; revised 1927); "Stain Removal from Fabrics, Home Methods," U.S. Department of Agriculture, Farmers' Bulletin No. 1474 (August 1926); G. H. Binger, "Successful Management of Farm Poultry," in *Nineteenth Biennial Report of the Kansas State Board of Agriculture* (Topeka: Kansas State Board of Agriculture, 1915), 670–79; "Home Economics," in *Twentieth Biennial Report of the Kansas State Board of Agriculture* (Topeka: Kansas State Board of Agriculture, 1917), 63–86.

29. *South Dakota Farmer*, April 10, 1908, p. 6; "Kitchen Clothes," *South Dakota Farmer Semi-Monthly*, December 24, 1915, p. 4; Goldie Robertson Funk, "Making Wash-Day Easier," *McCall's Magazine* (January 1918): 74.

30. Annie Hoffarth, "Paying the Preacher, The Women's Canning Club Brought the Dollars," *Farmer's Wife: A Woman's Farm Journal* 17 (April 1915): 319; Mae McGuire Telford, "Forehanded House Cleaners: They all Adopted One Woman's Magical Methods," *Farmer's Wife: A Woman's Farm Journal* 17 (April 1915): 320; *South Dakota Farmer*, November 23, 1906, p. 10.

31. Lillian May, "The Movie Man, Will You Help Him Choose Films for Your Boys and Girls?" *Farmer's Wife: A Woman's Farm Journal* 17 (April 1915): 314; "University Will Teach by Movies," *South Dakota Farmer Semi-Monthly*, October 27, 1916, p. 3; D. F. Houston, "Report of the Secretary," in *Yearbook of the United States Department of Agriculture, 1918* (Washington, D.C.: Government Printing Office, 1919), 53–54.

32. "Radio Programs, Station KSAC," Kansas State Agricultural College, Extension Service, Bulletin No. 55 (1927–28), 1–3.

33. Arthur Capper, *WIBW: The Capper Publications Radio Broadcasting Station* (Topeka: Capper Publications, ca. 1929), 5, 19; Arthur Capper, *WIBW: The Capper Publications Radio Broadcasting Station, Topeka, Kansas* (Topeka: Capper Publications, ca. 1928), 14; "Laura Ingalls Wilder," in *Current Biography, 1948*, ed. Anna Rothe (New York: W. Wilson & Co., 1949), 677.

34. "Selections from Aunt Sammy's Radio Recipes and USDA Favorites," U.S. Department of Agriculture, Agricultural Research Service, Home and Garden Bulletin No. 215 (August 1976), 1.

35. Nona Brown Thompson, "Teen-Age Teach," *Kansas History: A Journal of the Central Plains* 12 (Summer 1989): 129.

36. Strasser, *Never Done*, 210.

Chapter 3

1. "More Testimony," *Farmer's Wife: A Woman's Farm Journal* 17 (April 1915): 318.

2. "A Hundred Years," 45; Scott, *The Reluctant Farmer*, 119; Dorothy Schwieder, "The Iowa State College Cooperative Extension Service Through Two World Wars," *Agricultural History* 64 (Spring 1990): 224; Sanderson, *The Farmer and His Community*, 173–74; "The Woman's National Farm and Garden Association," *Journal of Home Economics* 25 (January 1933): 43; Anne M. Evans, "Women's Rural Organizations and Their Activities," U.S. Department of Agriculture, Bulletin No. 719 (August 29, 1918), 1, 3–4; *South Dakota Farmer*, August 2, 1907, p. 11; Mary I. Wood, *The History of the General Federation of Women's Clubs* (New York: General Federation of Women's Clubs, 1912), 155–57. (The General Federation was the forerunner of the National Federation of Women's Clubs.)

3. Tarbell, *Women at Work*, 78; Sanderson, *The Farmer and His Community*, 118; David Franklin Houston, "Report of the Secretary," in *Yearbook of the United States Department of Agriculture, 1914*, 50–51; "Helping Mothers in Erie County," *Farmer's Wife: A Woman's Farm Journal* 17 (April 1915): 310; "Kansas State Agricultural College, Extension Division, Annual Report for 1925, Dickinson County," 23, Extension Records, Courthouse, Dickinson County, Kans. (hereinafter cited as Extension, Dickinson Co.).

4. Women Members Committee chairman to Farm Bureau members, ca. 1922, Sedgwick County file, Cooperative Extension Service, box 2, Archives, KSU.

5. Maggie W. Barry, "Women's Organizations," in "Annual Report of Extension Work in Texas, 1924," 297–98, Archives, Texas A & M; Ronald S. Jones, *Good Homemakers—Good Neighbors: A History of Kansas Extension Homemakers Units, 1914–1982* (Manhattan: Kansas State University, 1982), 6; Leavenworth County file and Comanche County file, Cooperative Extension Service, box 1-B, Archives, KSU; Marlene Hightower, Cooperative Extension Service, to Anthony Crawford, April 23, 1991, Archives, KSU; Mary Elsie Border, "Kansas Annual Report, Dickinson County, November 1, 1929 to November 1, 1930," 6–7, Extension, Dickinson Co.

6. Charles E. Cassel, "Annual Report of County Agricultural Agent, State of Kansas, Finney County, Dec. 1, 1920–Nov. 30, 1921," 12, Finney County file, Cooperative Extension Service, box 1-B, Archives, KSU.

7. Ellen M. Batchelor, "The Procedure in Establishing Home Demonstration Agents in Kansas," 1, History of Home Economics Extension file, box 3; and "Kansas State Agricultural College, Extension Division, Annual Report for 1928, Home Economics Supervisors, from December 1, 1927 to November 30, 1928," Annual and Biennial Reports file, Cooperative Extension Service, box 7; both in Archives, KSU.

8. Mary Koch, "Food 'N Stuff: Stories of Our People," *Journal of the American Historical Society of Germans from Russia* 15 (Fall 1992): 44; Timothy J. Kloberdanz, "In the Land of *Inyan Woslata*: Plains Indian Influences on Reservation Whites," *Journal of the American Historical Society of Germans from Russia* 15 (Summer 1992): 22–24.

9. "State of Kansas, Annual Report of the Washington County Farm Bureau, 1917," Washington County file, box 2, and Francis L. Brown, "Annual Report of Home Demonstration Work in Kansas, 1919," 16, Annual and Biennial Reports file, box 7, and Montgomery County, Cooperative Extension Service, box 1-B, Archives, KSU.

10. Brown, "Annual Report of Home Demonstration Work in Kansas, 1919," 16; *The Ball Blue Book* (Ball Jar Company, 1930); Arnold, *Voices*, 142–43; "Negro Extension Workers, Home Demonstration," in "Annual Report of Extension Work in Texas, 1924," 645; Archives, Texas A & M; Sexton interview, October 1991.

11. Arnold, *Voices*, 141.

12. Rena Marie Farrell, "Stock Up the Pantry-Shelf for Winter," *Modern Homemaking* (September 1917): 16; Louise B. Moss, "Canning at Home," *Needlecraft Magazine* 17 (August 1926): 19-20, 25; Sexton interview, October 1991.

13. *South Dakota Farmer*, April 27, 1917, p. 11; "Women Can Help Conserve Food," *South Dakota Farmer Semi-Monthly*, June 8, 1917, p. 2.

14. "A Hundred Years," 45; "Give Special Farm Courses," *South Dakota Farmer Semi-Monthly*, June 8, 1917, p. 9; Wessell and Wessell, *4-H: An American Idea*, 31–32; "Girls Club Work," Riley County

file, Cooperative Extension Service, box 2, Archives, KSU; Teagarden and Johnson, *Extending the University*, 1: 60 and 4: 106; Rex C. Myers, "Homestead on the Range: The Emergence of Community in Eastern Montana, 1900–1925," *Great Plains Quarterly* 10 (Fall 1990): 223; Evans, "Women's Rural Organizations," 15.

15. Houston, "Report of the Secretary," in *Yearbook of the United States Department of Agriculture, 1918*, 22; Jones, "The South's First Black Farm Agents," 636–44; Schwieder, "The Iowa State College Cooperative Extension Service Through Two World Wars," 220, 223; Joan M. Jensen, *Promise to the Land: Essays on Rural Women* (Albuquerque: University of New Mexico Press, 1991), 223.

16. Penny Martelet, "The Woman's Land Army: World War I," in *Clio Was a Woman: Studies in the History of American Women*, eds. Mabel E. Deutrich and Virginia C. Purdy (Washington, D.C.: Howard University Press, 1980), 136; Alice Prescott Smith, "The Battalion of Life: Our Woman's Land Army and Its Work in the West," *Sunset: The Pacific Monthly* 41 (November 1918): 30–33.

17. *South Dakota Farmer*, May 24, 1918, p. 16; Mary Margaret Rowen, "Group Quilting in Kansas," *Kansas History: A Journal of the Central Plains* 13 (Spring 1990): 24–25; Evans, "Women's Rural Organizations," 8.

18. Ward, "Farm Woman's Problems," 10; Evans, "Women's Rural Organizations," 8.

19. Ola Powell Malcolm, "Women Market 4-H Brand Products in Increasing Volume," in *Yearbook of Agriculture, 1928* (Washington, D.C.: Government Printing Office, 1929), 614, 617–18. See also Jensen, "Crossing Ethnic Barriers," 169–81.

20. Evans, "Women's Rural Organizations," 8.

21. "Negro Extension Workers, Home Demonstration," in "Annual Report of Extension Work in Texas, 1924," 656; Mrs. M. E. V. Hunter, "Marketing," in "Annual Report of Extension Work in Texas, 1927," 681; and Mamie Lee Hayden, "Marketing and Home Industries," in "Annual Report of Extension Work in Texas, 1928," 464–65, 468, 470, 487, 489, 495; all in Archives, Texas A & M.

22. Anna Mary Landauer, "Leavenworth County History," 2, Native Sons and Daughters of Kansas Collection, Manuscripts, KSHS; Brown, "Annual Report of Home Demonstration Work in Kan-

sas," 56; Archives, KSU; "Home Improvements," in "Annual Report of Extension Work in Texas, 1924," 368, Archives, Texas A & M; Evans, "Women's Rural Organizations," 8.

23. "Flower Exchange," *Modern Homemaking* (September 1927): 29.

24. *Washington, Idaho and Oregon Farmer*, quoted in *South Dakota Farmer*, October 11, 1907, p. 10; William Alonzo Etherton, "The Farmhouse Improved," Kansas State Agricultural College, Bulletin No. 7, No. 1 (May 1, 1917), 71; T. N. Carver, "The Organization of a Rural Community," in *Yearbook of the United States Department of Agriculture, 1914*, 134–35.

25. Charles Alma Byers, "A Bungalow on A Ranch," *Sunset: The Pacific Monthly* 41 (November 1918): 50.

26. "Pretty Cottage of Five Rooms," *South Dakota Farmer Semi-Monthly*, May 26, 1916, p. 10; J. P. Martin, "New Tricks for Old Homes," *Household Magazine* 28 (May 1928): 10–11; Holt, *Time of Contrasts*, 19-20, 35.

27. Holt, *Time of Contrasts*, 35.

28. E. B. McCormick, "Housing the Worker on the Farm," in *Yearbook of the United States Department of Agriculture, 1918*, 347–56; Etherton, "The Farmhouse Improved," 60–61; Holt, *Time of Contrasts*, 37.

29. Holt, *Time of Contrasts*, 36; R. G. Kloeffler, "Water Heating in the Home," Kansas State Agricultural College, Bulletin No. 5 (June 1, 1921); F. F. Frazier, "Sewage Disposal for Country Homes," Kansas State Agricultural College, Engineering Experiment Station, Bulletin 5 (March 1916); John Daniel Walters, "The Water Supply of the Farmhouse," Kansas State Agricultural College, Engineering Experiment Station, Bulletin 4 (March 1916).

30. Ward, "Farm Woman's Problems," 9. Missouri study detailed in *South Dakota Farmer*, December 26, 1919, p. 5; Arnold, *Voices*, 195.

31. Ward, "Farm Woman's Problems," 8-9; Holt interview, November 1991; Mary Meeks Atkeson, "Woman in Rural Life and Rural Economy," in *America Through Women's Eyes*, ed. Mary R. Beard (New York: Macmillan Co., 1933), 406.

32. *Hays City [Kans.] Star-Sentinel*, August 20, 1885, p. 1; Ritter, *Letters of Louise Ritter*, 103.

33. Border, "Kansas Annual Report, Dickinson County," 73, Extension, Dickinson Co.; Sexton interview, October 1991.

34. Walter Stemmons, "What the Agricultural and Mechanical Col-

leges Does for the Farmers of Oklahoma," *Southwest Trail* 36 (April 1916): 10; "Sanitation" and "Home Improvements," in "Annual Report of Extension Work in Texas, 1924," 368–69, 381, Archives, Texas A & M; Montgomery County file, Cooperative Extension Service, box 2, Archives, KSU.

35. West, *Growing Up with the Country*, 58.
36. Woolrich and Howard, "The House on the Farm," 661–62.
37. Jensen, *Promise to the Land*, 263.
38. "A Hundred Years," 56; "Kansas State Agricultural College, Extension Division, Annual Report for 1928," 94, Archives KSU; "Kansas State Agricultural College, Extension Division, Annual Report for 1927, Dickinson County," 14, Extension, Dickinson Co.
39. "Home Improvement" and "Improved Kitchen Contest," in "Annual Report of Extension Work in Texas, 1924," 371–74, 376; and "Living Room Improvement," in "Annual Report of Extension Work in Texas, 1928," 449–51, Archives, Texas A & M.
40. Arnold, *Voices*, 133.
41. Alice M. Chalmers, "My College Daughter's Efficiency Ideas," *American Motherhood* 45 (July 1917): 12–13; *South Dakota Farmer*, January 11, 1918, p. 8, March 22, 1918, p. 5.
42. "Kansas State Agricultural College, Extension Division, Annual Report for 1928," 96, Archives, KSU.
43. Ibid., 98; *South Dakota Farmer*, December 26, 1919, p. 5; Boltz, "I Remember," 2; "The Homemaker," *Modern Homemaking* (September 1927): 18.
44. Homer E. Socolofsky, *Arthur Capper, Publisher, Politician, and Philanthropist* (Lawrence: University of Kansas Press, 1962), 121; Master Farm Homemaker Work Sheet, 1928–29 (St. Paul: *The Farmer's Wife*, 1929); and Master Farmer Homemaker Work Sheets for Mrs. C. D. Pottorff, Mrs. Edward Deschner, Mrs. James Clark, and Mrs. Mary R. Hollis, 1928–29, Master Farm Homemaker Work Sheets file, Cooperative Extension Service, box 10, Archives, KSU. For Spiegel advertisement for Gold Seal Congoleum, see *Modern Homemaking: The American Needlewoman* (September 1927): 32.
45. Master Farm Homemaker Work Sheets for Mrs. C. D. Pottorff, Mrs. Edward Deschner, Mrs. James Clark, and Mrs. Mary R. Hollis, 1928-29, Archives, KSU.
46. Coffey County file, Cooperative Extension Service, box 1-B, Archives, KSU; Cynthia Sturgis, "'How're You Gonna Keep 'Em

Down on the Farm?': Rural Women and the Urban Model in Utah," *Agricultural History* 60 (Spring 1986): 183; Landauer, "Leavenworth County History," 1; "Kansas State Agricultural College, Extension Division, Annual Report for 1925, Dickinson County," 20, Extension, Dickinson Co.; "Foods and Nutrition" in "Annual Report of Extension Work in Texas, 1924," 338, Archives, Texas A & M; Chapman Charmers EHU, interview with author, February 3, 1992; Atkeson, "Woman in Rural Life and Rural Economy," 405; Lulu Abbott and Rizpah Douglass, "If Illness Comes," Extension Circular 1022, Extension Service, University of Nebraska (November 1941), 7, 12, 14.

47. *Premium List for the Tenth Annual Indian Agricultural Fair, Mayetta, Kansas, August 1924* (n.p., 1924), 31; *South Dakota Farmer*, September 19, 1902, p. 7; "Foods and Nutrition" in "Annual Report of Extension Work in Texas, 1924," 329, Archives, Texas A & M; Leavenworth County file, Cooperative Extension Service, box 1-B, Archives, KSU.

48. Gayle R. Davis, "Women in the Quilt Culture: An Analysis of Social Boundaries and Role Satisfaction," *Kansas History: A Journal of the Central Plains* 13 (Spring 1990): 7; Evans, "Women's Rural Organizations," 1.

49. Balderston, *Lippincott's Home Manual of Housewifery*, 15–16; Hildegarde Kneeland, "Women on Farms Average 63 Hours' Work Weekly in Survey of 700 Homes," in *Yearbook of Agriculture, 1928*, 620–22; Ruth Schwartz Cowan, *More Work for Mother: The Ironies of Household Technology from the Open Hearth to the Microwave* (New York: Basic Books, Inc., 1983), 178; Joann Vanek, "Time Spent in Housework," in *A Heritage of Her Own: Towards a New Social History of American Women*, eds. Nancy F. Cott and Elizabeth Pleck (New York: Simon and Schuster, 1979), 500.

50. "The Needs of the Farm Woman," *South Dakota Farmer*, October 24, 1919, p. 6; Margaret Sexton, interview with author, February 11, 1992, Abilene, Kans.; J. W. McManigal, *Farm Town, A Memoir of the 1930s* (Brattleboro, Vt.: Stephen Greene Press, 1974), 68.

Chapter 4

1. Blanche Beal Lowe, "Growing Up in Kansas," *Kansas History: A Journal of the Central Plains* 8 (Spring 1985): 48.

2. Sexton interview, February 1992; Hamlin Garland, *A Daughter*

of the Middle Border (New York: Macmillan Co., 1921), 325; Arthur E. Hertzler, The Horse and Buggy Doctor (New York: Harper & Brothers, 1938), 118.

3. Abbott and Douglass, "If Illness Comes," 3. For fresh-air movement, see Jacob Riis, The Children of the Poor (New York: Scribner's Sons, 1892; reprinted, New York: Arno Press and the New York Times, 1971), 155; and The Children's Aid Society of New York: Its History, Plan and Results (New York: Wynkoop & Hallenbeck, 1893), 4. See also Anderson County Fair, 1894, poster, Kansas Museum of History, Topeka, Kans.

4. "Save the Youngest: Seven Charts on Maternal and Infant Mortality, With Explanatory Comment," Children's Bureau Publication No. 61 (1919), 2, 5; "Table Showing Total Number of Deaths from Conditions Related to Childbirth in the Death Registration Area," Maternal Mortality file, Central file, box 126, CB, RG 102, NA; Hertzler, Horse and Buggy Doctor, 119.

5. Mary Lee Adams, "Child Workers," 2, Agriculture file, Central file, box 205, CB, RG 102, NA.

6. Viola I. Paradise, "Maternity Care and the Welfare of Young Children in a Homesteading County in Montana," Rural Child Welfare Series No. 3, Children's Bureau Publication No. 34 (1919), 23, 75; South Dakota Farmer, August 30, 1907, p. 14.

7. Houston, "Report of the Secretary," in Yearbook of the United States Department of Agriculture, 1918, 72–73.

8. Samuel J. Crumbine, Frontier Doctor: The Autobiography of a Pioneer on the Frontier of Public Health (Philadelphia: Dorrance & Co., 1948), 158–59; Arthur E. Hertzler, The Doctor and His Patients: The American Domestic Scene as Viewed by the Family Doctor (New York: Harper & Brothers Publishing, 1940), 32; Chapman Charmers EHU interview, February 1992.

9. Carver, "Organization of a Rural Community," 129.

10. Paradise, "Maternity Care and the Welfare of Young Children, Montana," 8, 14; Florence Brown Sherbon and Elizabeth Moore, "Maternity and Infant Care in Two Rural Counties in Wisconsin," Rural Child Welfare Series No. 4, Children's Bureau Publication No. 46 (1919), 58.

11. Paradise, "Maternity Care and the Welfare of Young Children, Montana," 12, 31, 70; Sherbon and Moore, "Maternity and Infant Care in Wisconsin," 26, 32, 51; "Save the Youngest," 5; Hertzler, The Doctor and His Patients, 27; Sanderson, The Farmer

and His Community, 142–43; Joan M. Jensen, "The Death of Rosa: Sexuality in Rural America," *Agricultural History* 67 (Fall 1993): 3.

12. Paradise, "Maternity Care and the Welfare of Young Children, Montana," 60; Sherbon and Moore, "Maternity and Infant Care in Wisconsin," 28, 40.

13. Paradise, "Maternity Care and the Welfare of Young Children, Montana," 71; Sherbon and Moore, "Maternity and Infant Care in Wisconsin," 53, 92; Hertzler, *The Doctor and His Patients*, 31–32.

14. Arnold, *Voices*, 53.

15. E. McCullom, "Response," in *Nutritional Ages of Man: Proceedings of the Borden Centennial Symposium on Nutrition* (New York: The Borden Co., 1958), 124.

16. "Save the Youngest," 9–11.

17. Paradise, "Maternity Care and the Welfare of Young Children, Montana," 10–11; Sherbon and Moore, "Maternity and Infant Care in Wisconsin," 28, 44–45, 49; Mary Cornelia Wood Logan, "Grandma Logan's Story," 45, Mary Logan file, Manuscripts, KSHS.

18. Sandra Schackel, *Social Housekeepers: Women Shaping Public Policy in New Mexico, 1920–1940* (Albuquerque: University of New Mexico Press, 1992), 52–54; Ruth Landes, "The Ojibwa Woman," in *America's Working Women: A Documentary History—1600 to the Present*, eds. Rosalyn Baxandall, Linda Gordon, Susan Reverby (New York: Vintage Books, 1976), 8, 10.

19. Paradise, "Maternity Care and the Welfare of Young Children, Montana," 15; Elizabeth G. Fox, "Rural Problems," in "Standards of Child Welfare: A Report of the Children's Bureau Conferences, May and June 1919," Conference Series No. 1, Children's Bureau Publication No. 60 (1919), 187.

20. Paradise, "Maternity Care and the Welfare of Young Children, Montana," 10; Logan, "Grandma Logan's Story," 59–60; Hampsten, *Read This Only to Yourself*, 106.

21. Hampsten, *Read This Only to Yourself*, 109; Cooper, *Pivotal Decades*, 207.

22. *South Dakota Farmer*, May 4, 1906, p. 9; June 8, 1906, p. 9; August 3, 1906, p. 9; August 23, 1907, p. 9.

23. Ward, "Farm Woman's Problems," 5.

24. Green, "The Fourteenth Numbering of the People," 133.

25. Daniel Beekman, *The Mechanical Baby: A Popular History of the*

Theory and Practice of Child Raising (Westport, Conn.: Laurence Hill & Co., 1977), 109–12; Richard M. Smith, "Poverty, Nutrition and Growth," *Social Service Review* 1 (September 1927): 603; Elizabeth Thankful Bailey, "Your Healthy Baby: Acquiring Regular Habits," *Woman's World* (June 1930): 29; Hamilton Cravens, "Child-Saving in the Age of Professionalism, 1915–1930," in *American Childhood: A Research Guide and Historical Handbook*, eds. Joseph M. Hawes and N. Ray Hiner (Westport, Conn.: Greenwood Press, 1985), 417–25.

26. "What a Farmer's Wife Can Accomplish," *American Motherhood* 45 (October 1917): 251; *South Dakota Farmer*, July 10, 1908, p. 4, September 11, 1914.

27. Hampsten, *Read This Only to Yourself*, 47.

28. "U. S. Department of Labor, Children's Bureau—Exhibits," Women's Clubs file, Central file, box 139, CB, RG 102, NA; Anna Louise Strong, "Child-Welfare Exhibits: Types and Preparation," Miscellaneous Series No. 4, Children's Bureau Publication No. 14 (1915).

29. "Baby-Week Campaigns: Suggestions for Communities of Various Sizes," Miscellaneous Series No. 5, Children's Bureau Publication No. 15 (1915); "The Promotion of the Welfare and Hygiene of Maternity and Infancy," Children's Bureau Publication No. 137 (1924); Evans, "Women's Rural Organizations," 5; Brown, "Annual Report of Home Demonstration Work in Kansas," 40–41, Archives, KSU; Memorandum of Conference with W.R.P. Emerson, December 23, 1920, Tabulation of Cards file, Central file, box 143, CB, RG 102, NA; Crumbine, *Frontier Doctor*, 212.

30. *Farmer and Breeder*, October 15, 1920, p. 8; "Better Babies Standard Score Card," *Woman's Home Companion* (1929).

31. Ibid.; *Prize List of the Kansas State Fair, 1916* (Topeka: Kansas State Board of Agriculture, 1916), 119.

32. Bourquin Photograph Collection, "Better Baby" photo, 1917, Kansas Collection, KU; *Premium List: Johnson County Fair and Live Stock Association, Tecumseh, Nebraska, October 13–16, 1920* (Tecumseh: Johnson County Fair and Live Stock Association, 1920), 57; Strong, "Child-Welfare Exhibits: Types and Preparation," Appendix 5.

33. Lydia Roberts, "What Is Malnutrition? Hundreds of Thousands of American Children are Undernourished," Children's Year Follow-up Series No. 1, Children's Bureau Publication No. 59 (1920), 18.

34. "Does Your Child Pass?" Children's Conferences, Clinics, Tests file, Central file, box 142, CB, RG 102, NA; "The Promotion of the Welfare and Hygiene of Maternity and Infancy," Children's Bureau Publication No. 203 (1931).

35. "The Colored Unit," 1, Riley County file, Cooperative Extension Service, box 2, and Brown, "Annual Report of Home Demonstration Work in Kansas," 43, box 7, Archives, KSU; Harriet C. Andrews to Children's Bureau, Chicago Division, November 15, 1918, Children's Conferences, Clinics, Tests file, Central file, box 142, CB, RG 102, NA.

36. "Children's Year Weighing and Measuring Cards," and "Report, Committee in Charge of Examination, Florence, Texas, 1918," Children's Conferences, Clinics, Tests file, Central file, box 142, CB, RG 102, NA.

37. Kelly Miller, "Racial Factors," in "Standards of Child Welfare: A Report of the Children's Bureau Conferences, May and June 1919," Conference Series No. 1, Children's Bureau Publication No. 60 (1919), 66–67.

38. Mrs. C. J. Murphy to Julia Lathrop, June 12, 1919, and *Walla Walla Union*, 1919 (clipping), Children's Conferences, Clinics, Tests file, Central file, box 142, CB, RG 102, NA.

39. H. H. Watt to Julia Lathrop, June 24, 1918; Abby Williams Hill to Julia Lathrop, July 11, 1918; *Colfax [Ill.] Press*, July 25, 1918 (clipping); Memorandum for letter to Mr. Wm. Rhodes, August 5, 1918; Dr. Worth Ross to Julia Lathrop, July 5, 1918; Julia Lathrop to Dr. Worth Ross, July 9, 1918, Complaints file, Central file, box 143, CB, RG 102, NA; Edna Hatfield Edmondson to Jessica B. Peixotto, February 8, 1919, and Ina J. N. Perkins, Council of National Defense, to Edna Hatfield Edmondson, February 12, 1919, Children's Conferences, Clinics, Tests file, Central file, box 142, CB, Rg 102, NA.

40. *Prize List of the Kansas State Fair, 1916*, 119; Crumbine, *Frontier Doctor*, 213–24.

41. Florence Brown Sherbon to Julia Lathrop, July 1914, Iowa file, Central file, box 126, CB, RG 102, NA.

42. "The Promotion of the Welfare and Hygiene of Maternity and Infancy," (1924), 1–6, 17; "The Promotion of the Welfare and Hygiene of Maternity and Infancy," Children's Bureau Publication No. 203 (1931), 31–32, 36; Schackel, *Social Housekeepers*, 51–59; Mary Lyons-Barrett, "The Omaha Visiting Nurses Asso-

ciation During the 1920s and 1930s," *Nebraska History* 70 (Winter 1989): 286.

43. Jessica B. Peixotto to State Chairmen of Child Welfare, January 8, 1918, Children Conference, Clinics and Tests file, Central file, box 142, RG 102, CB, NA; "Annual Report in Foods and Nutrition," in "Annual Report of Extension Work in Texas, 1924," 334, Archives, Texas A & M; Frank K. Sanders, "Education as an Investment," in *Report of the Kansas State Board of Agriculture* (Topeka: Kansas State Board of Agriculture, 1912), 96; Navarre EHU, interview with author, February 13, 1992.

44. Tarbell, *Women at Work*, 79.

45. Jean Swift Dobbs, "Child Health Work at K.S.A.C.," *Home Economics News* 2 (December 1925): 35; "A Hundred Years," 9, 33, 56; Thomas F. Vance, et. al., "The Development of Children in the Home Management Houses of the Iowa State College," *Journal of Experimental Education* 2 (December 1933): 166–69.

46. Evans, "Women's Rural Organizations," 6.

47. Rena A Faubion, "Narrative Report, December 1, 1919–December 1, 1920," 2–3, in Annual Report of Project No. 13, Kansas State Agricultural College, Annual and Specific Reports, 1917–1950, Home Extension, Archives, KSU; Border, "Kansas Annual Report, Dickinson County," 12–13, 20–23.

48. Helen W. Atwater, "Food for Farm Families," in *United States Department of Agriculture Yearbook, 1920*, 471–83; Cravens, "Establishing the Science of Nutrition at the USDA," 127–29; Caroline L. Hunt, "Food for Young Children," U.S. Department of Agriculture, Farmer's Bulletin 717 (June 1917); Carrie Young, *Nothing to Do but Stay: My Pioneer Mother* (Iowa City: University of Iowa Press, 1991), 53–54; Henry T. Murray and John A. Murray, "Neighbors Helping Neighbors: Threshing in the Judith Basin," *Montana: The Magazine of Western History* 37 (Winter 1987): 59.

Chapter 5

1. John D. Hicks, "The Western Middle-West, 1900–1914," *Agricultural History* 20 (April 1946): 65–77; *Beatrice [Neb.] Daily Sun*, August 21, 1938, p. 11.

2. Bowers, "Country-Life Reforms, 1900–1920," 212; Dorothy Williams and Mary E. Skinner, "Work of Children on Illinois Farms," Children's Bureau Publication No. 168 (1926), 5–6, 8; Georgia Graves Bordwell, "Who Says White Folks Won't Work? Substi-

tuting American Families for Asiatics in California Orchards,"
Sunset: The Pacific Monthly 45 (December 1920): 104.

3. George K. Holmes, "Movememt from City and Town to Farms,"
in *Yearbook of the U.S. Department of Agriculture, 1914*, 257–58;
J. F. Jarrell, *The World and the Farmer* (Topeka: Atchison, Topeka
& Santa Fe, 1916), 8; David B. Danbom, "Romantic Agrarian-
ism in Twentieth-Century America," *Agricultural History* 65 (Fall
1991): 2–4.

4. "The Rural Church and Country Life," *South Dakota Farmer Semi-
Monthly*, December 10, 1915, p. 12; Arthur Capper, "Our After-
the-War Program, An Address Delivered at Assaria, Kansas,
November 28, 1918," 3, Library, KSHS.

5. Ward, "Farm Woman's Problems," 6; Sanderson, *The Farmer and
His Community*, 23; F. G. Stilgebouer, *Nebraska Pioneers: The Story
of Sixty-five Years of Pioneering in Southwest Nebraska, 1875–1940*
(Grand Rapids, Mich.: Wm. B. Eerdmans Publishing Co., 1944),
330; Garland, *A Daughter of the Middle Border*, ix, xi; Lowe, "Growing Up in Kansas," 49.

6. Ward, "Farm Woman's Problems," 6; Israel Herman Gorovitz,
"Some Aspects of the Child Labor Problem," *Social Service Re-
view* 2 (December 1928): 600; Branch, *Women and Wealth*, 69–70;
Jensen, *Promise to the Land*, 237. In addition, Nelson, *After the
West Was Won*, 42–48, notes women homesteaders as land specu-
lators.

7. William A. McKeever, "Training the Girl to Help in the Home,"
Home Training Bulletin No. 3 (1909), 14; Adams, "Child Workers," 7.

8. *South Dakota Farmer*, October 10, 1902, p. 15.

9. *South Dakota Farmer Semi-Monthly*, June 23, 1916, p. 1.

10. "'Opportunity Special' Meets With Unusual Success Throughout Kansas Wheat Belt," 54, clipping, Santa Fe Collection, Manuscripts, KSHS; Constance Libbey Menninger, "The Gospel of
Better Farming According to Santa Fe," *Kansas History: A Journal of the Central Plains* 10 (Spring 1987): 52–53, 55, 57.

11. "Kansas State Wheat Queen Contest, 1930," scrapbook, Archives,
KSU.

12. Lillian Montanye, "Make-Up in Moderation," *People's Home Journal* 44 (April 1929): 41; Calvert, *First Course in Home Making*,
160–61.

13. Sexton interview, October 1991; Dora R. Barnes, "Clothing," in

"Annual Report of Extension Work in Texas, 1924," 349–50, and "Clothing," in "Annual Report of Extension Work in Texas, 1927," 674, Archives, Texas A & M.

14. Retta Burns, "Travel Account, 1902," 1, Manuscripts, KSHS; "First Farm Survey of a Missouri County Made by the People Themselves Accurately Illustrates Conditions in Central Part of the State, Along Rock Island Lines," *Southwest Trail* 36 (September 1916): 10–11; Adams, "Child Workers," 2.

15. Kenneth E. Hendrickson, Jr., "Gilbert C. Fite, Interviewed by Kenneth E. Hendrickson, Jr.," *Heritage of the Great Plains* 22 (Fall 1989): 6; Young, *Nothing to Do but Stay: My Pioneer Mother*, 6; Sexton interview, February 1992; "This Land of Opportunity," *Harper's Weekly*, September 26, 1900, Agriculture clippings file, Library, KSHS.

16. Alvin Dille, "The Reorganization of the Country School," in *Yearbook of the United States Department of Agriculture, 1919*, 289–90, 296, 298.

17. Wayne E. Fuller, *The Old Country School: The Story of Rural Education in the Middle West* (Chicago: University of Chicago Press, 1988), 101, 107, 119, 222–26; Frank K. Sanders, "Education as an Investment," in *Report of the Kansas State Board of Agriculture* (Topeka: Kansas State Board of Agriculture, 1912), 94; *South Dakota Farmer*, June 3, 1904, p. 10, September 14, 1917, p. 9.

18. Bess M. Rowe, field editor, *Farmer's Wife*, to Helen V. Bary, April 11, 1924, General file, Central file, box 229, RG 102, CB, NA; Marian Allen, "School and Home," *Farmer's Wife: A Woman's Farm Journal* 17 (April 1915): 327; Wayne E. Fuller, "Making Better Farmers: The Study of Agriculture in Midwestern Country Schools, 1900–1923," *Agricultural History* 60 (Spring 1986): 167.

19. "A Model Rural School," in *Annual Report of the Office of Experiment Stations, 1910*, 383–86; Ila T. Knight, "Equipment and Use of the Home Economics Department in a Modern School," in *The American School and University, 1929–30* (New York: American School Publishing Co., 1929), 335–37.

20. "Radio Programs, Station KSAC," Kansas State Agriculture College Extension Service, Extension Bulletin 52 (1925–1926), 1–3; Alice Keith, "The Present and Future of Radio in Public Education," in *The American School and University, 1929-30*, 271–274.

21. Ann Oakley, *The Sociology of Housework* (New York: Pantheon

Books, 1974), 1–2, 41; *South Dakota Farmer,* January 26, 1906, p. 10; E. S. Goff, *The Principles of Plant Culture* (New York: Macmillan and Co., 1916); *Wisconsin Library Bulletin* 13 (January 1918 supplement): 154; Henry Jackson Waters, *The Essentials of Agriculture* (Boston: Ginn and Co., 1915), v, and *Essentials of the New Agriculture* (Boston: Ginn and Co., 1924), iv.

22. Joseph A. Cocannouer, *Trampling Out the Vintage* (Norman: University of Oklahoma Press, 1945), 79–80; Fuller, "Making Better Farmers," 156, 160; Alvin T. Steinel, "Most Striking Example of Modern Times of Cooperation in Public Service," *Southwest Trail* 32 (April 1912): 15; Tena Duis dress and sewing machine, exhibit and label, Gage County Historical Society Museum, Beatrice, Neb.

23. "Annual Report in Foods and Nutrition," in "Annual Report of Extension Work in Texas, 1924," 326, 328, and "Fairs," in "Annual Report of Extension Work in Texas, 1932," 674, Archives, Texas A & M; Evans, "Women's Rural Organizations," 9; *Premium List: Johnson County Fair and Live Stock Association, Tecumseh, Nebraska,* 49, 61.

24. Freda Irvin English memoir, 5–6, Archives, SSU; Shepperd, "The Possibilities of a Home-Maker's Course," 147, 149; LeAnn Francis, ed., *Bluegrass Memories: A Pictorial History of Iowa's Crestland Region* (Creston, Ia.: Creston News Adviser, 1990), 81.

25. Francis, *Bluegrass Memories,* 81; Girls' Yeast Bread Contest photograph, 328, in "Annual Report of Extension Work in Texas, 1924"; Cherokee County club girls photograph, 675, in "Annual Report of Extension Work in Texas, 1927"; McLennan County club girls photograph, 808, in "Annual Report of Extension Work in Texas, 1928," Archives, Texas A & M.

26. Bess V. Cunningham, "Some Human Values in Home Management," *Journal of Home Economics* 25 (April 1933): 272, 274.

27. Margaret M. Justin, "A Survey of Home Economics Courses in Kansas High Schools," *Home Economics News* 1 (December 1924): 6–7.

28. Ibid., 7.

29. T. E. Browne, "North Carolina: The Next Step in Education for North Carolina," *American Vocational Association News Bulletin* 1 (August 1926): 13; Nora Miller, "Out-of-School Girls in a Rural County," *Journal of Home Economics* 25 (June–July 1933): 463–64.

30. Calvert, *First Course in Home Making,* iii, 192–93, 307–13.

31. *Wisconsin Library Bulletin* 13 (January 1918 supplement): 154–55; "Your Own Library," *Farmer's Wife: A Woman's Farm Journal* 17 (April 1915): 324.

32. Treva E. Kaufman, "The Progress of Vocational Home Economics Education," *American Vocational Association News Bulletin* 3 (February 1928): 12.

33. Ibid., 14; "Domestic Science Class," *KERAHS* (Keats Rural High School newspaper), January 21, 1920, p. 3; Beulah I. Coon, "Home Economics Section," *American Vocational Association News Bulletin* 2 (February 1927): 26; Stella Moore, "Carol and 'Perky': Training in Vocational Home Economics Functions Today in Missouri High Schools," *American Vocational Association News Bulletin* 3 (February 1928): 18.

34. Rebecca J. Herring, "The Creation of Indian Farm Women: Field Matrons and Acculturation on the Kiowa-Comanche Reservation, 1895–1906," in *At Home on the Range: Essays on the History of Western Social and Domestic Life*, 42–43, 45; Clarice Snoddy, "The Social Adjustment of the American Indian" (1928), 13, Snoddy Papers, Manuscripts, KSHS.

35. *South Dakota Farmer*, September 25, 1914, p. 11; *Premium List for the Tenth Annual Indian Agricultural Fair, Mayetta*, Kansas (August 24, 1924), 1, 29, 37, 41, 43; The Bourquin Photograph Collection, Kansas Collection, KU, includes images of the 1917 Indian Produce Fair at the Kickapoo reservation.

36. "Program of Projects as Outlined by Miss Edna Groves, Supervisor of Home Economics," and "Sewing Room Order—1927–28," Pierre Indian School, box 36, file 812; Betz, ed., "Annual of the Fort Totten Indian Industrial School, Fort Totten, North Dakota, 1909–10," Fort Totten Indian Agency, file 820.3; and E. B. Meritt, BIA, to Axel Johnson, September 18, 1915, Omaha Agency files, box A-92, BIA, RG 75, NA–Central Plains. See also Snoddy, "Social Adjustment of the American Indians," 13, and Jensen, *Promise to the Land*, Ch. 8 for Seneca women.

37. Steven J. Crum, "Henry Roe Cloud, A Winnebago Indian Reformer: His Quest for American Indian Higher Education," *Kansas History: A Journal of the Central Plains* 11 (Autumn 1988): 171; Herring, "Creation of Indian Farm Women," 48.

38. Snoddy, "Social Adjustment of the American Indian," 16–17.

39. Cocannouer, *Trampling Out the Vintage*, 88; Vernon Runholt, oral history transcript, 8, Southwest Minnesota Historical Center;

Florence McKinney, "From 'Soddy' to Modern, 100 Years of Education," *Kansas Farmer: 100 Years of Kansas Agriculture, Commemorative Issue, 1861–1961*, January 21, 1961, p. 3C; Arnold, *Voices*, 17. West, *Growing Up with the Country*, 189, also notes that distance to school deterred attendance.

40. Wood, *History of the General Federation of Women's Clubs*, 232; "Ladies Literary League," typescript, 1, in author's possession; Evans, "Women's Rural Organizations," 9–11; "Club Work—Women" and "Community Work," both in "Annual Report of Extension Work in Texas, 1924," 308, 384, Archives, Texas A & M.

41. Joyce Henderson, "What a Club Means to the School and the Community," *Journal of Home Economics* 25 (April 1933): 294; Maurita Daniels, "What a Club Means to Its Members," *Journal of Home Economics* 25 (April 1933): 293.

42. "High School Home Economics Clubs," *Journal of Home Economics* 25 (April 1933): 292; "News Notes," *Journal of Home Economics* 25 (May 1933): 437–49, and 25 (October 1933): 649.

43. Alberta Young, "Making the Student Club Function," *Journal of Home Economics* 25 (April 1933): 296–97.

44. "History—Chronology for Kansas," and "Future Homemakers of America—Information Sheet," Kansas Association, FHA/HERO, Kansas State Department of Education, Topeka. Today, the national organization consists of FHA (Future Homemakers of America), emphasizing consumer homemaking education, and HERO (Home Economics Related Occupations), focusing on jobs and careers; young men are members and hold chapter, state, and national offices.

45. Freda Irvin English memoir, 7; Gladys Hasty Carroll, "Around the Family Table, a Page for Girls," *Household Magazine* 31 (October 1931): 52.

46. Minnie Miller Brown, "Black Women in American Agriculture," *Agricultural History* 50 (January 1976): 208; John R. Wennersten, "The Travail of Black Land-Grant Schools in the South, 1890–1917," *Agricultural History* 65 (Spring 1991): 61–62; E. Wilbur Bock, "Farmer's Daughter Effect: The Case of the Negro Female Professional," *Phylon* 30 (Spring 1969): 17–26.

Chapter 6

1. Sanderson, *The Farmer and His Community*, 119–20.
2. Alvin T. Steinel, "Story of a Plain Illinois Farmer Whose Heart

Is Big Enough for a Hundred Thousand Boys," *Southwest Trail* 32 (April 1912): 9, 12; Cooper, *Pivotal Decades*, 123–24.

3. Wessel and Wessel, *4-H: An American Idea*, 3–8; "Girls' Club Work," in "Annual Report of Extension Work in Texas, 1924," 304, Archives, Texas A & M.

4. Socolofsky, *Arthur Capper*, 117, 119–20; *Giving Boys and Girls a Greater Vision of Farm Life: Being an Illustrated Story of the Capper Pig, Poultry, and Corn Clubs* (Topeka: Capper Publications, ca. 1918), 10–11; John F. Case, *Facts About the Capper Pig Club* (Topeka: Capper Publications, ca. 1918), 4–7; Sexton interview, February 1992.

5. Mary A. Whedon, "Rural Club Activities," *Farmer's Wife: A Woman's Farm Journal* 17 (March 1915): 294.

6. Edward C. Johnson, "The Agricultural Agent and Farm Bureau Movement in Kansas," Kansas State Agricultural College, Division of College Extension, Bulletin No. 2 (May 1915), 8–12; R. W. Morrish, "Organization of Kansas Boys' and Girls' Clubs," Kansas State Agricultural College, Division of College Extension, Bulletin No. 30 (January 1922), 4–5.

7. Ibid.; Alvin T. Steinel, "One Hundred Thousand Boys and Girls in Uncle Sam's Great Outdoor Agricultural School in Fourteen Southern States," *Southwest Trail* 32 (December 1912): 6–7.

8. Alene Hinn, "Sewing Handbook for Girls," Kansas Agriculture College, Extension Bulletin No. 42 (April 1923); *Farmer and Breeder*, October 1, 1920, p. 5, October 15, 1920, p. 4.

9. "The Colored Unit," 2, Riley County file, box 2, and Brown, "Annual Report of Home Economics Work in Kansas," 57, and Sedgwick County file, box 2, Archives, KSU.

10. *Farmer and Breeder*, October 1, 1920, p. 7; Johnson, "Agricultural Agent and Farm Bureau Movement in Kansas," 11; John Farrar, *FFA at 25* (n.p.: Future Farmers of America, 1956), 20. Girls were readmitted into FFA in 1969.

11. Muriel Snyder, oral history transcript, 12, Wyoming file, American Agri-Women Collection, Agriculture Hall of Fame, Bonner Springs, Kans.; Arnold, *Voices*, 199.

12. Wessel and Wessel, *4-H: An American Idea*, 15–16; Steinel, "One Hundred Thousand Boys and Girls in Uncle Sam's Great Outdoor Agricultural School," 7; Scott, *The Reluctant Farmer*, 248–249, 251.

13. "Home Improvements," "Girls' Club Work," and "Clothing," in

"Annual Report of Extension Work in Texas, 1924," 304, 357, 365, 367–368, and Bernice Claytor, "Girls Home Improvement," in "Annual Report of Extension Work in Texas, 1930," 297, Archives, Texas A & M.

14. Houston, "Report of the Secretary," in *Yearbook of the United States Department of Agriculture, 1918*, 22; *South Dakota Farmer*, August 9, 1918, p. 7; C. B. Smith and George E. Farrell, "Boys and Girls Clubs Enrich Country Life," in *United States Department of Agriculture Yearbook, 1920* (Washington, D.C.: Government Printing Office, 1920), 490–91, 493–94.

15. A. N. Farmer and Janet Rankin Huntington, *Food Problems* (Boston: Ginn and Co., 1918), vi–vii; Johnson, "Agricultural Agent and Farm Bureau Movement in Kansas," 8–10. For Indian school 4-H examples, see Pierre Indian School reports, box 36, file 812, and Fort Totten Indian Industrial School annual reports, Fort Totten Indian Agency, file 820.3, both in BIA, RG 75, NA–Central Plains.

16. May, "The Movie Man," 314; "Radio Programs, Station KSAC," Kansas State Agriculture College, Extension Bulletin 55 (1927–28), 9; *Topeka [Kans.] Capital*, July 8, 1928, Agriculture clippings file, Library, KSHS.

17. Louise Ware, *Jacob A. Riis: Police Reporter, Reformer, Useful Citizen*, 109, 128, 162–63; Benjamin McArthur, "The Chicago Playground Movement: A Neglected Feature of Social Justice," *Social Service Review* 49 (1975): 377–79, 391; Dom Cavallo, "Social Reform and the Movement to Organize Children's Play During the Progressive Era," *History of Childhood Quarterly* 3 (1976): 509, 513; Wayne C. Nason, "Rural Planning—The Social Aspects," U.S. Department of Agriculture, Farmers Bulletin No. 1325 (May 1923): 1.

18. Kate Holladay Claghorn, "Juvenile Delinquency in Rural New York," Dependent, Defective, and Delinquent Classes Series No. 4, Children's Bureau Publications No. 32 (1918), 14–16; "Dependent and Delinquent Children in North Dakota and South Dakota," Children's Bureau Publication No. 160 (1926).

19. L. H. Weir and Abbie Condit, "The Leisure of the Child," in "Standards of Child Welfare: A Report of the Children's Bureau Conferences, May and June, 1919," Conference Series No. 1, Children's Bureau Publication No. 60 (1919), 55; "The Work of Child-Placing Agencies," Children's Bureau Publication No. 171 (1927), 65.

20. "Kansas State Agricultural College, Extension Division, Annual Report for 1927, Dickinson County, Supplement," 10, Extension, Dickinson Co.; Sanderson, *The Farmer and His Community*, 156–62; William A. McKeever, "A Modern Dictator for the Rural School," *Country Gentleman* 77 (December 7, 1912): 6; Ella Gardner and Caroline E. Legg, "Leisure-Time Activities of Rural Children in Selected Areas of West Virginia," Children's Bureau Publication No. 208 (1931), 27, 30, 39, 84.

21. Wayne C. Nason, "Rural Planning: The Social Aspects of Recreation Places," U.S. Department of Agriculture Farmers' Bulletin, No. 1388 (March 1924), 1–5, 10–13, 17–18; Carver, "Organization of a Rural Community," 130.

22. "Recreation," in "Annual Report of Extension Work in Texas, 1932," 421–422, Archives, Texas A & M.

23. Walter Burr, "Community Welfare in Kansas," Kansas State Agricultural College, Extension Bulletin No. 4 (October 1915), 15–16.

24. Nason, "Uses of Rural Community Buildings," 15.

25. "Dependent and Delinquent Children in North Dakota and South Dakota," 94; Sanderson, *The Farmer and His Community*, 159–60; *National 4-H Club Song Book* (Chicago: National Committee on Boys and Girls Club Work, 1954), 13, 16.

26. Mrs. A. H. Reeve, "The Exercise Problem of the Growing Child," *Popular Health Magazine* 5 (August 1927): 9–10.

27. "The Colored Unit," 2; "Colorado Takes Advance Step in Handling Boys' and Girls' Clubs," *Southwest Trail* 36 (June 1916): 12; "Short Courses and Encampments," in "Annual Report of Extension Work in Texas, 1927," 682, Archives, Texas A & M; Wessel and Wessel, *4-H: An American Idea*, 43; Mary A. Whedon, "Rural Club Activities: Happy Scout and Camp Fire Outings," *Farmer's Wife: A Woman's Farm Journal* 17 (April 1915): 327; Morrish, "Organization of Kansas Boys' and Girls' Clubs," 5; "National 4-H Club Camp," *Journal of Home Economics* 25 (October 1933): 723.

28. "Social and Labor Needs of Farm Women," U.S. Department of Agriculture, Report No. 103 (1914), reprinted in *America's Working Women: A Documentary History—1600 to the Present*, eds. Rosalyn Baxandall, Linda Gordon, Susan Reverby (New York: Vintage Books, 1976), 153–55.

29. "Encampments and Short Courses," in "Annual Report of Ex-

tension Work in Texas, 1924," 390–91, Archives, Texas A & M; Schackel, *Social Housekeepers*, 136–37; "Kansas Pioneers in Recreation for Farm Women," *Home Economics News* 2 (December 1925): 41; Border, "Kansas Annual Report, Dickinson Co., 1929–30," 79–80, Extension, Dickinson Co.; "A Hundred Years" 45; Sexton interview, October 1991.

30. Ada Beall Triggs to Julia Lathrop, November 29, 1915, Rural Child Welfare file, Central file, box 140, RG 102, CB, NA.

31. Alonzo B. See, *Schools* (n.p., 1928), 13–16; *The American School and University, 1929–30*, advertisements, 229, 240.

32. Mary Hurlbut Cordier, *Schoolwomen of the Prairies and Plains: Personal Narrative from Iowa, Kansas, and Nebraska, 1860–1920s* (Albuquerque: University of New Mexico Press, 1992), 113; Maude Elliott, "Pioneer School Teaching in the 20th Century," 11, Maude Elliott Papers, Kansas Collection, KU; Sexton interview, February 1992; Esther Lietz, interview with author, August 10, 1993, Topeka, Kans.; Charles R. Rankin, "Teaching: Opportunity and Limitation for Wyoming Women," *Western Historical Quarterly* 21 (May 1990): 155.

33. Louise F. Shields, Oregon Welfare Department, to Emma C. Lundburg, October 31, 1923; Grace Abbott to Paul Greer, *Omaha Bee*, June 25, 1923; W. W. Robb, Ft. Worth Welfare Association, to Marie Holt, November 17, 1922; Bordwell, "Who Says White Folks Won't Work," p. 28; Bettie Kessi, "Happy Harvest," *Pacific Homestead* (ca. 1923), clipping; and J. A. Churchill, Oregon Superintendent of Public Instruction, to Louise F. Shields, October 26, 1923; all in Agriculture file, Central file, box 205, RG 102, CB, NA.

34. Alice K. McFarland, "Child Labor in Kansas Sugar-Beet Fields, 1922," 2–4, Agriculture file, Central file, box 205, RG 102, CB, NA; Adams, "Child Workers," 8; Sara A. Brown and Robie O. Sargent, "Children in the Sugar Beet Fields of the North Platte Valley of Nebraska, 1923," *Nebraska History* 67 (Fall 1986): 256–303.

35. "The Federal Child-Labor Law," *School and Society* 6 (September 1, 1917): 256–57; "Child Labor, the Home and Liberty," *New Republic* 41 (December 3, 1924): 32–33; "Country Is Best Place," *South Dakota Farmer Semi-Monthly*, July 28, 1916, p. 7; William McKeever, "Teach Your Boy to Work Through Gardening," *Dearborn Independent* 26 (May 15, 1926): 8; William McKeever, *Farm Boys and Girls* (New York: Macmillan Co., 1913), 26.

36. Eleanor T. Marsh to A. I. Nichols, Capper Farm Publications,

September 8, 1923, Agriculture file, Central file, box 205, RG 102, CB, NA. In 1941 the U.S. Supreme Court upheld the child labor portion of Fair Labor Standards Act, but federal and state laws loosened during World War II. See Elizabeth S. Magee, "Impact of the War on Child Labor," *Annals of the American Academy of Political and Social Science* 236 (November 1944): 101–9.

37. Johnson, "Agricultural Agent and Farm Bureau Movement in Kansas," 12.

38. Jarrell, *The World and the Farmer*, 5; *South Dakota Farmer*, February 5, 1915, p. 10.

Conclusion

1. Mary R. Beard, "Introduction," in *America Through Women's Eyes*, 7.

2. Atkeson, "Woman and Rural Life and Rural Economy," 400; Paradise, "Maternity Care and the Welfare of Young Children, Montana," 14; Laurie K. Mercier, "Woman's Role in Montana Agriculture: 'You Had to Make Every Minute Count'," *Montana: The Magazine of Western History* 38 (Autumn 1988): 52; W. H. Olin, "Baker Quits Hogs When His Wife's Turkeys Win in Profit Race," *Capper's Farmer* No. 9 (September 1924): 5.

3. F. H. Newell, "National Efforts at Home Making," in *Annual Report of the Board of Regents of the Smithsonian Institution, 1922* (Washington, D.C.: Government Printing Office, 1924), 519; Caroline B. Sherman, "Rural Standards of Living," in *America through Women's Eyes*, 412-13; Henry Wallace, *Letters to the Farm Folk* (Des Moines, Ia.: Wallace Publishing Co., 1915), 26.

4. Amy Kelly, "Is the Farm Family a Successful Family?" *Home Economics News* 7 (November 1930): 3-4; Sanderson, *The Farmer and His Community*, 17.

5. Schlereth, *Victorian America*, 276-77; Gertrude Vaile, "Our Interpretation of the True Place of Family Life," *The Family* 4 (October 1923): 155.

6. Katie Lowry, "I Married a Farmer and, Oh, It Was Rough," in *Bittersweet Earth*, ed. Ellen Gray Massey (Norman: University of Oklahoma Press, 1985), 173; Arnold, *Voices*, 281.

7. Kelly, "Is the Farm Family a Successful Family?" 4.

8. "More Testimony," *Farmer's Wife: A Woman's Farm Journal* 17 (April 1915): 318.

9. Ibid.

10. Ibid.

11. Jensen, *Promise to the Land*, 238.

Bibliographical Essay

IN ASSEMBLING A BIBLIOGRAPHY RELEVANT TO agricultural history, rural reform, domestic economy, and the roles of women, it is obvious that while an overwhelming amount of published material exists for American agriculture, less has been published regarding rural women in particular.

For creating an overview of scientific farming and involvement of government and agricultural colleges, the following were important: Alan I. Marcus, *Agricultural Science and the Quest for Legitimacy* (Ames: Iowa State University Press, 1985); Roy V. Scott, *The Reluctant Farmer: The Rise of Agricultural Extension to 1914* (Urbana: University of Illinois Press, 1970); and Herman R. Allen, *Open Door to Learning: The Land-Grant System Enters Its Second Century* (Urbana: University of Illinois Press, 1963). Another study, not cited but allied to scientific farming and mechanization, is Richard G. Bremer, *Agricultural Change in an Urban Age: The Loup Country of Nebraska, 1910–1970*, University of Nebraska Studies, Series No. 51 (Lincoln: University of Nebraska, 1976).

Agricultural History contains a number of articles, cited in the text, that are relevant to this volume. Many articles, as well as the Marcus and Scott publications, refer to rural women in general. Other references are incidental, as is Douglas R. Hurt's *Indian Agriculture in* 233

America: Prehistory to the Present (Lawrence: University Press of Kansas, 1987). An account of agricultural development among native Americans, Hurt's book makes few references to women, and these are only woman-with-a-hoe stereotypes. For native American women and domestic economy education, Bureau of Indian Affairs records at the National Archives–Central Plains Region were most helpful, but two good studies are Rebecca J. Herring, "The Creation of Indian Farm Women: Field Matrons and Acculturation on the Kiowa-Comanche Reservation, 1895–1906," in *At Home on the Range: Essays on the History of Western Social and Domestic Life*, ed. John R. Wunder (Westport, Conn.: Greenwood Press, 1985) and the chapter, "Native American Women and Agriculture: A Seneca Case Study," in Joan M. Jensen, *Promise to the Land: Essays on Rural Women* (Albuquerque: University of New Mexico Press, 1991). A discussion of native American child rearing and education, as well as a bibliographical overview citing literature related to government Indian schools, can be found in Margaret Connell Szasz, "Native American Children," in *American Childhood: A Research Guide and Historical Handbook*, eds. Joseph M. Hawes and N. Ray Hiner (Westport, Conn.: Greenwood Press, 1985).

For rural women's experiences, one must turn to women's histories, edited letters, diaries and reminiscences, personal accounts, and studies. Many of these were found in manuscript and archival collections at universities and historical societies, but published material includes Carol Fairbanks and Sara B. Sundberg, *Farm Women on the Prairie Frontier: A Sourcebook for Canada and the United States* (Metuchen, N.J.: Scarecrow Press, 1983) and Carol Fairbanks and Bergine Haakenson, *Writings of Farm Women, 1840–1940: An Anthology* (New York: Garland Publishing, 1990). Both display an impressive array of female experience. The latter particularly demonstrates, as does Paula Nelson, *After the West Was Won: Homesteaders and Town-Builders in Western South Dakota, 1900–1917* (Iowa City: University of Iowa Press, 1986), that women sometimes were more interested in progressive improvements and scientific farming than were the men around them. These volumes also illustrate, as do so many others, that "frontier" and "farm women" project many mental and visual images.

Other important volumes are Elizabeth Hampsten, *Read This Only to Yourself: The Private Writings of Midwestern Women, 1880–1910* (Bloomington: University of Indiana Press, 1982); Eleanor Arnold, ed., *Voices of American Homemakers* (National Extension Homemakers Council, ca. 1986; reprinted, Bloomington: University of Indiana Press, 1993); Wava Haney and Jane Knowles, eds., *Women in Farming: Changing Roles, Changing Structures* (Boulder, Colo.: Westview Press, 1988); Theodora Martin, *The Sound of Our Own Voices: Women's Study Clubs, 1860–1910* (Boston: Beacon Press, 1987); Sandra Schackel, *Social Housekeepers: Women Shaping Public Policy in New Mexico, 1920–1940* (Albuquerque: University of New Mexico Press, 1992); and Sandra L. Myres, *Westering Women and the Frontier Experience, 1800–1915* (Albuquerque: University of New Mexico Press, 1982), particularly Chapter 6 (on frontier homemaking) and Chapter 9 (an examination of women's outlets for creative personal expression and financial gain). An excellent discussion of girls' farm work can be found in Elliott West, *Growing Up With the Country: Childhood on the Far Western Frontier* (Albuquerque: University of New Mexico Press, 1989), Chapter 4.

In the literature of women's studies on rural women, theoretical analysis is both diverse and divisive. Deborah Fink's *Open Country, Iowa: Rural Women, Tradition and Change* (Albany: State University of New York Press, 1986) and *Agrarian Women: Wives & Mothers in Rural Nebraska, 1880–1940* (Chapel Hill: University of North Carolina Press, 1992) emphasize subjugation and approximate methodology and interpretation found in studies of urban women. Fink's work is notable because it stands in rebuttal to those that argue that a partner relationship began on the frontier and extended into post-settlement days. Among those to suggest partnership are Laurie K.

Mercier, "Women's Role in Montana Agriculture: 'You had to Make Every Minute Count,'" *Montana: The Magazine of Western History* 38 (Autumn 1988): 50–61; Sarah Elbert, "The Farmer Takes a Wife: Women in America's Farming Family," in *Women, Households and Economy*, eds. Lourdes Beneria and Catharine R. Stimpson (New Brunswick, N.J.: Rutgers University Press, 1987), 173–197; and Seena Kohl, "Women's Participation on the North American Family Farm," *Women's Studies International Quarterly* 1 (1977): 47–54. In *Promise to the Land*, Jensen leans toward egalitarian patterns, not equal partnership.

Some writers in women's studies have departed from the paradigm of the Cult of True Womanhood, established by Barbara Welter's "The Cult of True Womanhood, 1820–1860," *American Quarterly* 18 (Summer 1966): 151–174. Lillian Schlissel, Vicki Ruiz, and Janice Monk in *Western Women: Their Land, Their Lives* (Albuquerque: University of New Mexico Press, 1988) question domestic ideology's influence, its impact upon minority women, and the ways historians have documented its transmission from dominant to minority cultures. Also addressing minority cultures, as well as questions of class, is Sarah Deutsch's *No Separate Refuge: Culture, Class and Gender on an Anglo-Hispanic Frontier* (New York: Oxford University Press, 1987).

Just as these publications raise issues, as well as awareness, earlier historial studies offer enlightenment and insights. These include the works of Mary Beard, who reconstructed women's history against a "myth" of female subjugation, against feminists who adopted and propogated the myth, and against historians, most of them men, who minimized or ignored women as subjects worthy of study. For a discussion see Berenice A. Carroll, "Mary Beard's *Woman as Force in History*: A Critique," in *Liberating Women's History: Theoretical and Critical Essays*, ed. Berenice A. Carroll (Urbana: University of Illinois Press, 1976), 26–41.

Useful accounts for this volume also include Darlene M. Ritter, ed., *The Letters of Louise Ritter from 1893–1925* (Fremont, Neb.: Siegenthaler-Ritter Publishers, 1980); Carrie Young, *Nothing to Do but Stay: My Pioneer Mother* (Iowa City: University of Iowa Press,

1991); Ellen Gray Massey, ed., *Bittersweet Earth* (Norman: University of Oklahoma Press, 1985); and Mary Hulbut Cordier, *Schoolwomen of the Prairies and Plains: Personal Narratives from Iowa, Kansas and Nebraska, 1860–1920s* (Albuquerque: University of New Mexico Press, 1992).

Not cited but noted here for consideration are June O. Underwood, "Civilizing Kansas: Women's Organizations, 1880–1920," *Kansas History: A Journal of the Central Plains* 7 (Winter 1984–85): 291–304; Marilyn Irvin Holt, "From Better Babies to 4-H: A Look at Rural America, 1900–1930," *Prologue: Quarterly of the National Archives* 24 (Fall 1992): 245–256; and Janet E. Schulte, "'Proving Up and Moving Up': Jewish Homesteading Activity in North Dakota, 1900–1920," *Great Plains Quarterly* 10 (Fall 1990): 228–244. For a comprehensive look at one radio station's homemaker programming, see Evelyn Birkby, *Neighboring on the Air: Cooking with the KMA Radio Homemakers* (Iowa City: University of Iowa Press, 1991); for a cultural history that connects women's roles to architectural changes see Gwendolyn Wright, *Building the American Dream: A Social History of Housing in America* (New York: Pantheon Books, 1981).

Three other volumes deserve mention, but for different reasons. The first, Rachel Ann Rosenfeld, *Farm Women: Work, Farm and Family in the United States* (Chapel Hill: University of North Carolina Press, 1985), is based on the 1980 Farm Women's Survey, conducted by the National Opinion Research Center in cooperation with the USDA; it illustrates that contemporary rural women's experiences resemble those of women of the past. The second volume, Norton Juster, *So Sweet to Labor, Rural Women in America, 1865–1895* (New York: Viking Press, 1979), is, as the title suggests, interested in nineteenth-century life; though it lacks interpretations of substance, the book is useful for its extensive use of illustrations and printed excerpts of what popular literature said about domesticity. Last, there is Ann Romines, *The Home Plot: Women, Writing & Domestic Ritual* (Amherst: University of Massachusetts Press, 1992), which examines American women's literary tradition of depicting domestic ritual.

Much of the material used for discussions of home economics and its application to rural life was taken from home extension files at state and county repositories. Two important archives were those at Kansas State University and Texas A & M University. Periodicals devoted to home economics or vocational education and popular women's magazines of the time were studied, and Children's Bureau records at the National Archives and Records Administration, Washington, D.C., were critical for examining child and maternal health and labor problems. Publications by agricultural colleges and the U.S. Department of Agriculture provided a core for the expert point of view and the types of advice offered rural residents; many of these materials were located at the Government Documents Library, University of Kansas. Among the most useful government publications were Anne M. Evans, "Women's Rural Organizations and Their Activities," Bulletin No. 719, U.S. Department of Agriculture, August 29, 1918; Florence E. Ward, "The Farm Woman's Problems," Circular 148, U.S. Department of Agriculture, November 1920; and George E. Farrell, "Status and Results of Boys' and Girls' Club Work, Northern and Western States," Circular 192, U.S. Department of Agriculture, 1920.

One farm newspaper was chosen as a study focus. Any number of agriculture newspapers would be of interest—*Prairie Farmer* in Illinois or the publications of Arthur Capper in Kansas or Missouri, to name just a few. The *South Dakota Farmer* was chosen, however, because of its many articles about farm women, domestic economy, and scientific farming. For general discussions of domesticity and home economics, the following were useful: Ruth Schwartz Cowan, *More Work for Mother: The Ironies of Household Technology from the Open Hearth to the Microwave* (New York: Basic Books, 1983); Barbara Ehrenreich and Deirdre English, *For Her Own Good: 150 Years of the Expert's Advice to Women* (Garden City, N.Y.: Anchor Press–Doubleday, 1978); Susan Strasser, *Never Done: A History of American Housework* (New York: Pantheon Books, 1982); Glenna Matthews, *"Just a Housewife": The Rise and Fall of Domesticity in America* (New York: Oxford

University Press, 1987); and Ann Oakley, *The Sociology of Housework* (New York: Pantheon Books, 1974). Another contemporary discussion of women as housewives that some may find useful, though it is of little relevance to rural women, is Helena Znaniecki Lopata, *Occupation: Housewife* (New York: Oxford University Press, 1971); its brief treatment of rural life refers to immigrant "neighboring" patterns and their relationships to Old World values.

Publications concerned with the progressive period and American culture are Susan J. Douglas, *Inventing American Broadcasting, 1899–1922* (Baltimore: Johns Hopkins University Press, 1989); William L. Bowers, *The Country Life Movement in America, 1900–1920* (New York: Kennikat Press, 1974); Alfred D. Chandler, Jr., *The Visible Hand: The Managerial Revolution in American Business* (Cambridge: Belknap Press of Harvard University Press, 1977); John Milton Cooper, Jr., *Pivotal Decades: The United States, 1900–1920* (New York: W. W. Norton & Co., 1990); and Adele Heller and Lois Rudnick, eds., *1915, The Cultural Moment* (New Brunswick, N.J.: Rutgers University Press, 1991). Additional readings of interest for the progressive period, but not cited in the text, include William L. O'Neill, *Divorce in the Progressive Era* (New Haven: Yale University Press, 1976), which notes the "reformer as expert" (p. 272) and the intensity with which Americans believed in a continuing upward spiral toward a better future; on the subject of divorce, O'Neill understands the progressives' devotion to scientific management and cites examples that identifed family troubles as simply "social inefficiency" (p. 265). Another examination of divorce is Elaine Tyler May, *Great Expectations: Marriage and Divorce in Post-Victorian America* (Chicago: University of Chicago Press, 1980), with its focus on early-twentieth-century Los Angeles, the emergence of suburban home life, and changing male-female relationships. And a volume with potential for comparative studies between America and the United Kingdom is Sheila Rowbotham, *Hidden From History: Rediscovering Women in History from the 17th Century to the Present* (New York: Pantheon Books, 1974);

Chapter 21 on motherhood and family discusses declining birth rates, maternal health, and child care during the early 1900s, and Chapter 22 considers Margaret Sanger, birth control, and abortion.

For progressive reforms in child labor and childhood experience there are Stephen B. Wood, *Constitutional Politics in the Progressive Era: Child Labor and the Law* (Chicago: University of Chicago Press, 1968), which concentrates on legal concepts but overlooks farm labor except in allied industries such as cotton milling in the South; Dominick J. Cavallo, "The Child in American Reform" (Ph.D. diss., State University of New York, Stony Brook, 1976), and *Muscles and Morals: Organized Playgrounds and Urban Reformers, 1890–1920* (Philadelphia: University of Pennsylvania Press, 1981); Louis John Covotsos, "Child Welfare and Social Progress: History of the U. S. Children's Bureau" (Ph.D. diss., University of Chicago, 1976). Other sources related to children but not cited in text are Susan Tiffin, *In Whose Best Interests? Child Welfare Reform in the Progressive Era* (Westport, Conn.: Greenwood Press, 1982), and Richard A. Meckel, *Save the Babies: America Public Health Reform and the Prevention of Infant Mortality, 1850–1929*, Henry E. Sigerist Series in the History of Medicine (Baltimore: John Hopkins University Press, 1990).

The research approach was to use materials that ranged from scholarly discussions to original documents to museum exhibits and photographs. Through these varied sources, a patchwork of experience and expectations emerged. Sometimes these meshed nicely; at other times, the fit was not so neat. That is as it should be. The note material and this essay suggest other possibilites for approaching further study of rural women. More can be done with practices in Indian schools and on reservations, and programs that separated women by race but not gender deserve more study, as do home extension programs and youth clubs appropriated by recovery programs during the 1930s. Although the national population is now predominately urban, agriculture and the agrarian dream still hold the imagination. Rural women, as part of that world, deserve attention and evaluation.

Index